D1571860

You must give birth to your images;
Fear not the strangeness you feel.
The future must enter you...
Long before it happens
                    —Rainer Maria Rilke

Martha Jones: Is that a city?
The Doctor: A city, or a hive, or a nest, or a conglomeration...
                    —Doctor Who, Season 3, Episode 12. Utopia

Let's be wonderfully awake
For what we are going to create,
To make happen,
In this mass co-scripting of the future.
                    —Ben Okri, Mental Fight

Nest City

HOW CITIZENS SERVE CITIES AND CITIES SERVE CITIZENS

BETH SANDERS

Published by
POPULUS Community Planning Inc.
Edmonton, Canada

Paperback ISBN 978-1-7771655-0-5
ebook ISBN 978-1-7771655-1-2

Cover and book design Judy Armstrong
Typeset in Gibson
Illustrations Amanda Schutz
Author photo Jane Purvis

www.bethsanders.ca

For those who have made,
make and will make,
our city nests.

And Mira and Evan.

C O N T E N T S

NEST CITY

F O R E W O R D

I first met Beth Sanders in late spring as the ice was melting on Lake Winnipeg in Manitoba, Canada. We met at a research retreat on the edges of the lake, in an intimate conclave of colleagues and mutual friends, exploring the interstitial zones of collective consciousness, emergence, and diversity generation.

As friends met strangers in the round of introductions, I heard, from across the room, Beth describe herself as a city planner who used three rules to guide her city development and planning team: "Take care of yourself, take care of others, and take care of this place." My heart jumped at these words, as they summarized the master code of care that I had built into the last chapter of my first book, which I was introducing to my peers at this same gathering. My eyes caught Beth's across the crowded room, and we knew we were destined to work together.

More than a decade later, I am inspired to offer a foreword to Beth's first book, *Nest City*—especially so because I discovered that the ethos that sparked our mutual attraction provides a satisfying denouement at the end of each chapter. Readers are invited to explore the impact of Nest-making Practices through the lenses of self, others, city, and care.

The subtitle to *Nest City* tells us of the path and passion of Beth's evolution from intelligent city planner to wise civic meshworker. Beth is a gifted guide, with on-the-street experience, who can reveal relevant, caring strategies for citizens to serve cities, and cities to serve citizens.

This book has already spawned a workshop series, online and face-to-face, where Beth invites members of what I call the four voices of the city (civic managers, civil society, business/innovators, and citizens) to re-value and reframe how they "work as love in action" in the nest they are building as a city.

Beth's exploration of nesting practices dynamically steers the reader through the city habitat they co-evolve as a living system. Her strong grasp of emergent systems is well informed by a nest that she knows well, Edmonton, Alberta, where she lives and works.

Beth is an astute observer of any city she visits, but she is also a valuable contributor to Edmonton's evolution as she brings tangible learnings to the city from other place she visits, and she dares to invite readers to spread their wings as they leap beyond the nest they have known into a whole new zone of unknowing. In doing so, Beth fearlessly challenges assumptions about traditional planning, opening doors to emergence, story making, messiness, and even happiness.

The engagement, interaction, and interbeing of the city that Beth describes make these qualities highly attractive—irresistible even. Such qualities arise from Beth's knack for storytelling—like the story of the family of geese that she and her son followed through the city from suburb to riverbank, holding up traffic, stopping a construction site, and endearing nature to every citizen who witnessed the "parade."

Nest City is a book for readers—whether they be professional planners or ordinary citizens—who want to fall in love with their city. Beth offers fresh lenses from which to appreciate their nest, new practices to improve city nest-making, and altered patterns to gain a better bird's eye view of the aliveness they are co-creating.

Nest City is an eminently practical book, enlivening the theory, action-research methodology, and complex challenges that I have explored in my *Integral City* book series. Beth has up-cycled my explorations with vibrant life by offering professional practices, illustrated with real-life anecdotes, charming graphics, heart-opening poetry, and clear prose.

If I hadn't found many ways to work with Beth in her path as professional planner, planning association leader, conference presenter, and workshop co-focaliser, *Nest City* would have galvanized me to meet the author and find ways to collaborate on how we inhabit cities and they inhabit us.

I consider myself truly blessed that Beth lives the nest-making practices of which she writes, and she so willingly and ably imparts her creativity through *Nest City*. I am always encouraged that Beth and I share the spirit of dedicating our work to the makers of cities. But I am equally moved right here and now to applaud Beth's nest building with such deep care for ourselves, each other, our places, and our planet (illustrating as well why Beth Sanders was the first Integral City Meshworker of the Year in 2013).

With gratitude and appreciation,

> **Marilyn Hamilton,** *PhD CPA/CGA (ret)*
> *Founder of Integral City Meshworks*
> *Author of* Integral City *book series*
> *Findhorn Foundation, Scotland, 2019*

PREFACE

In the days before this book becomes available to readers, I'm watching the coronavirus pandemic take over towns and cities and nations around our planet. The 2020 Olympic games have been canceled, but the flags of the world's nations are still top of mind. Who has the most cases, the most deaths, the most recoveries? Who is cheating on the numbers to make themselves look better? Where are the stories of hardship? Where are the stories of beauty and triumph, despite the odds? Where are the stories of devastating defeat? As a species, we are experiencing and watching our transformation in real time.

Humans alive today have not experienced a pandemic of this magnitude; if anyone was alive for the Spanish Flu in 1918 they were not old enough to remember it. In our lifetimes, when parts of the world have experienced a disaster or emergency, the rest of the world has been healthy and able to provide support. Yet as the COVID-19 pandemic sweeps across the planet, everyone is affected and we don't have the same means to support each other. This is happening at scale: nations are not able to help other nations and cities are not able to help other cities. And yet, on the ground, some citizens are able to help other citizens. We are not able to be physically close to each other, but we are able to sing to each other, buy groceries for each other, visit with neighbours we have never met, protect vulnerable populations. We are able, should we choose, to be kind to one another. We also, out of fear, defend ourselves from the realization that we cannot control the uncontrollable. From this fear we stockpile groceries, accept and sometimes espouse racist attitudes and behaviours, and deny the new rules that we need to follow to be safe.

Whether we want to or not, we are making the transition into a new world. In each of our lifetimes, most of us have experienced a significant transition: a loved one dies, disaster hits our community (flood, fire, economic downturn), work is lost, accident or illness strikes, etc. The difference is that we are all making this transition at the same time. All of us. Together. We are all going through the "disaster door," crossing a threshold, whether we want to or not. There is no going back.

In every place on our planet, the response to the coronavirus varies according to the local context. Strategies to slow the rate of infection and keep our physical distance from each other differ in accordance with local culture and infrastructure. Over the weeks, months, years, and lifetimes ahead, we will learn more about ourselves by examining the diverse ways we handled this emergency. At this time, the only perspective I have to offer is this: we are making a transition from "business as usual" to something new. The new is shaped by us. We have ourselves to rely on.

We are able to choose how to respond to the crisis. I do not propose that this is easy, or that you or I will be perfectly able to make conscious choices all of the time. Yet in conversation with a friend the other day, I noticed a simple truth: not all humans will survive this pandemic or the climate crisis. Both of these catastrophic events will end the lives of many humans, yet in both instances we do have the power to influence how quickly and how drastically events unfold. "Flattening the curve" applies to both the pandemic and the climate emergency.

Perhaps the purpose of the pandemic (if indeed there is one) is to show us that we are capable of snapping into action, that we have what it takes to address the world's climate emergency. The pandemic proves that we are adaptable and capable of quick change when needed. In less than a month, our cities have completely changed: the practices of self-isolation, keeping physical distance from each other, working from home, providing financial support to those who have lost work, and many other plans to aid in the continuous adjustments to come.

Nest City is released into a pandemic world of fear and possibility. While writing this preface, I paused to watch the season finale of *Star Trek: Picard*, the latest TV show in the *Star Trek* franchise. As with many episodes, a world needs to be saved. Jean-Luc Picard's words apply to us to today here on Earth: "Fear is an incompetent teacher. . . . To be alive is a responsibility, as well as a right." In this time of palpable danger, it takes extra effort to notice if the fear I experience is real and close, or not. For example, the risk is low that we will run out of toilet paper, and if we do, the consequences are not life-threatening. I have a choice: hunker down in fear or expand into new possibilities. Two questions guide me into possibility:

1. What is the quality of life I/we wish to have?
2. Under what conditions do I/we respond responsibly?

We are gifted with a reset. We will reinvent our work, and how we work, and this will regenerate our cities. We will choose to recalibrate the roles of government, business, community organizations, and citizens so we work better for each other. We will realign the relationships between our ecological, physical, social, and economic habitats so our cities are healthier. We will choose to make city nests that serve us well.

INTRODUCTION

*This is an invitation, not a recipe book. As you read this,
I encourage you to let the words enter into your experience as
a lake receives raindrops. Don't distance yourself by analyzing
what you read. Instead, feel the meaning rippling through you,
settling into the depths of your intelligence so that you enter
into a dialogue with the book …*
        —Risa Kaparo[1]

*You can't voluntarily cause an epiphany any more than you
can will a sneeze.
But you can voluntarily walk into a grain silo or an abandoned
house full of cats—thereby setting up the conditions for
a sneeze.*
        —Bruce Grierson[2]

NESTING INSTINCTS

One spring morning, my then 13-year-old son called me to come
see the geese walking to school. I didn't respond right away and
continued to fold laundry. He called again with more vigour, so
I joined him, beside his abandoned breakfast, at the kitchen
window. He wasn't joking—two adult geese and five yellow
goslings were making their way down the sidewalk. They crossed
the road, turned a corner, and started to head down another street.
This was usually the time when I head out for a walk to the ravine
that runs through my neighbourhood before I get to work, so
I followed the geese—they seemed to know where they were going.

Their route took them directly through a construction area where
city contractors were fixing pipes, sidewalks, and roads in our
neighbourhood. The geese stopped to tuck in between two houses
along the way, perhaps because of the noise, bustle, and vibration
of the construction site and heavy machinery. I zipped ahead to
tip off one of the workers and instantly, this 20-year-old wanted to
know where they were, spotted them, then went to talk to his boss.
Before I knew it, the contractors stopped their work. Being geese,
they didn't know that the road was closed; they waddled through
the construction site while the workers watched in silence.

The geese didn't know that the next two roads to cross were both four lanes of busy morning traffic. The 20-year-old construction worker, the 50-year-old construction boss, and I took it upon ourselves to step into traffic to clear their path. Drivers were raging mad; then thrilled.

We helped the city stop for a moment to make a safe crossing for the geese. We did not direct the geese; they knew where they were going. We just stepped out into traffic and followed our sense of direction as much as the geese did. We knew the initial reaction of the city would be the anger of morning commuters, yet knew it was the right thing to do. Sometimes what needs to be done needs an escort, a path cleared. (The 50-year-old construction boss walked with the geese to the ravine and down to the river to make sure they arrived safely. He followed a call from his heart.)

This notion of "escort"—being with what wants to happen, but not making it happen—is a new form of leadership. It is about letting what wants to happen happen. It is about revealing what wants to happen. It is a form of stewardship that does not protect and conserve, but rides alongside. It is a form of guiding that clears the way without directing the way. It is a form of leadership that understands that being part of something bigger than the personal—mine or yours—means following that something bigger. Moreover, it is a form of relationship that involves being in explicit relationship with something bigger.

David Whyte's *The Three Marriages: Reimagining Self, Work and Relationship* articulates the relationships we each have with self, work, and a significant other, each coming with spoken and unspoken vows. As I read Whyte's book, the voice inside my head kept calling out, "There's a fourth marriage: with **community**!" There are spoken and unspoken vows in our relationships with the communities in which we live—our neighbourhoods, towns, villages, and cities. What would it mean to be courageously smitten with our cities? What would it mean to have spoken and unspoken vows with our cities?

WORK IS LOVE IN ACTION

When I visited the Findhorn Ecovillage in Scotland two years ago, I often heard these words: "Work is love in action." They are the words that guide the essence of how an ecovillage has been organizing itself for fifty-five years. On my return from Scotland, a reader shared the words of her grandmother, "My work is my joy." Both of these perspectives embody the essence of this book: that the work we do, when done from a place of love and joy, is the force that generates and regenerates our cities. This happens in two ways. First, when work does not feel joyful, it is arduous and undesirable; but when we consider work to be love in action, it changes our relationship with the work and our world. When I stop the internal fighting about having to clean the dirty dishes or the toilet, or the tasks I find frustrating in running a small consultancy, and approach the work from a place of appreciation of helping my family and my company be in good working condition, I change my experience of my family and my work. I choose to not be filled with frustration and anger, but rather with a quiet sense of contribution. Second, when we have opportunities to do work that we love, we need to do that work. We need to allow ourselves to be escorted into the work that nourishes our hearts. We have to both surrender to work that must be done and exercise our spiritual authority to do the work we are called to do. What Whyte has to say about work applies to the city, too. While work is a place to find ourselves, it is also a place to lose ourselves in its wonderful undercurrents, a place to drown, losing all sense of our own voice, our own contributions and conversation.[3]

Our relationship with the city, like our relationship with work, is a constant conversation. Whyte describes his relationship with work this way:

> It is the back-and-forth between what I think is me and what I think is not me; it is the edge between what the world needs of me and what I need from the world. . . . [I]t is constantly changing and surprising me by its demands and needs but also by where it leads me, how much it teaches me, and especially, by how much tact, patience and maturity it demands of me.[4]

This is the same conversation the city asks of us, about our relationship with the city. It is in this conversation that we find out what the city needs of us, so it in turn can serve us well. A city is only as good as we make it—or remake it.

Nest City has emerged from my exploration of my relationship with my city, Edmonton, and the patterns I see in myself and others and their relationships with their cities. This is not a book about how to organize the physical world around us, about urban design or development economics. This is not a recipe, a list of ingredients that make a great city, rather it is an invitation to be in relationship with your city, wherever you are, which will make it great. In addition, it is about being in relationship with others while being in relationship with your city. Edmonton features prominently in *Nest City* because it is the city with which I am in closest relationship, but this is not a book about Edmonton. I invite you to explore your relationship with your city, listening to and discovering stories of you and your city as you read.

THE CITY IS OURS TO MAKE

Just as the geese had a clear sense of direction and purpose, I believe our cities have a clear sense of purpose and direction, to escort us to where we are going. Just as the geese did not know precisely where they were going, they did know—and we know—they are going somewhere. They have a sense of direction and I believe, if we tune in, we will find that we have a sense of direction, too. The city nests we make for ourselves are not only a survival instinct, but an evolutionary instinct in action. The more we explore this relationship, the better; in return, our cities will serve us.

Simply, our cities best serve us if they do more than help us survive—and serve us in our own evolutionary improvement. There are two aspects of this relationship that make the latter possible: first, if we don't like our cities, it is up to us to get to work to improve them; and second, the cities we make for ourselves will never be complete, our work will never be finished. We are in a relationship with our cities that is akin to a never-ending quest, which means we will always be asked to work to improve the city around us, whether we want to or not. So what would happen if the energy we use to fight the city around us was instead redirected into its improvement? What if we considered the things that endlessly frustrate us and make us angry and sad about our cities as an invitation to grow into new possibilities? It's up to us to improve our cities; they aren't made by anyone else.

The nest, as a metaphor for the city and the ideas in this book, offers insights at many (nested) scales. To start, imagine a nest you might make for yourself, a comfortable place where you feel safe. After a while, you might feel like it's time to leave, just as we often have the urge to leave home at 18, or leave our cities to explore the world at any age. It's also a place you can come back to as needed for food, rest, and comfort. I invite you to imagine your city as a nest too, a place that can both feel safe and a place from which to leap out into the world to do the work you are called to do.

This book is an invitation to experience that first leap out of the safety and security of the nest, allowing your wings to expand and truly unfurl as you drop into, and then rise up to meet the possibilities, known and unknown, before you. It is an invitation to explore the work we are called to do because it will make the world around us a better place. It is also an invitation to trust that if you do what you are called to do, and others do what they are called to do, that the diversity of what has our attention will serve us all well. We don't each have to work at everything and that's the beauty of the city and the diversity of our work—it ensures that collectively we have a wide range of tasks and skills covered off.

We all shape the cities we live in. Politicians, city planners, and business leaders are not solely responsible for dictating the experience of the city. The city is ours to make and remake as we need. We choose whether to be involved in this relationship unconsciously or consciously. Everything we do, from nanotechnology research to community garden building to working at the mall, shapes our experience. And in any of these areas of work, we see opportunities for improvement.

When you see room for improvement, you may find yourself feeling alone for a while, but if it is important enough to you, you will make it happen. And since humans are a social species, chances are you will find others interested in the improvement you seek, and you can create a social habitat for yourselves in which to thrive in your work. You can make a nest in which to nourish yourself and that serves as a platform from which to fly freely in the world doing your good work. You may even use your nest to welcome newcomers to your work and send them out into the world to build their own nests.

I invite you to return to the nest when you need to, to spend time with yourself and loved ones as you figure out what you are called to do, to protect dreams, to feed newly hatched ideas. Then again, as you have that figured out, you may leap back out again. Writ large, when you leap out of your nest, you are leaping into the bigger collective nest of the city. This is where you get to do the work you long to do, to experiment, play, explore, socialize, and find nourishment. This is where you fully engage in what it is to be human: out and about. And this is how the city gets the full benefit of you—and us—so it can serve us well in return. What we do changes what the city offers others. What others do changes what the city offers to us.

Humans "nest" together in cities, and in greater and greater numbers. I wonder what is possible if we enter into more conscious relationships with each other and the cities we live in? As integral evolutionary Terry Patten recognizes, it is not possible to explain the story of evolution or predict what will come, but "we can begin—for the first time in this great story—to consciously participate in it."[5] Conscious relationships with our cities provide a means to consciously participate in the story of evolution.

HOW *NEST CITY* IS ORGANIZED

Nest City reflects my personal learning journey to explore the relationship between cities and citizens. It is my work. As you read, you will learn about three things that happen as we organize ourselves in cites: we have a destination in mind, we embark on a learning journey, and we expect totally new things to emerge along the way. I learned that the destinations that we first envision are just a starting point; eventually they can add up to a sense of direction that serves better. This has been the experience of writing this book. I chose little things to write about (destinations) and after a while I knew I was writing a book but I didn't know quite what it was about. I chose to notice all the things I was learning along the way (journey) and trusted that something meaningful would reveal itself (emergence).

There was a moment when the writing snapped into place, and I knew I was writing a book in three parts. Part One: City Habitat Flight Path explores how cities come about, our practices and assumptions in organizing them, and what a thriving city looks and feels like. We don't know the precise form a city will take, neither its physical form nor its more subtle social, cultural, and economic experiences. The city is not predictable, but seems to have momentum of its own. Chapter One—Cities Are a Survival Skill explores how we organize our cities with evolving purposes, always connecting our work with our habitat. Chapter Two—The City Habitat is a Collective Endeavour identifies the dynamics of the economic, social, and physical habitats of the city and their connection to adaptability. Chapter Three—Cities are Evolutionary Systems lays out a framework for considering the evolutionary intelligence of the city. Chapter Four—Planning Is Work that Serves the City outlines how the function of planning our cities shifts to accommodate the complexity of today's cities.

Part Two: Nesting Materials explores three elements in organizing ourselves in cities: destination, journey, and emergence. Chapter Five—Destination: We Are Adrift and Alive articulates the evolutionary pull of improvement and the fundamental role of citizens in the city to do work that makes us feel alive. Chapter Six—Journey: Messy and Uneasy explores tension, the things that make us uneasy, as an evolutionary driver in city life and the essential role of quality social habitat. Chapter Seven—Emergence: Thresholds of (Un)known Possibility explores what it means to grow and perform new possibilities, with the courage to step into the unknown that beckons.

Part Three: Activating City Nestworks examines the relationship of those three elements with each other and declares the thresholds we face. To fully access the purpose of the city, we need to embrace city making, recognize the impacts of our civic practices, and tap into the soul of the city that wants to emerge. Chapter Eight—We Are City Makers explores how passion, happiness, and stories of possibility shape the city. We are asked to trust that we will lose nothing when we step into the unknown. Chapter Nine—We are Evolutionary Agents for the City discusses how conscious citizenship, involving a trust in the deeper knowing within us, relates to the cities we make for ourselves. Chapter Ten—We Ride the Winds of City Emergence articulates how the city emerges from both our actions and our inquiries. A Bird's Eye View, the concluding words of Nest City, reminds us of the power of our soul's desire.

Nest City is about how we shape the soul of our cities, which in turn shape us. The very soul of each of us that is the source of our ingenuity as a people lies both within us, and our cities. This is the very ingenuity that will lead us to our demise, to survive, or to thrive. The choice is ours. I invite you to eavesdrop and explore with me. Have a listen and see what makes sense for you. Use it to serve yourself, your work, and your city.

NEST-MAKING PRACTICE:
LEARNING ALONG WITH *NEST CITY*

At the conclusion of each chapter are some summative words and four questions to explore three scales of habitat—self, others, and city—and how to exhibit care. This pause at the end of each chapter gives you the opportunity to notice patterns and practices that can serve as "jumping off points" on your learning journey. The invitation is to circle up alone, with others, or with your city to see where these questions take you. You might write in a journal, paint, compose a song, or convene a gathering to debate and discuss, or simply sit and see what you notice. Noticing leads to new ways of thinking, making, and doing.

...lots of things that seem impossible to comprehend become more understandable if we identify the basic pattern and watch what it produces through repetition. It's a way of dealing with some complexities that otherwise are impenetrable...

—Jane Jacobs[6]

I like the feeling of combing out the tangles in things, of looking at the world around me and feeling I'm clearing the brush, bit by bit. This bit reclaimed from chaos, and this bit here, and that bit there.

—Annabel Lyon[7]

PART ONE
CITY HABITAT FLIGHT PATH

CHAPTER 1

As we see ourselves, so we act; as we act, so we tend to become.
It is a participatory universe. There is freedom at the very core of reality.
To be a conscious co-creator is not a metaphor; it is the power of
metamorphosis. We are designed to know the design and to participate
within it, as aspects of it, ourselves.
  —*Barbara Marx Hubbard*[8]

1

CITIES ARE A SURVIVAL SKILL

CITIES ARE OUR CREATION

Mayor Dennis O'Keefe opened a national city planning conference in his city of St. John's, Newfoundland, by inviting visitors to explore his "unplanned city." St. John's is crazy: houses perch on rocky slopes and hover perilously over the harbour; roads climb steep hills that every engineer I have worked with, if asked for approval, would scream rejection; streets connect and end with no discernable pattern, are impossibly skinny, too short, too curvy. The word "unplanned" implies some form of accidental or inadvertent city, but the more I learned about St. John's and its history, the more I realized that while unplanned, it was intentional, with each step in the city's evolution leaving a purposeful mark.

Mayor O'Keefe's remark might have slipped by me were it not for two things that captivated my attention while I took him up on his invitation to explore "unplanned" St. John's: the St. John's Port Authority is over five hundred years old and a map from the 1800s describes land ownership with the words, "from the high water mark to the back of the fish flakes." The city I live in, Edmonton, Alberta, shares St. John's colonial past, but more recent than 500 years ago, and on the Canadian Prairies we do not describe land by the location of fish flakes. Yet the essential story of how colonial settlement started in St. John's is not different from other North American cities.

In North America, Europeans arrived with the growth of European-based empires. The Truth and Reconciliation Commission of Canada (TRC) describes the phenomenon:

> *Starting in the sixteenth century, European states gained control of Indigenous peoples' lands throughout the world. It was an era of mass migration. Millions of Europeans arrived as colonial settlers in nearly every part of the world. Millions of Africans were transported in the European-led slave trade... Traders from India and China spread throughout the Red Sea and Indian Ocean, bringing with them indentured servants whose lives were little different from those of slaves. The activities of explorers, farmers, prospectors, trading companies, or missionaries often set the stage for expansionary wars, the negotiation and the breaking of Treaties, attempts at cultural assimilation, and the exploitation and marginalization of the original inhabitants of the colonized lands.[9]*

The cities of North America all stand on the lands of Indigenous people. The cities and citizens of Europe benefited from the growth of their empires in North America and elsewhere in the world.

The result of colonization was "usually disastrous for Indigenous people, while the chief beneficiaries of empire were colonists and their descendants."[10] This was settler colonialism, to gain control of the land of Indigenous people: colonial government "negotiated Treaties, waged wars of extinction, eliminated traditional landholding practices, disrupted families, and imposed a political and spiritual order that came complete with new values and cultural practices."[11] The cities of North America all stand on the lands of Indigenous people. The cities and citizens of Europe benefited from the growth of their empires in North America and elsewhere in the world. This is the context of our cities around Earth: colonized, colonizers, beneficiaries of colonization.

There is no single voice of Indigenous people in Canada or North America to tell us about the arrival of Europeans, but the Truth and Reconciliation Commission of Canada makes a clear statement:

> *Physical genocide is the mass killing of members of a targeted group, and biological genocide is the*

destruction of the group's reproductive capacity.
Cultural genocide is the destruction of those struc-
tures and practices that allow the group to continue
as a group. States that engage in cultural genocide
set out to destroy the political and social institutions
of the targeted group. Land is seized, and popula-
tions are forcibly transferred and their movement is
restricted. Languages are banned. Spiritual leaders
are persecuted, spiritual practices are forbidden,
and objects of spiritual value are confiscated and
destroyed. And, most significantly, families are dis-
rupted to prevent the transmission of cultural values
and identity from one generation to the next.

In its dealings with Aboriginal people, Canada did
all these things.[12]

The arrival of Europeans and their settlements and cities was an
act of colonization.

St John's began the work of recognizing this colonial story
explicitly in 2018 by starting city council meetings with this
acknowledgment:

We respectfully acknowledge the province of
Newfoundland and Labrador, of which the city
of St. John's is the capital city, as the ancestral
homelands of the Beothuk. Today, these lands are
home to a diverse population of Indigenous and
other peoples. We would like to acknowledge with
respect the diverse histories and cultures of the
Mi'kmaq, Innu, Inuit and Southern Inuit
of this province.[13]

This marks a starting point in colonizers' understanding that
North America was not "discovered." The history of human
settlement in North America does not start with the arrival of
Europeans. In my city of Edmonton, far west of St. Johns, we too
are beginning the work of acknowledging the diverse Indigenous
peoples whose ancestors have walked this land long before the
arrival of settlers like myself: the Cree, Dene, Saulteaux, Nakota
Sioux and Blackfoot peoples, as well as the Métis and Inuit.
Non-Indigenous people in my city are also beginning to better

understand the agreements made by the Canadian government with Indigenous governments—in Treaty 6 signed in 1876—and our violations of that Treaty. I acknowledge that the arrival of cities in North America was fostered by colonial strategies of European empires that exploited and marginalized original, Indigenous inhabitants. This is a legacy for cities—North American, European and any colonized/colonizer cities—to accept when we explore the primary question of *Nest City*: How do cities serve citizens, and how do citizens serve cities? Privilege and power, past and present, need to be acknowledged.

I offer these few pages as acknowledgement of my settler life and my settler perspective here in Treaty 6 and in the homeland of the Metis people, and more broadly in Canada and North America. I also acknowledge that there is a wealth of Indigenous knowledge about settlement and cities that I am not familiar with. As I write, I recognize that this book is an invitation to explore how we support and harm each other while we make cities. The arrival of settlers, towns, cities and industry has and continues to impact Indigenous people in harmful ways, such as physical and cultural genocide, racism and economic disparity. Readers: as you explore the stories of the cities you live in or visit, I encourage you to explore the parallel stories of Indigenous experience.

This book is an invitation to all citizens to explore how we support and harm each other while we make cities.

There is so much I don't know, so I humbly proceed with ideas for us to explore together. Let's explore how cities generate and regenerate themselves through our work—our efforts to improve them.

Mayor O'Keefe's Unplanned City

The purpose and shape of cities originate in a double-helix, DNA-like relationship between our value (or belief) systems and the world around us. This relationship is characterized by an unfolding pattern of stages of development of our cities, as there is at every scale of humanity, from the citizen, family, neighbourhood, organization, city-region, nation, continent, and planet. The journey is shaped by specific contexts, our "life conditions:" the times we live in (era); geographic place (physical conditions); challenges to existence (priorities, survival issues, threats to safety); and social circumstances (status, lineage, political systems).[14] Clare Graves' Spiral Dynamics theory of human development, as written and developed by Beck and

Cowan, provides an effective way to consider the growth and development of the city. Their—and my—spiral understanding is woven throughout this book. We are shaped by the habitat we settle in and our lives shape that same habitat. Our values and belief systems also affect our habitat, as they influence the decisions we make about the world around us. In other words, our city habitat is both given to us and created by us.

St. John's, on the most easterly point of land of North America, evolves over the course of its history. Changing life conditions, over time, guide the physical, social, and economic shape of the city.[15] In an era of colonial expansion five hundred years ago, the geography of St. John's was fundamental for colonial settlement: providing a sheltered, ice-free harbour that allowed people to survive harsh conditions and to harvest cod for trade in Europe. As power and might drove European colonial expansion, securing the Newfoundland fishery was a military imperative. Several wars culminated in English possession in 1762.

The early recorded physical shape of St. John's tells the story of European military life on the edge of North America. A map of St. John's from 1784 shows two forts (Townshend and William) and the town, consisting of a series of buildings along the harbour. Fourteen years later, a survey map[16] shows more fortification: numerous batteries, a block on Signal Hill, Fort Amherst, and Fort Waldegrave. The map also notes the hospital, courthouse, custom house, and church.

For the Empire, the purpose of this settlement of 3,244 people[17] was a military presence to stake its claim on the fishery. For people living in the settlement, the purpose was more immediate: creating the conditions for survival. The settlement was a means for survival and livelihood (of the Empire and individuals) by harvesting fish from the ocean for trade with Europe. Fishing was a dangerous way to make a living: from birth until death, endless hard work on land and water provided the basics needed to survive this harsh environment. The settlement was organized to meet both military and communal needs—a hospital, homes, wharves, public houses, and church—to support the settlement's ability to make meaning of life and hardship. The dual value of the settlement is in its ability to be a military presence and a place for residents to survive and thrive.

By the end of the 1800s, Newfoundland had secured its position as the world's largest exporter of salt cod.[18] In St. John's, this meant more houses, docks, fish flakes, wharves and boats at the edge of the water. The businesses that support this work also emerged: pharmacies, offices, stores, warehouses, trades, and suppliers. In 1856[19], a map of St. John's shows a much larger physical settlement to accommodate a population of 30,000[20], almost ten times that of a 1798 map.

Mayor O'Keefe's unplanned city, tis seen in today's St. John's between the water and New Gower Street, appears. However, the map itself reveals extensive order and thoughtfulness: everything the settlement needs is on hand. Fortifications protect the settlement and British imperial interests, while wharves and docks accommodate the fishery. Land and buildings are organized to accommodate: authority and government (government house and grounds, custom house, courthouse, public wharf); various spiritual needs; services, such as confectionary, hotels, auction mart, fishing rooms; future needs of a telegraph company; land transportation networks; and an aqueduct to provide a clean water supply.

The early settlers of St. John's and the authorities supporting them provided sufficient order to meet the needs of the emerging city. The activities of fishing, preserving, storing, and shipping the catch required a town to support the industry. As years passed, citizens and governments both noticed when conditions changed and something new was needed, or things no longer needed were discarded. And so the city evolved, constantly adjusting to changing life conditions.

One hundred and fifty years after the founding of the unplanned city, geography continued to play a significant role: in 1901, Marconi sent the first transatlantic (wireless) telegraph from Cornwall, England to Signal Hill. During the Second World War, the fortifications were used once again, this time to protect transatlantic shipping routes and North America's easternmost point of land from the attack of German U-boats. Torpedo nets were set up across the narrows to protect the harbour. New gun batteries were placed at Fort Amherst, and an American military base, Fort Pepperell, was built. The territorial impulse expanded from the British Empire to the Allied Forces.

The activities that defined St. John's in its earliest days also changed over time. The demand for salt cod declined, and the demand for frozen fish in the mid-1900s resulted in industrialized fishing practices. A subsequent decline of fish stocks, due to over-fishing, resulted in a fishing moratorium in 1992 and economic hardship ensues. The late 1990s brought offshore oil production, reaching a peak of 134 million barrels of oil for Newfoundland and Labrador in 2007.[21] As a result, St. John's became the primary offshore energy supply and service centre for east coast Canada, according to the Port of St. John's.[22] Today, the port serves a new industry—tourism--with cruise ships regularly visiting St. John's as part of their "Operation Titanic," "Voyage of the Vikings," and "Top of the World" expeditions.

St. John's continues to adjust and organize as conditions change. While fish flakes no longer surround the harbour, the unplanned city centre survives as a cultural hub and tourism asset. St. John's Port Authority continues to serve local, regional, and international trade. Its mission is to provide reliable, economic, and efficient port services in support of Canadian trade, fostering regional economic development and serving Newfoundland and Labrador's distribution requirements.

St. John's sits where land meets water, connecting the past with the present and the future. The sheltered, ice-free port was strategically located five hundred years ago and remains strategic today. This port city has always been about connections, a meeting place. It served as a rendezvous site and safe harbour for European nations five hundred years ago. It supported the connection between Europe and North America through the fishery. It connects communities by providing supplies and services with other Newfoundland and Labrador communities, with Canada and the United States, and continues to serve ships crossing the Atlantic Ocean from points all around the world. And to be all of that, St. John's became a city.

The shape of St. John's is derived from its geography, its purpose, and the activities within St. John's and its connection to other cities. It may not have been planned to be what it is today, but each stage of its development has been intentional, responding to its life conditions. The double-helix relationship between a settlement and its life conditions (the times, geography, survival needs, and culture) means we shape our habitat while our habitat shapes us.

Growing Cities

We create cities to serve citizens and we are growing our cities dramatically, in numbers and size. In 1800 only one city on our planet had over one million inhabitants: Beijing. Move ahead to 1900; now there are twelve cities with over one million inhabitants. Skip ahead again. This time to 1950. In only fifty years, the number of cities with over one million inhabitants has increased almost seven fold to eighty-three cities. Astonishingly, in 2019, 575 cities now surpass one million inhabitants.[23]

Our cities are more numerous and larger in scale. In 1950 only two of the world's cities were home to over ten million people: Tokyo and New York.[24] Mexico City joined the ranks in 1975. In November 2019, thirty-four cities had over ten million inhabitants and thirteen of those cities were larger than twenty million, with Tokyo arriving at an unprecedented 40.2 million and Guangzhou, China, reaching 45.6 million inhabitants.[25]

The increase of the world's population is as dramatic. World population in 1800 was 0.978 billion;[26] world population in November 2019 was 7.742 billion.[27] It took two thousand years to grow our first billion people[28] and only twelve years to grow our most recent billion.[29] Over fifty per cent of the world's population lives in cities today and in thirty years, sixty-six per cent of the world's population is expected to live in cities.[30] The question is this: Are cities growing people, or are people growing cities?

Think, Make, Do

We know that three archeological shifts took place around sixty thousand years ago:

> First, the tools used by humans became far more diverse and made more efficient use of stone and other materials. Second, art makes its first appearance, with a presumed leap in conceptual thought. And finally, it is around this time that humans began to exploit food resources in a far more efficient way. All in all, the evidence points to a major change in human behaviour.[31]

These shifts mark the point where we began to think new things, make new things, and do new things.

Anthropologists surmise that advancements in our language skills sixty thousand years ago allowed us to develop complex social networks; this was almost certainly a spark that transformed our ancestors' behaviour.[32] A change in the ways we communicated altered our social behaviour and with it our culture, tipping the scales to learn new things and drive our capacity to migrate across the planet.

Learning—thinking, making, and doing new things—sparked the initial migration, and it continued to spark the emergence of independent settlements, agriculture, and civilizations. Consider Ronald Wright:

> *By 3,000 years ago, civilizations had arisen in at least seven places: Mesopotamia, Egypt, the Mediterranean, India, China, Mexico and Peru. Archaeology shows that only about half of these had received their crops and cultural stimuli from others. The rest had built themselves up from scratch without suspecting that anyone else in the world was doing the same. This compelling parallelism of ideas, processes, and forms tells us something important: that given certain broad conditions, human societies everywhere will move towards greater size, complexity, and environmental demand.*[33]

Three broad conditions allowed for migration across the planet, the simultaneous development of independent civilizations, and current city growth. The first is our capacity and interest to create new work—to think, make, and do new things. The second is our capacity to create a social habitat that supports the generation of new work. The third is our capacity to respond to—and create—a physical habitat that supports our social habitat and the generation of new work. These three conditions are dynamically intertwined: work recreates social and physical habitats; social habitat recreates work and physical habitat; physical habitat recreates work and social habitat. The relationship between our work, social, and physical habitats sparked our migration from village, to villages and towns, to cities.

While our ancestors experienced whole new physical worlds as they migrated, the world we live in today is physically changing as well. Our cities are growing in size and number, but so too is how they look and feel. Each generation lives in an entirely new world—the work is different, our social habitat is different, the physical environment we build for ourselves is different. And every change brings more change. As cities become more complex, the consequences of changes are harder to track, unpredictable and unimaginable. We are travelling in an unknown world, still on the journey our ancestors began with their migration from villages to cities.

We are living in new times; we have never been here before. Yet despite not knowing exactly what's happening or what's to come, we are headed in a direction: we migrated across the planet, we migrated into cities, and now we are growing our cities.

New Work Creates Cities

The human journey continues to be sparked by thinking, making and doing new things. Physicist Geoffrey West found that as a city grows, it becomes more innovative. A city ten times the size of a neighbouring city is seventeen times more innovative. A metropolis fifty times bigger than a town is 130 times more innovative.[34] Writer Steven Johnson contends that the city propels and drives innovation because it is an environment that boosts creation, diffusion, and adoption of good ideas.[35] His conclusion about West's work: in one crucial way, "human-built cities broke from the patterns of biological life: as cities get bigger, they generate ideas at a faster clip…despite all the noise and crowding and distraction, the average resident of a metropolis…[is]…more creative."[36] As a species, we have an impulse to innovate, to seek new ideas and new ways of doing things. We strive to improve the quality of our lives, and we do this in cities.

In cities we learn and grow; we continue our quest to improve life.

Consider that innovation is simply new work, and the constant generation of new work is how we adapt to our changing world. If our work stayed the same, our species would not have travelled and settled across the planet. New work—innovation—allows us to evolve. The habitats we build for ourselves have evolved with us, for they are the result of our work.

In cities we learn and grow; we continue our quest to improve life. First and foremost, the work we do as individuals, and as a species, is about survival. We work to house, feed and clothe our families, and to meet recreational and material interests.

But work, when we generate new ways of thinking, making and doing, offers something larger: opportunities for self, family, neighbourhood, city, nation, and species to adapt to the changing world.

Before cities, I imagine these kinds of work: find and prepare food; provide and maintain shelter; look after children; look after the physical and spiritual well-being of the people; and provide wisdom and leadership. Work in today's cities includes these and many other kinds of work, from cashiering to nanotechnology research. All iterations of new work in cities come about when our basic needs are met—when we have time to explore, invent and pursue our passions. Or when our basic needs are not met—when we are compelled to explore, invent and pursue our passions for tangible improvement. Both versions are work in service to the community around us, love in action.

Work is ubiquitous: we work all day, every day. Paid or unpaid, work is simply what we do as we make our way through life. It may be hard: a drudgery, or a grind. When something succeeds or functions well, we say it "works." To get the results we seek, we need to be willing to put in effort and "work at it." We have a desire to "work things through" so they "work better," perhaps more easily. The truth is, work is a "work out."

Our work is what we offer the world, whether to make ends meet or because we love doing what we do.

Our work is what we offer the world, whether to make ends meet or because we love doing what we do. We each offer knowledge and skills to others, who in turn offer us both the goods and services we need and opportunities to do our work. When we search for new work, it becomes a learning impulse, a desire to find new and better ways of doing things that are of interest and offer improvement. If we choose, we develop newness in our cities. Writer and city activist Jane Jacobs termed this relationship between our work and the world "our economic life."

Our economic life informs and influences everything about us. It is an exchange that involves much more than money. It can be a simple exchange between me and another (Figure A) or more complex sets of transactions between me and the wider economy, others like me (Figure B). The full complexity of these exchanges, whether paid or unpaid, informs and influences everything we do. As I write, my paid work includes chairing a series of meetings where city employees and stakeholders are writing

design guidelines for new neighbourhoods. My full work life also includes writing, shovelling my neighbour's sidewalk, taking my turn to get my son and his friends to soccer practice, and doing my share of housework. While not paid for some work, I do get something in return: I have a good relationship with my neighbour who keeps an eye on our home; my son's teammates' families take turns driving to practices; and my whole family contributes to the physical well-being of our home so we are all able to participate fully in life. This dance between self and other, and what we offer to each other, is our economic life.

It is easy to spot new work. Just pick up a magazine, flip through your favourite newspaper or news site: the London Waste and Recycling Board is establishing a circular economy to keep products circulating at their highest value for as long as possible; research is underway to find economically viable ways to use the paper mill sludge that has polluted a Finnish lake[37]; leaders of the Siksika First Nation and the town of Strathmore are confronting racial tensions after the killing of a young Indigenous man.[38] This is work that explicitly responds to the physical and ecological world around us.

Cities are engines of innovation; innovation is the engine of cities. New work offers something far greater than we imagine: we

create the conditions for more people to create new work and follow their passion. Our evolutionary journey hinges on new work—the ideas and implementation—in response to changing life conditions. New work generates, and regenerates, cities and the capacities we need to adapt to our changing world. People are growing cities and cities are growing people.

WE ORGANIZE OUR CITIES

Cities Organize Purposefully
There was no master plan for St. John's; its shape and character were not determined by a single dream, or a single person, or even a single authority. At the scale of nation, its first purpose was military might. On the ground, at the edge of the ocean, at the edge of a continent, its purpose was survival, and once immediate needs were met, people began organizing themselves. Colonial authorities and the people living in St. John's gave it shape. Military personnel, governors, port authority officials, businessmen, church leaders, servants, and the patterns of how families met their needs all shaped the city. They organized themselves to make sure they had what they needed to persist and prosper as individuals, as a settlement, and as an Empire.

Collectively, they knew what it would take to run the fishery from the port of St. John's, and they did it. The city and citizens evolved, hand in hand.

The overriding purpose of a city is to integrate the needs of its people with its context, to create a habitat in which people survive and thrive. The story of St. John's reveals how what we see and value in the world expands, how a city's purpose changes and the new iterations of cities build upon each other in a rising spiral relationship (Figure C). St. John's exemplifies five purposes, that build upon what precedes, of settlement and cities:

1. Individual survival: in an ice-free harbour with food and fresh water, and materials to build shelter, to ensure the most basic needs are met.

2. Collective survival: by living together to ensure the collective survives.

3. Power and might: in the political might vested in the establishment of St. John's.

4. Authority and moral codes: in the form of churches, a custom house, law and order.

5. Prosperity: the port of St. John's is a "strategic hub for synergy and innovation," that takes advantage of a broad network of business operating from the port.[39]

As each of these purposes emerge, they transcend and include the preceding purposes, and each in its own trajectory shapes St. John's over time. Three more purposes of the city are evident, as we understand higher levels of complexity in the world and in cities, in more general terms:

6. Diversity of knowledge: by creating the conditions for us to fully access our diverse knowledge. We are growing into an understanding that city hall is not the only player that organizes a city but that there are many others involved: chambers of commerce, community foundations, advocacy groups, developers and builders, health authorities, school systems, provincial and federal governments, citizens, and so on. All and each of these players shape our complex cities and they are increasingly demanding a role in the process of creating our cities, though we have yet to organize for this purpose

7. Systemic flow: by creating a habitat in which we can see the value of the first six, recognizing that they all have

strengths on which we can draw. Cities help us see ourselves and our relationships with our habitat.

8. Global life force: in becoming a planet of cities, we become what scientist and futurist James Lovelock senses we are growing into: Gaia's reflective organ .[40] (Best described by Marilyn Hamilton.)

The city's purposes correspond to a pattern of unfolding, evolutionary intelligence identified by Clare Graves, Don Beck, and Christopher Cowan. Marilyn Hamilton applies this pattern of evolutionary thought to cities, where each stage of our development—and our cities' development—comes with different values, priorities, purposes, and structures. The spiral will be explored further in Chapter Three.

Corresponding Modes of Purpose and Organizing
Each city purpose has a corresponding mode of organizing. The first four levels of organizing (Figure D) are evident in early St. John's: reacting (survival), gathering (collective survival), doing (power and might), and planning (authority and moral codes).

Once our survival needs are met, we are able to expand our view and consider others. We gather with others, in homes, pubs and churches, to make meaning of what has happened and what will happen. Working together, the emphasis begins to shift from survival to thriving. When work needs to be done, it gets done. Docks and fish flakes are built where it works. In St. John's, the "doing" also takes place at the scale of nations: the British, French, Spanish, and Portuguese all want to claim and secure access to the fishery. Their purpose is to build kingdoms and lay claim to territory.

When the "doing" feels sufficiently unruly, structure emerges— in the case of St. John's, the Port Authority, government house, custom house, courthouse. As time goes on, hints of plans take root in St. John's, with authority to make sure they are implemented. Early maps of St. John's reveal early planning: pipes for water supply, custom house (and its rules), road construction, and property ownership. For local government this meant standards for activities such as construction and licenses. A calming blanket of order begins to cover the city. Over time, when rules begin to feel constricting, we look for ways to be entrepreneurial and creative, strategizing how to work without

Figure C
City
Purposes

Figure contents: GLOBAL LIFE FORCE · Systemic flow · DIVERSITY of KNOWLEDGE · PROSPERITY · AUTHORITY & MORAL CODE · Military & economic POWER · SURVIVAL · COLLECTIVE SURVIVAL

the rigid silos that come with standards and rules. When the opportunities that come with strategy and entrepreneurial creativity generate inequalities, hierarchies begin to flatten, to fully engage and benefit from the diversity of perspectives available. Over time, when listening gets more attention than decision-making, the lack of hierarchy feels like we are floating, that nothing gets done. As before, it is time to reach for a new mode of organizing.

An epic leap takes place in our development as we reach beyond these first six modes of organizing—with a desire to integrate these ways of being. Three additional modes of organizing are discussed further in Chapter Three. For now, we can see that they each surface in our cities, and we organize as appropriate in response to our life conditions.

CITIES ARE A SURVIVAL SKILL

The economic life of our cities, and our own economic well-being, depends on the changing conditions around us. Whether conscious or unconscious, our ability to adapt is the force that drives the creation, and re-creation, of cities. The qualities we see in a person, an organization, a city, a nation, or humanity shift and adjust over time in reaction to change. Response at any scale—self, family, city, nation, planet—can vary dramatically; there is no

recipe for adaptation. Each system finds the response that works for the circumstances.

Drawing on the work of 19th-century embryologists and evolutionists, Jane Jacobs highlights the patterns that surround the generation of new work, informing us about the economic well-being of cities and how they come about. New work begins with a new idea, a new way of thinking that may later lead to a new way of doing things. The clues I discern from Jacobs' work[41] fall into three categories: habitat, relationship, and scale.

Habitat
Our habitat shapes our work and as our habitat changes, our work changes with it. More specifically, this is a cycle that does not end: the city habitat shapes us, we shape our city habitat, the city habitat shapes us, and so on. For example, when fuel prices rise, we seek new technologies for fuel efficiency. When a child is born, our work within the family shifts. When a resource is discovered, we find ways to extract and make use of it. When the global economic marketplace struggles, we look for new ways to organize ourselves. New work arrives in response to our habitat—our economic, social, and physical contexts of time and place. Our work shapes our habitat, and our habitat shapes our work.

Relationship

New work is purposeful. It responds to change, either predictable or inexplicable. To begin, all new work builds on previous new work that has become conventional or commonplace. It offers something different and may become the next commonplace work upon which future new work can be built. As Jacobs puts it, new work has lineage and will serve in turn as the basis for more new work. Further, the development of new work depends on the co-development of other new work;[42] there is significant interdependence. Nothing happens in isolation.

Scales of Time and Space

The development of new work is not a tidy linear process, rather an endless mesh of interconnections that are seen and unseen, an open-ended process that creates diversity and increased complexity. Layers of interconnection result in greater diversity and complexity.[43] This pattern takes place at all scales of time and space: at the scale of self, family, city, nation, or planet; an hour, a day, a lifetime, or three thousand years. Each rise in scale brings new understanding and more complexity, to which we respond. These responses create more complexity to which we respond, and so on.

Hamilton describes this phenomenon of cities and scale by imagining a nested holarchy[44] of city systems (Figure E) where each holon (circle) is both a part and a whole system responding to its own life conditions. She says, "The city as a human system is a nest of systems; one cannot just look at the city as a whole or integral system without recognizing that it is made up of a series of whole systems."[45]

The work of each individual combines to become the economic life of the entire city (Figure F). The self is nested in the city. For Jacobs, the "development" of new work means qualitative change in the city—new kinds of work, a greater diversity of work, new ways of working. The cumulative effect of these adjustments is a world that becomes larger in scale and more complex. This is exactly what we see in our migration from village to towns to cities: an increase in scale and complexity. In terms of time, we are now able to see this journey from "deeper" time, back to our ancestral village.

A city with a well-developed economic life—where new work is created in response to changing conditions, in relationship with other work at various scales of complexity—is a city that adjusts, adapts, and evolves.

A city with a well-developed economic life—where new work is created in response to changing conditions, in relationship with other work at various scales of complexity—is a city that adjusts, adapts, and evolves. For each of us, our work—and our approach to it—adds diversity to the economic life of our cities. For Jacobs, new work is the development of the economic life of each of us for all of us.

MAKE THE CITY NEST WE NEED

Every species relies on an appropriate physical habitat for its health; without the right amount of water, the right temperature, the right light, a species will fail. Every species has a social habitat, too—a solitary life or one in community. For example, the hen duck sits on her eggs, while the drake hangs out with other drakes. For swans and geese, both parents stay to look after the eggs and young. In contrast, the mother brown-headed cowbird leaves her eggs in the nests of other birds to raise on her behalf; her young do not even meet her. Each species' habitat is unique: the food it eats, the shelter it finds or creates, and the role it plays in the lives of other species in its habitat. A species and its habitat are inseparable—humans are no exception.

We must be in good relationship with each other for our city habitat to work well for us.

The majority of humans live in city habitats, with many more in regular relationship with cities. I think of these cities as nests of various sizes in which thousands or millions of people live. And each city nest is intricately connected to the larger and smaller nests around it. Small towns and settlements are in relationship to larger cities, as small cities are in relationship with bigger cities, and vice versa. It is a complex network—or "nestwork"— of relationships between cities, towns and all of humanity, as well as relationships within cities between people (citizens, families, neighbourhoods, organizations).

The city nest is many things: shelter and a place to call home; a place to nurture our young; a place to grow up and mature; a place to explore the world, with the wide range of work we do; a place to leave so we can explore other aspects of the world; and a place to which we can return when we feel it is time. We must be in good relationship with each other for our city habitat to work well for us. Moreover, the times demand we awaken to the relationship between our city nests and the physical, social and economic world in which we find ourselves.

At the core of the city nest, and unique to our species, is our economic life—what we think, make, and do; how we innovate and generate new work; and how we create and recreate our city nests. We, and our city nests, have evolved hand in hand as we find new ways to think, make, and do. Our work is in response to our habitat—both the physical world of Earth and the nests we build for ourselves.

For Jane Jacobs, developing new work (thinking) takes place in response to habitat, as does implementing new work (making and doing). For Jacobs, this is the quantitative expansion of economic life. All settlements and cities begin with the implementation of new work, with at least one useful inheritance from Earth's past development and expansion.[46] For our ancestors, it may have been the use of bone, making a longer lasting hunting tool that allowed hunters to explore. Settlement at St. John's, Newfoundland, drew on vast cod stocks and a geography that placed the sheltered, ice-free harbour at the easternmost point of North America. The initial resources for settlement economies, writes Jacobs, are "earned by combining gift resources with human effort."[47] Starting with physical resources and geography, new work continues to emerge into the cities we know today.

Each generation builds on the work of previous generations, and how we do our work physically changes our habitat: cities.

Figure F
*Our Collective
Work in City
Habitat*

Our choices every day affect our physical habitat. Just as when we mine coal or farm, when we build (or rebuild) neighbourhoods, art galleries, and freeways, we change our habitat. Each generation receives a habitat, and each day, month, year, and lifetime we continue to recreate it. And then we create more new work to adjust to the new habitat we have created. Cities, simply, are the habitat we build to create the conditions for new work and innovation.

Our physical habitat evolves, with us, from the physical resource inheritance that starts a settlement to the very cities we create and all the diverse physical changes they bring with them. Our physical habitat transforms with us and remains the basis for our economic life. Cities create the conditions for us to pursue new work. Despite the rules or regulations we set up governing "what happens where" in cities, we self-organize to create habitats for new work. Steven Johnson says: "Cities bring minds together and put them into coherent slots. Cobblers gather near cobblers, and button-makers near other button-makers. Ideas and goods flow readily within these clusters, leading to productive cross-pollination, ensuring that good ideas don't die out."[48] People look for habitats that will support their desire and ability to pursue their work.

The city is a natural habitat that we both inherit and create with each generation. Our economic life is a force that sparks the creation of, and our migration to, cities. As Geoffrey West found, people collectively become more innovative as our cities get larger, because "good ideas...want to connect, fuse, recombine."[49] Cities are engines we have created for innovation—and our evolution. We make the habitat that serves our survival.

We also make the habitat that threatens our survival. Herbert Giardet, author of *Creating Regenerative Cities* and co-founder of the World Future Council, points out that humanity is building prosperous economies across the world, but at the expense of our physical habitat; we are harming the very habitat we need to survive.[50] This is taking place in, through, and from our cities. He invites us to think, make, and do in new ways, rather than rest in current economic practices that threaten the future of humanity because they threaten the natural world on which we depend. Simply: rather than thinking isolation, linear, and independent, the invitation is to start thinking ecosystem, circular, and interdependent because the latter ways of thinking allow us to create economic and ecological systems—our cities—that are regenerative, resilient, and adaptable. This means allowing ourselves to be moved to make the new work we long to do to improve our lives, because wanting to is enough, and because doing so is responsive to our self and city around us. This is responsible.

Would we change how we organize our cities if we were to make conscious choices?

If cities power innovation and our evolution, and if we make cities, we can explicitly choose what we would like our cities to be. Would we change how we organize our cities if we were to make conscious choices?

We Are a Planet of Cities

Settlements and cities have started and thrived when their physical, social, and economic habitats were in alignment. They declined—and ended—when the habitat changed and the city didn't, or couldn't, adjust.

Ancient civilizations met their demise because they couldn't adjust to changing life conditions: weather, food supply, environmental disasters, or economic conditions. Life conditions for a city can change quickly, such as wildfires in British Columbia that burned 3.3 million acres or and the Camp Fire in northern

California (153 thousand acres) that destroyed almost nineteen structures and killed 86 people in 2018, or Hurricane Sandy's destruction in New York City in 2012, or the tsunamis that hit Indonesia in 2004 and Japan in 2011. Life conditions can change over years or decades, and over large geographies, as with the North American drought of the 1930s.

Until recently, we have accepted that Earth's natural systems will, from time to time, upset a city's built habitats. We manage fire and earthquakes and snow loads with building codes. We build our cities in areas that are not prone to flooding. We build water and wastewater systems that provide clean drinking water and safely treat our wastewater. There are so many choices we make to create city habitats that work for us, yet it is always possible that events will still overtake us—that's life on Earth.

James Lovelock first articulated Earth system science, which became Gaia Theory, in the 1960s. Seeing Earth as a living system, he defined our home as "not the house or the street or the nation where we live, but the Earth itself."[51] Earth, or Gaia, is an emergent system on which climate and organisms are tightly coupled and evolve together.[52] As things change, we adjust to them. Gaia does the same. When we change her, we expect her to adjust. Lovelock's point is that Earth will self-regulate to survive, and she doesn't care if we survive or not. So if we wish to survive, we need to heighten our abilities to adapt to the changing world. To do that, we need to heighten our abilities to notice our habitat and our effect on our habitat.

Using any metric, it is impossible to ignore that the world is no longer the place with which we have become familiar; it is constantly changing. The staggering rates of population growth are enough for me to see that we are in an age of change, but I need only look at how our lives have changed in my fifty years. When I was a teenager my family bought one of the first desktop computers. Today, everyone in my home has several "computing devices," much more powerful, much smaller, and, more importantly, connected to the big wide world.

We are constantly adapting to the new world we create around us. The very nature of cities is changing because of our work, our economic life. The systems we put in place to organize ourselves, consciously and unconsciously, are in flux. The cities we build and how we build them are changing. The economic systems we create are changing. Our social systems and how we communicate are changing. We create the systems and structures that in turn create who we are. We shape our world in our day-to-day lives, with families and neighbours, with organizations, with cities and nations, and with the rest of humanity.

James Lovelock, Bill McKibben, Jared Diamond, and Tim Flannery argue that as a species we have overextended ourselves; we have overused our inheritance and threaten our own existence. The result may be an overcorrection, as nature does with any species that reaches too high a population, a possibility not difficult to imagine given our population growth. Perhaps, unlike earlier civilizations, we will cultivate our capacity to be conscious of the condition of our habitat and adapt. The stakes, though, are higher this time. This time the context to which we must adapt is not local in scale, but planetary. Our species, through our city-habitats, spans the planet. The well-being of all cities depends on the well-being of all other cities.

We face change that we have created for ourselves, and we must adapt. The good news is that adaptability is what got us here: new work, new ways of thinking, making, and doing. Yet to be adaptable, we need to be aware of that to which we must adapt. It means that we must be in relationship with our habitats—physical, social, and economic. This relationship is a survival skill we can hone, and in doing so citizens and cities will continue to evolve, as we have, in a more informed, conscious way.

THE IDEAS TAKING F L I G H T

1. While cities are not planned to be what they are today, they are intentional.

2. The number of cities, and the population of our cities, is growing dramatically.

3. The shape of a city is derived from its geography, its purpose, and the activities within and in connection to other cities and settlements. As each purpose for a city emerges, there is a corresponding mode of organizing that serves that purpose.

4. New work—new ways of thinking, making and doing— generates and regenerates our cities and allows us to adapt to our changing world, the world we are changing. This is a survival skill for the human species:

    a. Our habitat shapes our work, our work shapes our habitat, and as our habitat changes, our work changes and adapts with it.

    b. New work is purposefully in response to predictable or inexplicable changes to the world around us.

    c. For each of us, our work—and our approach to it—adds the necessary diversity to the economic life of our cities, at any scale.

5. The city is a natural habitat that we both inherit and create with each generation. Citizens and city nests have evolved hand in hand as we find new ways to think, make, and do. The times demand that we awaken to the relationship between our cities and us, and examine the well-being of our physical, social and economic habitats.

6. The cities we make for ourselves power innovation and our evolution and we can explicitly choose what we want our cities to be for us. Would we change how we organize our cities if we were to make conscious choices?

7. We face changes that we have created for ourselves and we must adapt. The good news is that adaptability is what got us here: new work, new ways of thinking, making, and doing.

8. Being in relationship with our cities is a survival skill.

NEST-MAKING PRACTICE
Noticing The Work In The City

I made no vows, but vows
Were then made for me
> *—William Wordsworth*

For David Whyte in **The Three Marriages**, Wordsworth's words reveal that "life comes to find us as much as we go out to find it."[53] Further,

> *life can find you only if you are paying real attention to some-*
> *thing other than your own concerns, if you can hear and see*
> *the essence of otherness in the world, if you can treat the world*
> *as if it is not just a backdrop to your own journey, if you can*
> *have a relationship with the world that isn't based on triumph-*
> *ing over it or complaining about it.*[54]

The world around us is the city. It provides us with a place to **do** the work we long to do, as well as a place to **look for and find** the work we long to do.

Finding the work that aligns with the essence of who we are can be immediately apparent for some of us. For others, it is a life-long journey, a quest to find out who we are deep inside. The time this takes is not relevant. For all of us, there is a contract that operates behind the scenes: there is a place for all of us—and our contributions through our work—in the city. When we offer ourselves, we make the city better for all of us.

REFLECT

Take a moment with a journal or sketchbook and see where the following questions take you. There are no wrong or right answers.

Self—What do I think, make, and do? What do I offer to others with my work (paid or unpaid)? What is the work I do with love?

Other—What is the work of others around me? Who loves the work they do? Who does not work with love? How does love of work affect what they offer to me and others and the city?

City—On the whole, what does the city offer to me as a citizen? What does it offer for all of us?

Care—In what ways does the work I do care for others? How does the work of care for me?

> **Reminder:** *"city" means the city-habitat we make for ourselves, the community around us, not our municipal government (often referred to as "the City").*

The imagination and its ability to discern bigger underlying patterns is just as important if not more important than a firm grasp of the details of what we want. The mighty interior wish is more important than mere outward details...
        —David Whyte[55]

THE CITY HABITAT IS A COLLECTIVE ENDEAVOUR

LEARNING AT WORK

A Guiding Truth of Many Truths

On a crisp September morning in 1991, in the yellow glow of fall and draped in frosty breath, I waited with excitement and trepidation for the bus that would take me to my first day of school in a new city. I was in Winnipeg on a whim; guided by intuition, I had applied for and been accepted into the city planning program in the Faculty of Architecture at the University of Manitoba. I had no idea what city planning was and wondered if I'd made the right decision. As I voraciously read Jane Jacobs' *Death and Life of Great American Cities* on my commute that day—and every day for days to come—I knew I *had* made the right choice. Even though I knew nothing about city planning, I knew this work would feed my soul. At 21 years old, Jane Jacobs served as the spark to help me find my passion: to learn about, understand and support the relationship we have with cities and with each other in our cities. At city planning school, I began to notice the work I was called to.

As I read Jacobs' ideas about cities and how they work, I kept thinking that, surely, planners were no longer the overzealous and heartless bureaucrats she'd encountered in the 1950s, uninterested in the vibrancy of cities and in the connection between citizens and their cities. In 1961, she observed:

> So many of the problems need never have arisen. If only well-meaning officials in departments of the city government or in freewheeling authorities knew intimately, and cared about, the streets or districts which there schemes so vitally effect—or if they knew in the least what the citizens of that place consider of value in their lives, and why. So many of the conflicts would never occur if planners and other supposed experts understood in the least how cities work and respected those workings.[56]

In the 29 years since that first bus ride, I have come to see the validity of her observation, though in today's context the nuance of that warning has changed. We are all—planners and citizens alike—mistaken to think that the creation of cities is the responsibility of the planners. True, planners have a role to play, but theirs is one of many specialized areas of work that contribute to the growth of a city. We are all responsible for the cities we create.

While I was a city planning student, two of my professors died. They both left me with important insight into how cities work. Professor Kent Gerecke taught me "the truth of many truths"—that many truths exist simultaneously. While previous classes had been on field trips to New York, Chicago, and Barcelona, he took my class to Saskatoon, Saskatchewan. We were a grumpy bus load of students in their early 20s, furious to be going to such a mundane place until we saw the magic that Gerecke could see: the system of systems at work in a city. We met people we would never have met in Chicago: the mayor, the president of the Chamber of Commerce, the head of the social housing agency, a draft dodger, a spectacular artist, and an environmentalist. We learned about the many perspectives from which people know their city and city life. Everyone we met held a piece of the truth.

Professor Christine McKee taught me about shepherding and guiding. My antennae were tuned to participatory design, a way of working I couldn't explore in the city planning program, so I drifted over to landscape architecture for a semester, only to be told that citizens are not smart enough to design our cities.

Professor McKee was the head of the city planning program and graciously accommodated my departure and my return. She made room for my learning journey, and did so without judgement. At her funeral, I learned more about her character and left inspired to choose to do the work I want, even if I didn't know exactly what it was. She showed me that the approach we take to our work as planners is as important, if not more so, as the work itself.

Both Gerecke and McKee revealed and modelled ways of experiencing the city that were counter-cultural. Instead of looking at the city as an objective science—exactly what Jacobs rebelled against—I learned to look at my knowledge as a planner as only one part of a city's bigger "truth." I also learned that, at times, the role of a planner is to shepherd or guide, not to decree exactly what to do and how to do it. Rather a planner can help people understand where they want to go and help them get there.

After completing my master's degree, I landed my first job as a planner with a planning district, serving a city of 40,000 (Brandon, Canada) and the two surrounding rural municipalities (Elton and Cornwallis). Here, I made the connection between Gerecke's and McKee's lessons—to be a good shepherd or guide, it was necessary to acknowledge that I only hold part of the truth and it was going to be necessary to build strong relationships. My first boss, Ron McCullough, understood the importance of healthy relationships among the players in his city and city-region. He knew the poor relationship between the development approvals office and its two main clients—people who want permission to develop their land and people who want to stop or change development of land—had to change. As McCullough put it, even though we were "the only game in town"—the government agency that everyone had to come to for permission to build and develop—we did not have to behave like we were the only game in town. That, for McCullough, was a choice. We can "beat people up" when they come in the door, or we can welcome them and help them reach their desires. McCullough knew that strong relationships between citizens and the building community were vital. His work to be helpful to the people he served, and support and guide his employees to do the same, was infectious—and helpful.

Similarly, McCullough was flexible in his approach to serving three diverse municipalities: one urban, and grappling with how to be the best city it could be; one rural, with a strong and clear focus on farming and agriculture; another rural, with much poorer quality agricultural land and desperate to be more connected to urban life. McCullough showed me—and the politicians we worked with—that all three "personalities" are valid, and he found ways to help them work together. When a big pork processing plant came to town, McCullough, along with other civic-minded players, played a key role in pulling together the public institutions (city government, school, and health officials) that were needed to accommodate the development and the arrival of many new citizens who would be employed by the plant and the business or service organizations that support the plant. He connected people from across the systems of the communities and found room for them to be heard, both within himself and others. He helped people talk to each other, enabling the city and region to take wise action.

As I worked with McCullough, I learned about the technical plans and rules guiding the physical development of our cities and regions. I learned how these rules influence the physical shape of our cities, but also how they relate to the economic and social worlds around us. Rules about hog barns, for example, need to balance the profitability of the farms with the environmental impact on land, water, and neighbours, as well as the quality of life for the hogs themselves. Construction standards affect the financial bottom line for builders and homeowners, while community standards provide safety and aesthetics guidelines. Hours and hours of public hearings, where I supported the citizens who needed to know how to participate and the politicians who wanted to understand the rules and how to change them to get what they wanted, taught me what the rules do, how they fit with a community's desires, and how organizing our cities is a subjective, highly political activity. I learned that it is necessary for the city—as a whole community— to know where it wants to go, then determine the rules that will provide the needed guidance to get there. The planner can help the city understand its direction, then propose the rules that will lead to that future.

No One Has Control

When I moved to Fort McMurray, Canada in 2005, in the heart of the burgeoning oil sands, I learned the value of moving slow, rather than frantically, to respond effectively to the challenges the community was facing. When I became general manager of the planning and development department, the city was in its sixth consecutive year of over nine per cent annual population growth. "Fort Mac" was growing so fast that infrastructure development could not keep up. The city and region did not have enough permanent or temporary housing for all the new workers, not enough schools for the kids, not enough room in the hospital. The housing that was in place was too expensive for public sector employees, making it a challenge to hire municipal, school, police, and health workers. Working for the municipality and living in the community, I saw and experienced intense pressure to resolve the community's stress.

In my first week on the job, the planning and development department presented a new, financially risky bylaw amendment to council for approval, laying out who would pay for city infrastructure as the city grew. The current bylaw was dramatically out of date, with a price tag for infrastructure that was far too low and that saw city government, i.e., citizens, paying far more than their fair share and the development community paying far less than its fair share. Council was in the middle of a public hearing about the proposed changes. Not surprisingly, the development community felt that the document was flawed, inaccurate, and full of errors. I leaned over to ask my new staff if the development community had been consulted on the new bylaw. They had not. I asked council to send the bylaw back to administration (me) for further review and consultation.

Here's what happened. The development community designated two representatives, each with eyes for details, people they would trust to take their city government to task. I grabbed my engineer. Then we sat and listened to each other while we pored over the document, line by line. We found operating principles that we agreed on. We found the places in the document that aligned with these principles and worked on the places where they didn't. This was an arduous task but worth the effort. When the revised bylaw was presented to council a year later, the development community supported the bylaw *and* were paying more infrastructure costs. No one was off the hook and it was clear who was paying for what.

While we took a year to finalize a document that suited both parties' needs, the process cemented an effective relationship that proved to be a solid foundation on which to add simple upgrades in the years to come, and even work on other initiatives. While some of my colleagues had difficulty working with the development community representatives, I found them open to building a positive relationship with their city government. Clear—and shared—objectives lead to clear and sensible rules that support transparent political processes. We moved slow enough to build good relationships, and as a result we created an accurate and fair quality document in a short amount of time. (A year for a controversial off-site levy bylaw is fast.) We understood that neither of us, the municipal government or a developer, had control over how things would unfold in the city. We chose to work together to better serve the city we were making.

No one person or one entity has control over what happens; everyone has responsibility for little bits and pieces. No one has the single ability to plan a city and make that plan come about.

The Citizen is in Relationship with the City

I see now that it was the citizen in me, as much as the city planner I would become, that drew me to Jacobs' work. Jacobs shaped the cities she lived in by being an active citizen and by fighting heartless bureaucratic planners who were set to build massive transportation routes through neighbourhoods. Her very simple descriptions of street life, and the value of that life to citizens, has resonated with her readers and followers for decades. They in turn have shaped streets and neighbourhoods well beyond those she lived in.

As I work with cities grappling to organize themselves in a way that will best meet their needs, I encounter diverse interests, agendas, and perspectives that make the re-creating of a city a messy and frustrating endeavour. City making is not a mechanical process with simple, linear steps. On the contrary, it is complex, uncertain, unpredictable—and often the "right path" is not clear. No one person or one entity has control over what happens; everyone has responsibility for little bits and pieces. No one has the single ability to plan a city and make that plan come about.

Order emerges from chaos, however, and Jacobs teases out some patterns for us. She knows that active sidewalks encourage people to interact with each other, generating resiliency and innovation. She knows that economic quality of life is critical to a city's existence. She knows that our choices shape cities, and in return our cities shape us; we are in a reciprocal relationship with our habitat. The patterns she highlights have helped me identify a question that is at the heart of this book. **How can we organize ourselves in cities so that we purposefully create habitats that learn and grow along with us?**

To contemplate this question, we must weave together three threads, each of which must be healthy: our self, our relationship with others, and our city. As individuals, we must be healthy for the collective population to be healthy. Where we can, we must aim to work in areas we are passionate about because this makes us feel alive. The quality of our relationships with each other—the social habitat we create—also nourishes us and enables us to do the work we love. And when these first two threads are healthy, then the city we make as a result allows us to thrive rather than merely survive. When we feel alive, our city comes alive, and when our city comes alive we feel more alive. This is, in fact, a pattern that goes back to the beginning of cities.

CITY WORK BELONGS TO ALL

In Integral City, Marilyn Hamilton offers a simple way to see where we all fit in city life. She builds on Ken Wilber's integral theory framework, which invites us to see—and integrate into our ways of knowing of and being in the world—all of the relationships between and among the individual and collective experiences of the world around us and the world within. He suggests a way to see a complete view of the world, his *Theory of Everything* (the title of one of his books), that Hamilton applies to the city. The result is a complete—or integral—view of the city that considers four perspectives (Figure G[57]), each of which offers an essential role in city life. If any of these views are missing from how we look at cities, we are not looking at the whole city.

In very simple terms, to consider a whole city, four perspectives need to be considered. First, **civic managers**, the elected officials and staff who are responsible for looking after the public interest, are our local government, school boards, and health authorities. In many ways, they regulate citizen behaviour. Second, **civic**

builders and developers, those who build the cities we live in, are the developers, builders, and contractors who build the structures of our city. They are the business community. Third, our **civic organizations** offer a different perspective as the service organizations, not-for-profits, and community organizations. They are the collective conscience and culture of the city. And fourth, perhaps the most familiar perspective, of individual citizens, the people who live in our communities. Each of us has a perspective of the city in a way that no one else does. Each of us needs from, and offers to, the city something different.

As citizens, we often find ourselves using more than one of these voices. I frequently work for local governments, so I identify with the civic manager perspective, but I recognize other voices in my choices as well. I was a civic builder when I decided to renovate my home, rather than knock it down and rebuild; on a small scale I contributed to the built environment of my street. I'm also a volunteer with my neighbourhood association working on quality of life matters in our neighbourhood. As a citizen, I willingly pay property taxes as an investment in the collective services I receive. I also chose to send my children to neighbourhood schools because I value schools as a place to create a sense of community with neighbours, and for schools to remain open, they need to have students in them. (These are my choices, my relationship with my city, but not necessarily the right choices for you.)

Figure G
What Integral City
Perspectives Explore

Each of these perspectives plays a role in the creation and re-creation of our communities and cities; they are most often separate from each other in silos, interacting only when necessary. Usually, we fight with each other. Imagine, for example, citizens in conflict with city hall or a developer, or a ratepayer community organization with city hall, or an environmental group with a developer. We are always in relationship with each other, often with tension and the purposes of the city, and the levels of organizing in the city, evolving within and between these relationships. The city is a dance of perspectives, purposes, and modes of organizing.

How we experience the city, through our individual life conditions, shapes what we value, what we find important. The necessary tension in cities, that pulls us into conflict and new realities, is a result of the variety of life conditions experienced by the inhabitants of the city; citizens do not have a uniform experience of the city.

As we organize ourselves in cities, citizens attend to our collective needs, according to what we find important in our experience of the city: volunteers serve at a food bank to help hungry people in survival mode; new immigrants assemble to cultivate a sense of belonging and identity in a new place; the fire department responds to emergencies in "do" mode; municipal governments establish order with bylaws regulating on-street parking; the chamber of commerce seeks strategic economic advantage; social justice groups demand participative decision-making processes. As a whole, we undertake these activities to organize ourselves and create habitats in which we will thrive. In this diversity of work, we are serving our personal passions and the needs of others in our city—all because we respond to our economic, social, and physical habitats.

What we value shapes the purpose we see for the city and thus shapes how we organize ourselves.

What we value—whether survival, belonging, power, authority, entrepreneurialism, diversity, or some way of finding room for each of these—shapes the purpose we see for the city and thus shapes how we organize ourselves. The integral city model also reminds us that we all have a legitimate and vital role to play in city life. City builders organize themselves to physically construct our city. Civic organizations organize the social and cultural life in our cities; they look after various non-physical qualities of our cities and hold us to account. Citizens, in our day-to-day experience, bring life to the city with every choice we make, particularly when we follow our passions in our work—whether paid or unpaid. Civic managers create the minimal critical structure on which cities sit, with pipes, roads, buildings and rules; they are our municipal government, health services, and schools. Each of the city's voices shape the city, all at once, creating a world of messiness and uncertainty because no one entity has control of a city. Improving our cities is work that belongs to all of us all at once.

CITY HABITAT INTERACTIONS ENABLE DYNAMIC STEERING

Three City Habitats

As discussed in Chapter One, the large, evolutionary purpose of a city is to create a habitat in which citizens generate new ways to think, make, and do. We build nests that spur improvement, that motivate us to spread our wings and try new activities and experiences. The city nest occupies three essential habitats: economic, social, and physical— nests within nests, nests interwoven.

Figure H
City Habitat

Economic Life Is the Heart

Our economic life, the sphere in which we exchange our work with one another, particularly new work, is at the heart of the dynamic that creates and recreates cities (Figure H). At a minimum, we work to ensure personal well-being of self and family. If no one did any work, we would not exist. We have to make an effort to survive; it doesn't just happen.

The location of our work varies greatly: some people work at home, others in the fields or the barn, on a construction site, in an office, or on a train. Largely, our work is a transaction; we get something in return for the work we do. At a survival level, work may be building shelter and growing food for our families. When we can't perform these survival tasks ourselves, we work for others who can share those skills with us. As work becomes specialized in cities, we receive money for our work that we exchange for shelter, food, clothing, and if affluent enough, the enjoyment of a myriad goods and services. When we volunteer for community events or work in our homes, money is not involved at all. But that is still work. Paid and unpaid work is everywhere.

The common thread in our work lives is a transaction with others. As a species, we do not live alone, but within a vast series of interconnections. At the scale of the city, our economic life is the accumulation of all our work, combining and interacting, transacting. Our work creates our physical, social, and economic worlds; this is what builds our cities. We inherit our physical habitat, but our work changes it. We all build and create: individually we plant flowers, maintain our homes, build garages; collectively we build highways, swimming pools, airports, and social technologies. Our work—past, present and new—makes our cities.

Physical Habitat Holds It All

The largest nest in Figure H is the physical habitat in which we live, the habitat we are given when we arrive in the world and the habitat we make and remake with our work. A city's existence hangs on its physical, environmental context, starting with what Jacobs calls an "inheritance:" a natural resource with which to develop work.

Living in Alberta, Canada, my province's economic life relies on oil and gas resources, a resource we have developed for generations.

The economic life of most of the province relates to this resource as we develop new, specialized work to construct oil wells, mines, processing facilities, equipment, roads and pipelines over the landscape. We have grown cities and built new cities to accommodate the extraction of oil and gas for cities across the planet.

In my prairie city, agriculture came first, which was then buttressed by oil and gas extraction. Today my city actively seeks to diversify our economy, building upon these initial resources and create new work. And as we work, we recreate the physical world around us; sometimes we do so with an awareness of the impact our work has on the physical well-being of the planet; other times we do not.

We constantly create new work, which in turn creates the conditions for more diverse work, generating more change to which we must adapt.

An important note: the physical habitat of a city includes more than the environment within the city's boundaries. It includes all the resources we draw on for city life: food and water, materials for shelter, energy generation, and the long-distance transportation of resources. Land, water, and air across the planet are connected to my city's life, as are the human and other inhabitants of the planet. The city reaches outward, and the wild, remote, and rural reaches inward, inextricably linked. Our physical habitat scales from the immediately local to our planet and beyond.

New work in relation to our habitat continues to be an operating principle, whether we are responding to changes we are making, such as the shift in cities to accommodate modes of transportation other than the car, and changes that happen to us, like climate change. Along the way, we constantly create new work, which in turn creates the conditions for more diverse work, generating more change to which we must adapt.

Social Habitat Is Our Contract

Between our economic life and our physical habitat lies our social habitat the place where we allow—or disallow—connections with our economic life and physical habitat. Here, we create the conditions, individually and collectively, to notice what is happening around us and integrate our world with our work, our work with our world. This is where we integrate our cities with our work, our work with our cities.

We are social creatures who gather and work together. Whether implicit or explicit, the reason we gather is to create the conditions for finding new and improved ways of doing things. Together, rather than alone, we physically create cities to face our challenges, but we also create a social habitat conducive to facing the challenges.

The quality of our social life—our social habitat—affects our economic life and our ability to create the conditions in which we can thrive. In cities, we organize ourselves socially, creating the world in which we live. We continually make new connections between citizens and work, and the more our social habitat fosters connections, the more resilient we become.

In the social habitat, there are written and unwritten agreements of care needed in this collective endeavour. The quality of this environment dictates the quality of communication we have between our economic life and our physical habitat. Even when conflict erupts, this contract remains in place; that we are in relationship with each other is unavoidable. We have three choices: not to look after self, others, and the world around us; selectively look after self, others, and the world around us; or look after self, others, and the world around us. Like a valve in the heart, the choices are closed, blocked, or open. Only the latter ensures that life thrives.

That we are in relationship with each other is unavoidable.

The Relationships Between the Habitats
The city dynamic consists of endless feedback loops, going in all directions all at once (Figure I)—threads and twigs of different length and breadth interwoven between and among the nests we create and recreate. Looking at cities from an evolutionary perspective, our physical habitat holds everything. Within that, we have evolved socially to create opportunities for new work, a feature of our economic life that generates cities, and in turn recreates our physical habitat. Each nest is essential, with a distinct role to play.

I have layered these nests together, building on the lineage of our current understanding of sustainable development, rooted in the World Commission on Environment and Development's 1987 report, *Our Common Future*. Known as the Brundtland Commission, this report inserted into our collective consciousness the relationship between economic development and ecological

Figure I
City
Habitat
Dynamic
Activity

disaster. This is typically displayed as a Venn diagram, noting the relationship between economic, environmental and social pillars as separate and overlapping considerations, with a sweet spot—sustainability—in the middle. (Put "sustainable development Venn diagram" in your search engine.) I have rearranged these as nested, concentric circles to demonstrate that no single aspect of our lives operates independently, even partially. No parts of our economic life and social habitat exist in isolation of our physical habitat. It is not possible, for example, to look at economy and ecology (physical habitat) without the social; all is interwoven and interconnected.

Three relationships occur within the city habitat: between economic life and social habitat, between social habitat and physical habitat, and between economic life and physical habitat through social habitat.

Economic Life and Social Habitat

In the relationship between economic life and social habitat, we make personal investments to come up with ideas and turn them into new work. Likewise, we organize ourselves in ways that shape our collective investments in the idea—the labour we put to it, the skills we put to it, or the "human potentialities," as Jacobs says, shape the idea. In the workplace or in a community, for example, new ways of thinking, making, and doing emerge when they are welcomed; they likely remain invisible or non-existent if the social habitat is hostile.

At a societal level, sometimes we are not ready for new things until our context changes. For example, sixty years ago, my home was built with no insulation. Energy prices were low and the notion of human-caused climate change did not exist. In contrast, today we have building codes with minimal requirements for energy efficiency and government grants to upgrade older homes.

As our social habitat changes, so does our work. And as our work changes, so does our social habitat. Nowhere is this more clear than the adjustments we have made to life with computers, the Internet, and social media.

Social Habitat and Physical Habitat

The relationship between the social habitat and the physical habitat reflects the relationship between self and the human-made and natural worlds. Here, we notice our physical world, how it works, how it changes, and where we fit. This includes the social relationship we each have with the city we build.

The city does two things: it encourages us to weave ourselves among each other while simultaneously encouraging us to keep our distance.

The city does two things: it encourages us to weave ourselves among each other while simultaneously encouraging us to keep our distance. We design transportation systems that allow thousands and millions of people to live in a centralized area and at the same time create space between us. We design parks that allow people to congregate for public events and that also allow small groups of people or individuals to enjoy quiet. We design buildings and streets with both public and private spaces, providing social space and private refuge. The city asks us to be individuals and a collective in myriad ways and it does so with physical structures we make for ourselves.

Our physical world, however, is more than the city we make; it is also the physical habitat within which the city is located. The city is part of the natural world, even hundreds or thousands years after the original settlement, because we are always in relationship to the world around us. This can be seen, for example, in a study on flooding in Ontario, Canada, that notes that flood damage has replaced fire damage as the number one cause of household insurance claims in that province. Historic levels of precipitation are expected as a result of climate change and urban and rural communities are looking for ways to increase their resiliency: policies need to change to improve capacity to prepare and recover from flooding; efforts are fragmented and cause concern about their effectiveness; financial capacity is in question; and community and political buy-in is needed to address both present and future flood risks.[58] Acknowledging flooding as a consequence of our actions demands emotional maturity before we will be able to take responsibility and action. Even more emotional maturity: accepting that our local actions have devastating and life-threatening consequences in other areas of the planet. An unhealthy social habitat renders us unable to see and understand the challenges we face. A healthy habitat does not ensure we see everything, but allows us to look and anticipate as best we can.

Just as our social habitat affects our view of the physical world around us, the physical habitat can help create healthy social habitats. When we have a relationship with the natural, wild world, either in the city or outside the city, we observe how nature works—which is also our nature. In addition, noticing how the physical world we make serves us well, or harms us, is vital. For example, do we design transportation systems that keep people safe and cause no harm to the natural world? If we destroy the natural world in the making of our cities, we have destroyed the fundamental habitat on which we rely.

Economic Life and Physical Habitat

The relationship between our economic life—our work—and our physical habitat is only as healthy as the feedback that flows between the two, and the quality of our cities depends on this flow. This relationship is unique because it requires travelling through the social habitat. Our social habitat creates the conditions for a relationship *with* our physical habitat and our economic life and *between* our physical habitat and our economic life. In this relationship, we recognize explicitly that the city affects our work and that our work affects our city. We boldly look for feedback to link these three spheres.

When we allow ourselves to see the physical world and the challenge posed by flooding, for example, as above, our work will shift. Scientists will dig into the issues and the implications;

others will advocate for better understanding in our communities, some of whom will serve as political leaders. Government administrators will change policies and programs to meet the new societal understanding, and engineers, architects, and developers will build the physical changes we need in our cities, from installing sewer back-up valves, increasing the capacity of pipes to carry storm water or relocating some communities.

Each Relationship Involves Social Habitat

Each of these relationships involves our social habitat, where there are degrees of mutual support and information exchange. As a whole, the city is a habitat that encompasses our economic, social, and physical habitats. Our social habitat allows the new work that creates and recreates our cities to take place in the context of our physical habitat. This means that new work is needed to create a social sphere that allows the necessary data to flow between our physical environment and our economic life. The quality of the relationship between our economic life and our social and physical habitats shapes our ability to generate cities that meet our economic, social, and physical needs.

To continue with the flooding example, if we choose to close off our social habitat, we will not see the requirements of our physical world, or we will not see the new requirements of our work, our contribution to our economic habitat. Our social habitat is a place where we brave hearing about the consequences of our actions and organize ourselves in response to our life conditions. Social habitat is an essential aspect to city making.

More Interactions Mean More Adaptability

The more activity between the city habitats, the more responsive citizens are to the needs of the city, and the more responsive the city is to the needs of its inhabitants. In Figure I, therefore, an abundance of thread and twigs means more communities are interacting with each other. If nest infrastructure is sparse, economic life—our work—is not adapting to meet the demands of changing social and physical habitats.

The interweaving of habitats allows information to move, but this movement is not enough. The quality of our economic life and social habitat must enable receiving information and, further, to be open to integrating the information and finding appropriate ways to adapt and act on it. We must individually and collectively be prepared to *be changed* by our *changing* world; we must be prepared to think, make, and do new things. Jacobs' work reveals three patterns about the way that new work functions:

- The development of new work allows the creation of new ideas to respond to life conditions.

- The expansion of new work allows the implementation of new ideas in response to life conditions.

- A habitat that is conducive to change and adjustment is needed to link the development and expansion of new work.

When our social habitat allows us to deepen into the work we long to do, to the improvements we long to enact, we tune into the world around us. This interaction grows our ability to create and recreate cities. Allowing our work to respond and adjust to the ways we experience life becomes, then, a survival skill. With this skill we can adjust our path; without it we cannot.

When our social habitat allows us to deepen into the work we long to do, to the improvements we long to enact, we tune into the world around us.

We need to approach our city systems in ways that allow for feedback and adjustment. Brian Robertson describes this as "dynamic steering,"[59] where regular, real feedback leads to immediate adjustments, whether at the scale of citizen or planet. Imagine the system is you, riding a bicycle. As you move along, you start to tip, so you adjust your balance or your speed to remain upright. Ahead, you see a pothole and you adjust, steering around the hazard in the road. Even though you can't predict the hazards, you adjust your response when you need to.

We usually operate in a predict-and-control stance—we anticipate what is going to happen and make adjustments before events unfold, assuming that future events will follow a similar course as past events and require a similar response. However, a predict-and-control mode does not allow for appropriate responses to life conditions because only minimal feedback takes place between the habitats of the city. Imagine riding a bicycle with your arms out stiff in front of you; you aren't able to respond to your surroundings—at least not comfortably.

Cities need to be responsive. Just like when riding a bicycle, we need to be aware of our surroundings—the bumps and turns along the way—while simultaneously keeping our eyes on where we are going. Our ability to notice when we have moved off track—and to get back on track—matters. Our ability to do the work at hand matters. Are we building the right kind of infrastructure? Are we properly maintaining the infrastructure we have? Do we have the right balance of roads and public transportation? Our approach to our work matters.

In today's cities, with today's challenges, we have an opportunity to be explicit about the cities we are creating and how they shape us in return. It is time to integrate our economic, social, and physical worlds in ways that respond to the changing conditions in our world. We need to learn to dynamically steer our cities into the future in a way that allows them to flourish. Learning to be more adaptable than we have been in the past is key. We need to be open to feedback and willing to take action. There is lots of work to do.

Organize for Adaptability
Adaptability ensures we survive and thrive. Consider the staggering rate of population and city growth, or the symptoms of climate change, for example. We are going to have to adjust, and quickly. That means we have to welcome change, quickly examine the necessary adjustments, and take timely, appropriate action. Getting bogged down in distractions is not helpful—we have to grow our capacity to adapt and improve.

1. City work belongs to everyone. No one person or one entity has control over what happens in the city. No one has the single ability to plan a city and make that plan come about. Everyone has responsibility for the various bits and pieces.

2. Citizens know about the city and city life from many perspectives; each perspective holds a piece of the truth. In *Integral City*, Marilyn Hamilton offers four perspectives:

    a. Civic managers create the minimal critical structure on which cities sit: pipes and roads, buildings and rules.

    b. Civic builders and developers organize themselves to physically construct and be the business of our cities.

    c. Civic organizations organize the social and cultural life in our cities; they look after various non-physical qualities of our cities and hold us to account.

    d. Citizens bring life to our cities with every choice they make, particularly when they follow their passion in their work (paid or unpaid).

3. Three city habitats require particular attention, and the more activity between them, the more responsive citizens are to the needs of the city, and the more responsive the city is to the needs of its inhabitants:

    •   Our economic life, the sphere in which we exchange our work with one another, particularly new work, is the force that creates and recreates cities.

    •   Our physical habitat holds everything. A city's physical well-being relies on our relationship with our physical habitat, the one we are given when we arrive in the world and the one we make and remake with our work. The work we do is in relationship with our physical habitat.

- Our social habitat, in which we name and act upon the agreement of care we share with each other in the collective work of city making. Our social habitat creates the conditions for a relationship with our physical habitat and our economic life and between our physical habitat and our economic life.

4. The city affects our work and our work affects our city. In this never-ending relationship that shapes our cities—and us—we choose (or not) to look after self, others and the world around us.

NEST-MAKING PRACTICE
Being Dynamically Stable

Our city habitat constantly presents us with challenges that compel us to take action, to improve ourselves and our cities. In the messiness of life, we are invited to be dynamically stable and to steer well. To do this, we need to willingly receive feedback and explicitly seek feedback, even if what we learn is difficult to hear. Honest feedback is needed for us as citizens and as a city.

Being open to and aware of the world around us takes courage because it allows us to see ourselves, others and the city fully and honestly. We might hear we need to change what we think, make, and do because it's no longer working. We might have to change our work. We might have to move in a new direction, and as a result we might have to change how we organize. We might have to give up most of what we know about our work and the identity we associate with that work, either as self or as a city. Being dynamically stable means we are willing to look at the changing conditions around us and be willing to make adjustments. It also means that we are willing to choose a clear destination and provide ourselves with the support we need to make the journey. It means we choose to consciously create our nest city.

REFLECT

Take a moment with a journal or sketchbook and see where the following questions take you. There are no wrong or right answers.

Self—What do I appreciate in the city around me? What brings me joy? What improvements do I see are needed in the city around me? How does my experience of the city—the joy and improvements—shape my work in subtle or dramatic ways? What is the work I long to do?

Other—What work are others doing to bring me joy in my city? What work are they doing to improve my experience of city life? How are they organizing themselves?

City—What efforts does my city make to bring the four city voices (civic institutions, city builders and developers, civic organizations, and citizens) together to help the city see itself? What are we collectively called to respond to?

Care—What support do I need to allow honest feedback? What do others need? What does my city need?

> *Reminder: "city" means the city-habitat we make for ourselves, the community around us, not our municipal government (often referred to as "the City").*

*[L]ots of things that seem impossible to comprehend become more un-
derstandable if we identify the basic pattern and watch what it produces
through repetition. It's a way of dealing with some complexities that
otherwise are impenetrable.*
　　　—Jane Jacobs[60]

*I...find it useful to speak of an evolutionary impulse that is active across
every domain of existence—from matter to life to mind and spirit. It is
significant that this impulse operates...toward the seemingly miraculous
emergence of new potentials—tending over time toward greater complexity, more sophisticated forms of intelligence, and more powerful forms of
cooperation.*
　　　—Terry Patten[61]

3

CITIES ARE EVOLUTIONARY SYSTEMS

EVOLUTIONARY BURST

Organizing ourselves into and within cities is a process that requires organizing intelligence. There is no recipe to thrive, no plan per se, but as evolutionary pattern-thinker Don Beck would say, there are patterns in the life conditions. Beck and Christopher Cowan, drawing on Clare Graves's work from the 1970s, introduced the Spiral Dynamics theory, revealing how organizing principles emerge in humans and how they bolster our social systems. [62] In Chapter One, we saw the Spiral in the evolving layers of purpose and modes of organizing when we looked at the story of St. John's, Newfoundland. In this chapter, we consider Spiral Dynamics as a model to explore human evolution and connect this model to cities.

If the purpose of cities is to support the growth and evolution of citizens, then it is necessary to understand the evolutionary forces in play. For example, in the past decade, the nature of our engagement with self, other, and the city has evolved significantly: our relationships with each other via smartphones, texting, and social media have been rewired. We are in contact with each other, locally and globally, in ways unforeseen only a few years ago; information is distributed quickly and we are both more informed and more misinformed than ever before. We use social media to organize ourselves—to share information, to get to know each other, to rally, to have fun, and to protest. Social media does not remove our desire to create cities that serve us well or minimize our desire for face-to-face contact. In many ways, it helps us see ourselves and our cities better. We hunger for contact, and technology is providing another way for us to connect and communicate. Just as communication sparked an evolutionary burst in humanity sixty thousand years ago and the printing press almost six hundred years ago, the digital age is sparking another evolutionary burst now.

We are also in the process of reorganizing the energy sources that power our cities, moving from fossil fuels to non-carbon-based energy. We are imagining how our cities can best work when they are home to millions and millions more people. It's time to ask ourselves: What needs our attention, so the sparks of evolutionary bursts do not turn into fires that consume us?

What needs our attention, so the sparks of evolutionary bursts do not turn into fires that consume us?

The evolution of the city of St. John's highlights patterns of human activity that reveal its citizens' evolutionary intelligence. Here's where Beck and Cowan's work in Spiral Dynamics helps us see human organizing principles in relation to social systems. Imagine the double-helix spiral of our DNA and the work that has been done to catalogue our genes—the codes that guide our physical being. Now imagine a similar spiral that catalogues our cultural codes, our organizing principles. These principles, found in the value systems that emerge as we evolve, have been coined value memes, or vMemes for short (sounds like genes).[63]

vMemes are codes—behavioural instructions passed from one generation to the next, social artifacts, and value-laden symbols that sustain social systems. They embrace our worldviews, our assumptions about how the world works, and the rationale for our decision-making.[64] We evolve and grow through these vMemes as individuals, families, cultures, workplaces, cities, nations, and humanity.

Beck and Cowan's vMemes are reflected in the evolving purposes of St. John's and the corresponding modes of organizing described in Chapter One. The first six vMemes, represented by the colours Beige through Green in Table 1[65], focus on subsistence. Beige forms the base and is explicitly about surviving. When our basic needs are met, we survive together and make sense of the magical world in groups (Purple). When resources become scarce, our groups compete for independence (Red). When we need stability, rules, institutions, and protocols emerge (Blue). When those rules get in the way, entrepreneurial, creative spirits arise (Orange). When uncomfortable with the achievement orientation of Orange, Green emerges and seeks caring and socially responsible communities. These first six vMemes have little tolerance for each other: we see great conflict between the values of competition and community and between the power of the individual versus the role of the collective.

A monumental leap takes place in our development as we reach the seventh vMeme, Yellow, with a desire to integrate the first six. Turquoise, the eighth vMeme, embodies further integration and a new, larger experience of the world. A ninth vMeme, Coral, is emerging and researchers are working to identify and define this set of values and how it shows up in the world.

THE vMeme	WHAT IS THE VALUE	WHAT IT LOOKS LIKE
CORAL	To be determined	To be determined
8 TURQUOISE wholeness	Experience the holistic existence through mind and spirit	Paying attention to whole Earth dynamics and macro-level actions, being part of a larger, conscious whole
7 YELLOW integration	Live fully and responsively as what you are and learn to become	Adapting to change through connected, big-picture views, living in ways that focus energy
6 GREEN community	Seek peace within the inner self and explore, with others, the caring dimensions of community	Fostering the well-being of people, building consensus, responding to feelings, cultivating socially responsible community
5 ORANGE achievement	Act in your own self-interest by playing the game to win	Displaying symbols of success, recognizing individual for their achievements, welcoming challenges for improvement, focusing on possibility
4 BLUE purpose	Acknowledge left has meaning, direction and purpose with predetermined outcomes	Adhering to traditions and absolute belief in one right way, honouring loyalty, obeying family
3 RED impulse	Be what you are, do what you want	Storytelling about heroes, celebrating feats of conquest, respecting power
2 PURPLE magic	Keep spirits happy and the group's nest warm and safe	Observing rituals, finding reassurance, expressing enthusiasm in life's mystery, belonging
1 BEIGE survival	Do what you must to stay alive	Staying alive through innate sensory equipment, meeting sustenance needs

Table 1
The vMemes

Clare Graves value systems, adapted from Cowan and Beck

In city life, vMemes occur naturally. No vMeme is "better" than another, and, as my Spiral Dynamics colleague Marilyn Hamilton says, they each have "their dignities and disasters." They are useful, though, because they help us understand different perspectives of the world and its complexity. They give us clues about people's behaviours and motivations as we navigate city life. They tell us about the types of thinking that naturally occur in us. As a body of work, Spiral Dynamics recognizes patterns, allowing for a deeper understanding of the role of cities—and ourselves—in human development.

Table 2
Modes of
Organizing
Using vMemes

In Chapter One, we noticed how different modes of organizing emerged as the purpose of a city evolved. We saw how the ways we think—our worldviews, our vMemes—shape our city's economic, social, and physical habitats. Table 2[66] provides further insight into modes of organizing using vMemes.

THE vMEME	THINKING	STRUCTURES	PROCESS	MODE OF ORGANIZATION	ILLUSTRATION
CORAL					
8 TURQUOISE wholeness	HOLISTIC	GLOBAL	FLOWING AND ECOLOGICAL	HARMONIZE	
7 YELLOW integration	SYSTEMIC	INTERACTIVE	INTEGRATIVE	INTEGRATE	
6 GREEN community	RELATIVISTIC	EGALITARIAN	CONSENSUAL	FLOAT	
5 ORANGE achievement	MULTIPLISTIC	DELEGATIVE	STRATEGIC	STRATEGIZE	
4 BLUE purpose	ABSOLUTIST	PYRAMIDAL	AUTHORITARIAN	PLAN	
3 RED impulse	EGOCENTRIC	IMPERIAL	EXPLOITATIVE	DO	
2 PURPLE magic	ANIMISTIC	GROUP	CIRCULAR	GATHER	
1 BEIGE survival	AUTOMATIC	LOOSE THREADS	SURVIVALISTIC	REACT	

Clare Graves value systems, adapted from Cowan and Beck

FRAMING PRINCIPLES

Beck and Cowan use seven principles to describe the Spiral's core intelligence: the patterns in our emerging value systems.[67] Let's take a closer look at each of these principles and how they apply to human systems at any scale, including cities.

....

PRINCIPLE 1
Humans are able to create new vMemes

Looking back over the history of the human species,[68] we see that fifty thousand years ago people formed tribes and experienced magic, art, and spirits (Purple). Ten thousand years ago, warlords, conquest, and discovery dominated (Red). Five thousand years ago, literature, monotheism, and purpose emerged (Blue). Mobility, individualism, and economics came to the fore one thousand years ago (Orange), while 150 years ago, human rights, liberty, and collectivism emerged (Green). Only fifty years ago, complexity, chaos, and interconnections surfaced (Yellow), and an eighth level, emerged thirty years ago with a new discourse on globalism and eco-consciousness (Turquoise). As humanity grows and develops, we create new values, new worldviews. It is assumed a ninth level, Coral, is possible and likely. With time, the traits that define it will emerge.

The creation of new vMemes is exemplified in the ideas of city historian Lewis Mumford,[69] who notes a progression in human life from movement to settlement, which brought a "deliberate remolding of the environment" to create the village, which includes the "embryonic structure of the city" (Purple). With the development of agricultural societies, the role of the hunter changed from securing food to protecting the village; skills shifted from slaughtering game to "the more highly organized vocation of regimenting or slaughtering other men" (Red). As villages grew, they transformed into towns and then cities; the city was the essential organ of "accumulative activity." The first cities were ruled by kings and monarchs (Red) and were often built as walled fortresses. In these cities, "specialized work became for the first time an all-day, year-round occupation."[70] And as more people inhabited these cities, rules of law and order (Blue) surfaced, with cities recognized as "the seat of law and justice, reason and equity … To appeal from irrational custom or lawless violence, one must seek the protection of the court of law in the city."[71]

The city also became a tool for colonization and imperialist expansion. For example, from the seventh century BC to the fourth, the small, self-contained towns of Greece "sent out colonies in every direction, and in particular to Sicily and to Italy: they ranged from Marseille at the mouth of the Rhone to Naucratis in the delta of the Nile, and eastward to the shores of the Black Sea."[72] In more recent times, this same story repeats itself as the imperial forces arrived on the shores of North America to start the colonial story of St. John's, with which we are already familiar. The story of the city is thousands of years old and it reflects this first principle—that we are able to create new vMemes.

PRINCIPLE 2
Life conditions awaken vMemes

vMemes are not scripted; they are a result of dynamic interaction between our internal states and our external world—our life conditions. The age we live in, the place we inhabit, the problems we face, and the social circumstances we find ourselves in shape our beliefs, ideas, and values. (See Table 3[73]).

When I was a child, it was socially acceptable to "drink and drive." Party-goers wouldn't think twice about getting in their cars and driving after a night of drinking. In the 1980s, as I was learning to drive and had access to alcohol, anti-drinking and driving campaigns began to increase awareness of the preventable deaths caused by drunk driving. Slowly, as stories of hardship and sadness emerged, it was no longer acceptable to drive drunk. The lawlessness of drivers deciding if they were fit to drive (Red) gave way to standards, tests, and rules (Blue). At the same time, penalties became more severe, including possible jail time, if drivers were under the influence of alcohol. Today, similar regulations ensure that drivers are not distracted by mobile phones, a new rule in response to the changing world around us (Blue).

PRINCIPLE 3
vMemes alternate between "me" and "we"

Imagine a pendulum swinging between two poles. At one pole, I define myself as a freestanding individual, and at the other I define myself in terms of my group (Table 4[74]). When focused on the individual, I generate hierarchies to establish my position, and when focused on the collective, hierarchies are flattened and I blend in; I become part of the whole. There is a necessary relationship between these two poles in that the more the pendulum swings toward one, the more it is propelled toward the other.

When I reflect on my settler lineage on the Canadian Prairies, I can imagine the drive for a new life that propelled my ancestors to leave their homeland in Europe to come to North America. My Norwegian ancestors settled in a place where other Norwegians had settled, providing a sense of belonging (Purple) among waves of immigrants from other cultures, colonizing the territory of Indigenous peoples at the invitation of the Canadian government. My great-grandfather could see battles of cultures for power (Red) and he realized that with our white skin we were at an advantage and able to blend in within a generation. He changed the family name to sound more like the dominant English settler culture, and he did not teach his children to speak Norwegian, so they sounded like dominant English settler culture. The identity of my family (Red) took a backseat to the need to blend in with the dominant culture (Blue).

The influx of European settlers in the 19th and early-20th centuries was followed by waves of immigrants from around the world. Today in Edmonton, at workplaces and in schools, an amazing mix of cultures can be seen simply in our names. My great-grandfather's notion of blending in is no longer so urgent. While there is still a pecking order of cultures (Orange), they are blending, and there is far more tolerance for diversity (Green) in ways that allow individuals to stay connected to their culture.

As a city, Edmonton has matured to a point where its leaders and citizens are contemplating what it means to be—as a settler culture—living in a place that is the original territory of Indigenous peoples and subject to Treaty 6, an agreement signed by First Nations leaders and the Queen of England and her commissioners in 1876. The "us and them" of Indigenous and non-Indigenous people, an I/me/mine perspective, is becoming more visible, as are the harmful consequences of colonial forces against

Indigenous peoples. We are finding a way to understand the truths of our past and present relationships and to reconcile hurts known and unknown, allowing us to reach into our shared humanity. As we grow and as we swing back and forth between individual and collective orientations, we bring what we have learned, expanding our understanding of the world.

THe vmeme

	IF THE LIFE CONDITIONS ARE . . .	EXPECT PEOPLE TO . . .
CORAL		
8 TURQUOISE wholeness	a single living entity	see the order beneath the earth's chaos
7 YELLOW integration	at risk of chaotic collapse	learn how to be free but also principled
6 GREEN community	shared habitat of all humanity	join community to experience shared growth
5 ORANGE achievement	full of viable alternatives	pragmatically test for advantages to succeed
4 BLUE purpose	directed by a higher power	obey higher authority and be faithful to the Truth
3 RED impulse	tough and dangerous	fight to survive in spite of what others want
2 PURPLE magic	mysterious and frightening	placate spirits and join together for safety
1 BEIGE survival	a state of nature	act much like other animals

Clare Graves value systems, adapted from Cowan and Beck

INDIVIDUAL ⟷ COLLECTIVE

Table 4
The Memetic
Poles of
Me and We

put self ahead of best interest of group	**CORAL** To Be Determined	put self ahead of best interest of group
rely on external inputs, feedback from others		**TURQUOISE** Sense Of Oneness — trust internal judgements
explore external world	**YELLOW** Most Knowledge And Complexity	
	GREEN Assembly Of Common Interests	repair the inner world and be at peace to accept the inevitable
take charge and control of external world	**ORANGE** Most Status	
	BLUE Congregation Of Believers	
	RED Most Powerful	
	PURPLE Series Of Belonging	
	BEIGE Most Fit	

Clare Graves value systems, adapted from Cowan and Beck

PRINCIPLE 4
Memes emerge in waves

Beck and Cowan describe the fourth principle best:

> New vMeme systems come in like waves to a beach. Each has its own ascending surge.... At the same time, each also overlaps the receding waves of the previous system as they fade. Sometimes the interference generated as new systems compete in their ascendancies slows the overall Spiral's momentum, even shoving it backwards. At other times, the vMeme waves resonate and reinforce one another to speed the evolution of thinking along.[75]

As Edmonton becomes more culturally diverse, the changes this diversity brings feels threatening for some. In 1974, Edmonton City Council started a practice of beginning their council meetings with a Christian prayer. In the mid-1990s this practice shifted to reflect the various faiths of Edmontonians. In 2015, the Supreme Court of Canada ruled it unconstitutional to pray in council chambers, a place where decisions are made for all citizens. Council stopped the practice and considered starting meetings with a moment of reflection instead. I was hired to engage with community stakeholders to determine how to implement this idea.

Most stakeholders pitched in to figure out how this change could be an opportunity to acknowledge Edmonton's diversity for a minute or two at the start of council meetings, in a new way, without prayers. A handful of people, however, were saddened and angry, feeling their "right" to have a prayer had been taken away or that Canadian heritage was being eroded by the new cultures. Instead of exploring the gifts of cultural diversity (Green), they felt threatened, feeling the need to protect their turf (Red). In contrast, many stakeholders were looking forward to a moment of reflection as a means for the city to see itself (although, in the end, City Council decided not to have a moment of reflection). Something new was happening, and despite resistance, a wave of forces pulled us in a new direction and prayers at council meetings ceased. Before long, another wave will come, pushing us again.

....

PRINCIPLE 5
Higher levels of complexity emerge as we grow and develop

As we grow and develop, we experience and can handle—both inside ourselves and in the outside world—higher levels of complexity. We become more multi-faceted, our organizations take diverse forms, the big picture becomes bigger, we experience wider spans of influence, and time frames we comprehend are further extended.[76] As we move up the Spiral, more choices present themselves; there are more ways to do things, more ways to be, more ways to show emotion, and more ways to be in human relationships.

When I was a teenager in the 1980s we didn't talk about homosexuality in school. In university, I had friends who were "out," who lived their lives as couples the same way my soon-to-be-husband and I did, but they only did so in places where they felt safe to do so. There was a strong sense of right and wrong in the moral code of the times (Blue), where homosexuality was wrong; there were regular beatings of men who "looked" gay. Today, my teenagers are in schools that welcome people who identify as lesbian, gay, bisexual, transgender, queer, questioning and two-spirited. The school is mandated to be safe for all students, regardless of sexual orientation or gender identity. The binary simplicity of male and female and male–female relationships has grown into a wide range of combinations. We are making room for more diversity and complexity in our cities (and there will always be room for improvement). Changing how we think is changing us and our cities.

PRINCIPLE 6
vMemes co-exist

We have the capacity to think in different ways about different things at the same time. For example, in my work with the inaugural Edmonton Food Council (EFC), I noticed the passion of the council members (Red) and the diversity of skills (Green) they brought to reach their goal of a vibrant food and urban agriculture scene in Edmonton (Blue). When the EFC first met, I guided them in developing processes to create and nurture their relationships (Purple) and their creativity (Orange). They looked at food as a survival need (Beige) and an energy system (Yellow). How brightly each vMeme shines depends on life conditions—when we gather, there are moments I inject just enough rules and structure (Blue) to keep us on track and support their emerging work. vMemes are not trade-offs; each contributes to dynamic and effective work to improve our city.

PRINCIPLE 7
A momentous leap after the first six levels

The first six vMemes—Beige through Green—represent a first tier of human development and focus on human subsistence. The leap to the seventh vMeme indicates a shift from subsistence to "being," which means appreciating the wisdom of each of the first six vMemes. Beck and Cowan advise that the momentous leap is characterized by a dropping away of fears and compulsion, an increase in conceptual space, an ability to learn a great deal from many sources, and a trend toward getting much more done with much less energy and fewer resources.[77] Clare Graves says:

> After being hobbled by the more narrow animal-like
> needs, by the imperative need for sustenance
> (Beige), the fear of spirits (Purple) and other pred-
> atory men (Red), by the fear of trespass upon the
> ordained order (Blue), by the fear of his greediness

(Orange), and the fear of social disapproval (Green),
suddenly human cognition is free. Now with his
energies free for cognitive activation, man focuses
upon his self and his world (Yellow, Turquoise, etc.).[78]

The crossing into Yellow brings a significantly expanded view of self and the city.

I see the first six vMemes reflected in the work of Edmonton's city council: their dedication to ending poverty (Beige); their work to craft a sense of belonging and identity through heritage, the arts, and sport (Purple and Red); the rigour they apply when deciding to spend money only on essential needs (Blue); their decisions to support the business community to take advantage of economic development opportunities (Orange); and their desire to consult with and engage a wider variety of citizens and stakeholders in their decision-making (Green). City Council's budget discussions puts these priorities in conflict with each other. In rare moments, they are able to see that there is a time and place for each of these values; they don't need to be in conflict with each other and this provides them with a much wider view of the city and their work (Yellow).

MOVEMENT ON THE SPIRAL

When cars first came into use in the late 19th century, few rules were needed. In those early days, not many people were driving yet and cars did not go very fast. As they became more common and their speed increased, life conditions changed dramatically. The world of impulse (Red) led to accidents, injury, and death. It became clear that rules were needed (Blue): speed limits, laws of the road, enforcement, road design standards, and so on. A change came about and progress was made up the Spiral. When a forest fire destroyed most of the town of Slave Lake, Alberta, in May 2011, rules of the road became less important than residents' safety. Life conditions changed quickly because of the fire, and citizens moved down the Spiral to ensure their survival, an appropriate response to the circumstances.

Movement up and down the Spiral takes place when life conditions change, compelling us to change. Change can happen in three ways: expand and broaden our perspective and understanding, while still including all the levels below, and move up the Spiral; constrict and hunker down, and move down the Spiral; or adjust to life conditions and stay put. Movement on the Spiral depends on the degree to which we are open to change and, of course, the specific situation. At times, even if we are very open to change, it may be fully appropriate to maintain the status quo. The trick is to be aware of what the circumstances demand. The easy route may be to avoid change and hunker down. The tough route may be to face your fears. This is difficult for us as individuals, let alone as collectives the size of cities. If we choose to consciously make cities that work well for citizens, we need to undertake this important work.

We find it difficult to change our current ways of being. We like to tinker, to stay where we are, rather than make big changes, but current circumstances demand that we meet the world with more bravery. We need to expand our awareness and understanding to meet more complex challenges in life conditions, such as the climate crisis, a pandemic, seemingly intractable social matters like homelessness and addictions, and race-based power imbalances due to white privilege. Will we choose to hunker down or to expand upward into new possibilities?

Graves called the expansive movement up the Spiral a never-ending quest. Our evolutionary growth, however, is not a given. Beck and Cowan suggest that upward movement on the Spiral, the broadening of our awareness and understanding, is subject to six conditions, which offer insight into our development as citizens and cities.

....

CONDITION 1
Open to the potential for change

Not all people—or cities—are equally open to or even capable of or prepared for change. Normally, humans operate in a consistent, enduring steady way and we tend to stay in these zones of comfort unless we experience turbulence.[79] The potential for change revolves around thinking that is open; the ability to operate under more complex life conditions; and being free from restrictive patterns, "sink-holes," and "baggage." Are we open to living closer to each other so we can reduce greenhouse gas emissions or are we attached to single-family dwellings?

CONDITION 2
Presence of solutions for unresolved problems or threats

At each vMeme, we reach a stage where we can adequately manage the problems at that vMeme. This offers us comfort and balance, allowing us to direct excess energy to explore the next, more complex system.[80] When our challenges are met, we start to see new unresolved problems or threats, but we cannot fully reach that next vMeme until we solve those problems. As we see the threats posed by fossil fuel consumption, solutions are present in alternative, renewable energy sources.

CONDITION 3
Presence of dissonance

As Beck and Cowan explain, "Change does not occur unless the boat rocks."[81] Waves of some kind must jostle the steady-state system, causing awareness of a growing gap between new life conditions and how we handle the problems of previous life conditions. When current solutions fail to solve the problems of emerging conditions, new thinking may be stimulated or a release of energy may liberate the emergence of the next vMeme. Despite all the efforts in my city to keep pedestrians safe, record numbers of pedestrian–car incidents occur, many of them fatal. There is a growing understanding that our current road design does not meet the needs of all users of the street.

CONDITION 4
Ability to eliminate, bypass, neutralize, or reframe barriers

Effectively handling barriers to change is a way to provide a solid foundation on which to build change. To do so, we need to be conscious of risks, consequences, and the pain of removing barriers; we also need to expose excuses and rationalizations that make it difficult to implement change. Both external and internal obstacles slow our progress up the Spiral.[82] There are external barriers to consider: "It's the developers' fault; that's why we have a sprawling city." "The bloody bureaucracy holds us down." There are also internal barriers to consider: "The only way I can move around the city is by car." "It works fine the way it is."

CONDITION 5
Awareness of thinking patterns

When moving from one vMeme to another, we step into new ways of thinking, new ways of seeing ourselves and the world.[83] Before we can act on the new thinking pattern, it needs to become part of the collective consciousness; people need to have a sense of what things might be like for them in changed circumstances. New thinking patterns can take place when we initiate personal exploration of how systems change; look for answers that address today's conditions rather than past conditions; identify and demonstrate alternatives toward which we can reach; and recognize new life conditions and the changes that need to be made to address new conditions.[84] The energy systems of the city have changed over the last hundred years, from coal and firewood to electricity and gas to alternate energy sources that are tangible examples of what a new thinking pattern might feel like.

CONDITION 6
Support for transition

A supportive culture allows new awareness to germinate and grow. Assistance is needed to support the clumsiness of new growth, the confusion and false starts. Sometimes, those who make or propose change are perceived as a threat to those who do not understand what is happening and who may feel left out; turf battles and new obstacles may need to be dealt with.[85] This is a time when change is integrated and incorporated into the system in question. When the Supreme Court of Canada declared it unconstitutional to have a prayer at the beginning of city council meetings, most welcomed Edmonton's decision to replace the prayer with a moment of reflection, while a vocal minority felt left out and fought the decision.

Meeting these six conditions does not make growth certain—sometimes, most conditions are met but expansion does not occur. On the other hand, only some conditions may be met and change occurs anyway. These conditions highlight the mindset we must operate from in order to respond to the changing world around us—the internal social habitat, if you will, that is within each of us at the scale of the individual, family, organization, nation, and humanity.

The chasm between how we experience the world and the possibilities we see for how the world can be propels us forward. As citizens, we do not see the needed improvements in the city at the same time, in the same way, nor are we required to before attempting to work to make those improvements. The six conditions for movement up the Spiral highlight what we choose to notice, examine, and explore. We are on a never-ending quest to improve the world around us, a quest that always involves obstacles and our varied responses to them. The learning we are engaged in is not clean or easy; it is full of fault lines. Cities and citizens are always at a threshold of new understanding.

EVOLUTIONARY CITY INTELLIGENCE

Understanding that we work in growing complexity, with varied values and priorities, is crucial for the physical city we build, the work we do, and the social habitat we create in our cities.

The Spiral serves as a crucial map that helps us understand and chart evolutionary intelligence. We adapt to life conditions and provide structures that support new levels of complexity. As the purpose of a human settlement evolves, we respond by shifting and adjusting our values and priorities. As a map, the Spiral shows us what people value, what motivates them, what they see as improvement. And it plays out explicitly in our cities.

Imagine the Spiral alive across the whole city: a symphony of voices each expressing where they are at any moment. The Spiral allows us to see priorities clearly. When a tsunami or super typhoon hits, we hunker down in survival mode (Beige). When our hometown hockey team wins a big game, we experience a surge of elation and pride (Red). When a drunk driver kills a bus load of school children, we call for a recalibration of rules (Blue). When we are hired for a big job at the top of the corporate ladder, we revel in our achievement (Orange). When we realize that the voices of the powerful are the only ones heard in city decision-making, we begin to look for ways to hear, empower, and incorporate the marginalized voices of the city (Green). As we integrate these value systems and see their value together rather than in competition with each other, the flex and flow emerges (Yellow), allowing us to see a bigger view of city life. Turquoise is bigger yet, connecting city life to planetary matters. Coral, a ninth emerging level, is one we are only beginning to sense.

Understanding that we work in growing complexity, with varied values and priorities, is crucial for the physical city we build, the work we do, and the social habitat we create in our cities. This understanding changes the way we talk about how we organize ourselves in our cities, and their design.

The Spiral map, when used to look at the whole city system of systems, can be applied in scalar[86] and fractal[87] ways. Our work, our habitat and the city-habitat dynamic (Figures A, B and I) are the same regardless of scale. The image and concept of our work evolving in response to our habitat—social and physical—also applies to individuals, families, neighbourhoods, cities, and so on. The nested hierarchy (Figure E) offers another way of mapping our cities, reminding us that cities are systems made of systems and part of larger expanding systems.

The Spiral map, combined with the scalar and fractal nature of how cities are generated and regenerated, becomes more powerful yet with the addition of the four Integral City perspectives (Figure G), another essential map. This map serves as a simple way to determine if the basic elements of the city system are present: civic managers, civic builders and developers, civic organizations and citizens. Any contemplation of a city without all four of these perspectives is incomplete; in order to create cities as habitats in which we thrive, integral intelligence—intelligence that is complete and contains all fundamental aspects—is crucial.

Evolutionary city intelligence can be charted by values, by scale, by quadrant. Our work, as people committed to making cities that serve citizens and citizens that serve cities, applies to many scales and in many directions at once. Understanding cities as whole systems means using new maps—new to city system thinking—to chart our understanding and create the conditions for our evolution.

Evolutionary Intelligence in a Sentence
In 2012, I worked with Marilyn Hamilton to design and host the Integral City 2.0 online conference. Six hundred participants from six continents attended—all of them curious about how to design a new operating system for their cities. Over twelve days, and with the support of sixty visionary thought leaders, designers, and practitioners, we explored the twelve "evolutionary intelligences

for the human hive" that Hamilton had articulated in her book, *Integral City*:

1. Ecosphere intelligence: locating places for the human hive
2. Emerging intelligence: seeing wholeness in the human hive
3. Integral intelligence: charting patterns of the human hive
4. Living intelligence: living and dying in the human hive
5. Inner intelligence: conscious capacity in the human hive
6. Outer intelligence: embodying right action in the human hive
7. Building intelligence: creating structures that flex and flow in the human hive
8. Story intelligence: feeding each other in the human hive
9. Inquiry intelligence: releasing potential in the human hive
10. Meshing intelligence: enabling order and creativity in the human hive
11. Navigating intelligence: directional intelligence for the human hive
12. Evolving intelligence: imagining the future for human hives

One of my roles during the conference was to capture the main ideas of each day; in doing this work I distilled her twelve evolutionary intelligences into one sentence:

> *Seeing the entire city as a habitat made up of many alive, evolving "wholes" that need nourishment allows us to create cities that serve citizens well and citizens that serve cities well.*

Let me unpack this sentence using each of the twelve evolutionary intelligences.

"Seeing the entire city" means using maps, like the four described above (the Spiral, nested hierarchy of city systems, four city voices, and scalar and fractal relationships), to look at the city as a whole—using integral intelligence. Cities grow out of our evolving interaction with our habitat.

When we think of cities as **"alive,"** we use ecosphere intelligence, recognizing our relationship with our habitat and adjusting and growing with it as life conditions change. When we engage our living intelligence, we see that the city is alive because it survives; it connects with its environment and it regenerates. If it doesn't do this, it does not survive or thrive, but dies.

When we consider the city as a habitat made up of **"evolving wholes,"** we see its complexity. The city is made up of many whole, identifiable systems: citizens, families, organizations, neighbourhoods, and so on. The city survives just as each of these systems survives, has a relationship with its environment as these systems do, and regenerates as these systems do. The city system and other systems—within and beyond—are always in relationship with each other, which creates the conditions for our evolving intelligence. The back-and-forth between cities and citizens, for example, fuels the development of all wholes, at all scales.

Cities and citizens alike **"need nourishment"** to thrive. Inquiry intelligence allows us to unlock the potential of cities by simply noticing and appreciating what works in cities and the work needed to get more of it. Inquiry also gives us the opportunity to imagine what we need beyond fixing—an activity that keeps our attention on old problems and away from new possibilities. Curiosity about and inquiry into what naturally needs to happen next nourishes possibility. Endlessly asking and exploring questions nurtures citizens and cities.

The connections we make in cities, and the quality and quantity of those connections, also nourish the city. This is meshing intelligence, our capacity to make catalytic connections within and between whole systems. These relationships are self-organizing and hierarchical at the same time, and the health of both within and between systems fuels the city. Looking at cities as alive, evolving wholes with needs allows us to navigate toward a destination while we create our cities. Our navigating intelligence allows us to inhabit two behaviours—aiming for a destination and discerning whether we are on course to that destination. This intelligence is about feedback loops that allow us to see whether our actions are helping or harming our journey. This intelligence asks if we know where we want to go and what "getting there" looks like. At this point, we navigate toward "**cities that serve citizens well, and citizens that serve cities well.**"

1. As a human settlement's purpose evolves, we shift and adjust our values and priorities to organize ourselves in response to changing conditions.

2. Understanding that we live and work in growing complexity, that we live with varied values and priorities in this complexity—often in conflict—changes how we talk about our city (social habitat), the work we do (economic life), and how we design our city (physical habitat).

3. The Spiral and the value memes (vMemes) first proposed by Clare Graves give us clues about what people value, what they see as improvement, their behaviours and motivations (and our own) as we navigate city life.

4. vMemes are codes—behavioural instructions that are passed on from one generation to the next, social artifacts, and value-laden symbols that bolster our social systems. These vMemes serve as indicators of how we evolve and grow as individuals, families, cultures, workplaces, cities, nations, and humanity.

5. As a body of work, Spiral Dynamics reveals patterns in human development and allows for a deeper view of the role of cities— and citizens—in human development.

6. Upward movement on the Spiral only occurs in the right conditions.

7. Evolutionary intelligence can be charted by values, by scale, and by quadrant. Our work, as people keen on making cities that serve citizens and citizens that serve cities, occurs at many scales and in many directions at once. Understanding cities as whole systems means using new maps—new to city system

thinking—to chart our understanding and create the conditions for our evolution.

8. The twelve evolutionary intelligences for cities identified by Marilyn Hamilton can be summarized in one sentence: Seeing the entire city as a habitat made up of many alive, evolving "wholes" that need nourishment allows us to create cities that serve citizens well and citizens that serve cities well.

9. Maps and models help us see and explore the evolutionary patterns that are in play in our cities.

To organize cities that serve citizens well, citizens must organize with levels of complexity that match the challenges they face. Cultivating evolutionary intelligence is an endless practice of:

- Discerning the difference between "the city" we make for ourselves and "the City" that is our municipal government
- Seeing the entire city—the good and the bad; the economic, social, and physical; and the diverse perspectives in the city
- Seeing the city as alive
- Noticing the layers of whole systems within and around the city that are themselves growing and evolving
- Inquiring into and nourishing what works well in the city
- Naming the direction in which we are moving
- Acting with the knowledge that our choices shape the city, and the city in return shapes us

NEST-MAKING PRACTICE
Being Dynamically Stable

It means being certain amidst uncertainty. It means trusting ambiguity and seeing clearly in ambiguity. It means embracing the gifts of differing opinions. It means being the citizens we are called to be to have cities that serve us all well. It means courageously having a direction in mind, even if only a hint of a destination. It means accepting that individuals and humanity are on a learning journey. It means being open to the future that is wanting to come into being and trusting that the future we want is the future we can have. It means organizing ourselves and our habitat—our nest cities—to thrive.

REFLECT

Take a moment with a journal or sketchbook and see where the following questions take you. There are no wrong or right answers.

Self—In what ways do I practise expanding my evolutionary intelligence? What systems am I a part of in my city? How do I nourish my relationship with these systems?

Other—What parts of my city are alive with possibility? What nourishes that possibility? How do I connect the systems of the city?

City—In what direction do different city systems want to go? In what direction does my city want to go as a whole?

Care—In what ways does my city care for itself? In what ways do different city systems look after each other's needs?

> **Reminder:** "city" means the city-habitat we make for ourselves, the community around us, not our municipal government (often referred to as "the City").

CHAPTER 4

So it is with this moment.
A gigantic death
And an enormous birth.
This mighty moment
In timelessness
                    — Ben Okri[88]

4 PLANNING IS WORK THAT SERVES THE CITY

PLANNING IS NEW WORK

In Canada, "city planning" began in 1914 when the federal government's Commission of Conservation hired Britain's Thomas Adams as its town planning advisor.[89] His work supported the creation of town planning legislation across Canada and heralded in a new area of work distinct from surveying and engineering because of its additional focus on improving civic conditions.[90] This was the beginning of a structure (legislation) and a profession dedicated to bring order to settlements across Canada, work that emerged with the fourth purpose of the city, as indicated in the Spiral model (plan) and the fourth level of organizing (authority and moral codes).

In 1919, five years after Adams' arrival, the Town Planning Institute of Canada was established. (It was renamed the Canadian Institute of Planners in 1974.) Today, the formal act of planning municipal land use is established by the provinces and territorial governments and includes zoning bylaws, area structure plans, municipal development plans, and official community plans. In their work, planners help organize social and community services, build economic capacity, address transportation and infrastructure needs, manage cultural and heritage resources, and ensure environmental protection. In recent decades, the profession has evolved and is now regulated by many provincial governments, including explicit expectations that city planners protect the public interest.

The Canadian Institute of Planners defines planning as "the scientific, aesthetic, and orderly disposition of land, resources, facilities and services with a view to securing the physical, economic and social efficiency, health and well-being of urban and rural communities."[91] While complicated, this definition articulates the planning profession's intention—and role—to help the city be the best it can be for its citizens.

Planning communities—even just thinking about planning them—has played a critical role in how our communities look and feel today. Gerald Hodge and David L. A. Gordon, authors of *Planning Canadian Communities*, the country's primary text for city planning students, note: "[T]he regard for planning and making plans is strong. Even in...contentious situations, the essential debate is not about the need for planning, but for better planning—not whether but how it should be done."[92] Citizens, developers and builders, community organizations, various public institutions, and politicians—everyone has ideas about how planning can be improved. And they are right—there are many improvements to be made. Today's challenge is to shift the way we look at planning and planners, recognizing it is not up to planners alone to make the improvements we desire in our cities.

The formal act of planning practiced today, with zoning bylaws and area structure plans, was developed in response to life conditions of a certain time, geography, challenge, and social circumstances. The activities fit the era in which Adams worked. Planners used to be (and some still are, as appropriate) the people who write the plans for political approval. As policy writers, they take direction from city council or propose policy to city council. They are obligated to seek out the views of the public and stakeholders and synthesize what they hear with what they know to make recommendations to council. The policy may be a transportation plan, a facility plan for a school division, or a plan for future neighbourhoods or industrial subdivisions.

We, as the public, assign great responsibility to this profession, but we often do so in error, because while professional planners shape and influence our cities, they do not have as much control as we ascribe to them. In today's world, the work of organizing a city belongs to many; the work of organizing ourselves to thrive belongs to all of us. The planning profession is one of many kinds of work in the city. Planners do not have a recipe, or even The Recipe, let alone all the ingredients to organize a city. In Marilyn Hamilton's model of the *Integral City*, city planners are primarily civic managers, regulating the city, or civic builders and developers who construct the structures of the city. Formally, planners are part of two perspectives—civic manager and civic builders.

Making A City Is A Complex Endeavour
In 1922, Adams stated, "Cities do not grow—all of them are planned."[93] His words suggest cities are built the way buildings are built, with a complete set of plans. This linear thinking is too simple for today's world and the complexity of city making. In *Getting to Maybe*, Frances Westley, Brenda Zimmerman, and Michael Quinn Patton[94] explain that by changing the way we see, we can change the world. Their insights apply to city making: we are active participants in shaping the world around us, and when it comes to city making, we are active participants, not builders following a fixed, predetermined plan.

In *Getting to Maybe*, the authors identify three kinds of challenges: simple, complicated, and complex (Table 5[95]). *Simple* challenges are, well, simple, with clear causes and effects. With practice and good skills, the same outcome can be created over and over again, like baking a cake. With a recipe, even the uninitiated will likely be able to complete the task. In contrast, a *complicated* challenge requires expertise to be successfully addressed. Formulas and calculations replace the simple recipe; we're not baking a cake any more, we're sending a rocket to the moon. Precision is required; a detailed blueprint lays out precise relationships, with known consequences. In a *complex* challenge, linear cause-and-effect relationships are no longer in play. For example, when raising a child, the uniqueness of each child eliminates the usefulness of a recipe or a blueprint; there is no one single way to respond to the needs of any child, let alone all children.

Table 5
Three
Kinds of
Challenges

SIMPLE	COMPLICATED	COMPLEX
BAKING A CAKE OR ESTABLISHING ST. JOHN'S	SENDING A ROCKET TO THE MOON OR BUILDING A BRIDGE	RAISING A CHILD OR MAKING A CITY
Certain elements are essential: safe harbour, fresh water supply	Rigid protocols or formulas are needed	Rigid protocols are no longer effective
Similar elements of other successful settlements can be tested in a new setting	Building one bridge increases the likelihood that the next bridge will also be a success	Experience is no guarantee of success
No particular expertise is required, but experience increases success rate	High levels of expertise and training in a variety of fields are necessary for success	Experience is of value when responsive to conditions
Similar living conditions will allow for other safe settlements nearly all the time	Key elements of each bridge **must** be identical to succeed more than once	Recipes and blueprints are not particularly helpful
The best conditions give good results every time	There is a high degree of certainty and outcome	Outcomes are uncertain despite planning
A good settlement notes the quantity and nature of the "parts" needed and specifies the order in which to combine them, but there is room for experimentation	Success depends on a blueprint that directs both the development of separate parts and specifies the exact relationship in which to assemble them	Relationships are the essence of the city

The trajectory in this simple model parallels the trajectory of a spiral, starting with simple ways of organizing ourselves and moving to complicated and complex ways of organizing. When colonial St. John's was settled, the intent was simple: find a safe place for shelter. Over time, as more people arrived and the settlement grew, their water needs were addressed by a complicated system of pipes for water and wastewater. In today's context, cities are no longer simple or complicated endeavours, rather a complex network of relationships and uncertain outcomes.

Simple and complicated challenges are a part of the everyday fabric of city life: organizing a community picnic or designing a new bridge to replace a worn-out one. In the 1920s, Adams saw the city as a series of complicated challenges that could be met with a comprehensive set of plans, a very "Blue view" of the world that was linear and mechanistic, a consistent view for his times. Adams' approach today is insufficient; cities grow and behave in complex ways, inconsistent with the plans; we prepare that imagine the city as a series of simple and complicated challenges. Our expectations of cities, our plans for them, and the plans' purposes have all changed. We no longer plan our cities, we guide their development. For cities to meet the needs of their citizens, we need to adjust our relationship with our cities and our expectations of planning professionals.

The Value Of Plans Is In Their Direction

City plans serve a purpose; they document our shared understanding of where we want our cities to go and how they will get there. They describe our shared intentions and intended actions to reach our goals. Planning supports a city's efforts to notice, adjust, and organize so that the city fulfills its purpose as a habitat serving its inhabitants. This understanding is essential for decision-makers at every level—in our local governments, business communities, civic organizations, and among citizens— to ensure our cities function with expanded focus, broadened purposes, and less concentrated decision-making processes. City planners are most relevant when co-creating the conditions for citizens and cities to see and respond to life conditions, to ensure we survive and thrive.

Hodge and Gordon assert that the purpose of a city plan is "achieving a goal desired by its citizens...community planning is about attaining a *preferred* future, built and natural environment."[96] They cite two reasons for making community plans: to solve some problems associated with its development and/or to achieve some preferred form of development.[97] This is civic manager work that makes a meaningful contribution to cities.

In today's world, professional planners are responsible for creating the plans that will ensure a city's preferred state is realized. Citizens, civil society, civic builders, and developers, along with politicians, provide feedback to planners through formal public engagement activities. What makes cities more complex is the understanding that city hall is not the only player who organizes a city, but that many others are involved. Numerous organizations, activities, and events shape the city without city hall's direction. Environmental groups have had an influence on our tolerance for weeds. Arts foundations find the funds to build new museums and art galleries. Business leaders join forces to advance technology research and innovation. The university hospital chooses to emphasize health research and expands its facilities. School boards decide to allow families to choose their schools. Citizens choose where to live in relation to employment, schools, and services. All of these players shape today's cities.

More and more frequently, citizens, civil society, civic builders, and developers are demanding a role in the process of planning our communities. As a result, the role of the plan and the planner has evolved. City plans are no longer simply the blueprints that early land surveyors and engineers prepared for orderly development. A new kind of work is required that supports an expanded view of what it takes to make cities healthy habitats for citizens.

I've been asking myself for years if "planning" is the right word to describe this work that takes place in our cities. If its definition means more than a tidy, linear, mechanical, rational practice, it can be the right word. The purpose of planning, as an organizing activity, is now about integrating new and emerging voices and values of a city. In order to build the city nest that citizens need to thrive, we need to organize ourselves in ways that match the complexity of today's life conditions. Some of this work takes the form of planning as we know it, other ways of planning are emerging that are non-linear and messy, yet full of purpose.

Two kinds of planning support cities: in one, planners provide answers to citizens in a traditional, linear form of technical planning expertise; in the other, planners support the creation of a social habitat in which the whole city becomes more aware of itself, through exploration, so it can respond purposefully and appropriately to life conditions. The tension between the two is this: planners have expert knowledge and we all have expert knowledge. The specific expertise of planners is sometimes needed. This is "top down" activity, which is the right approach under certain circumstances. Planners also need to acknowledge that a city organizes itself and that they can support the city in these efforts. At a minimum, this means being a conversation convenor and host, scribing and documenting shared understandings as they emerge. Professional planners need to understand what their cities need of them, recognizing situations where *listening* skills are more important than *telling* skills. It also means noticing the difference between what "the planners know" and what is being asked of them. This is the next evolutionary step for the planning profession—a profession in service to cities and their inhabitants.

Planning today is about a clear, shared sense of direction that allows for learning and adjustment along the way and that recognizes that we do not always know exactly where we will end up. The value of plans is in their intention and common direction, not their end point. The planning profession is called to be conscious of collective intention and purpose, yet not to endeavour to have control, for that may sabotage the potency of possibility in the city.

The ways we organize ourselves in the city has entered a new age that Thomas L. Friedman, in *Thank You for Being Late*, refers to as the "age of accelerations." Friedman describes a new culture of politics and the need to consciously choose, consensually wherever possible, to focus on the following attitudes as we govern ourselves: embrace diversity; assume ownership over the future and one's own problems; recognize that a healthy community is a network of healthy ecosystems on top of ecosystems each thriving on its own and nourished by the whole; and approach politics and problem-solving with a mindset that is entrepreneurial, hybrid, and non-dogmatic. At the heart of this conscious decision making, ideas blend and evolve, creating resilience and propulsion no matter whose "side" they come from.[98] The city is the perfect place to activate and practice these choices.

As we all actively engage in city life, the many purposes of the city emerge, as do the many modes of organizing to meet those purposes. Planning is only one mode of organizing. No one has control of the city, yet everyone has a role to play.

Citizens Are City Planners

In the summer of 2007, I walked away from my dream job in Fort McMurray. I was working with what poet John O'Donohue describes as "vacant endurance;" I was pouring myself into my job, yet my soul was calling for something else. I desired to remain connected to my work as a city planner, yet sought much more. At one point in my turmoil, I came across this checklist for a summer music camp that metaphorically (and literally in the end) rocked my world:

Checklist: What to bring each day to summer music camp:

- Your instrument in good working condition
- An open, respectful attitude
- A willingness to learn and try new things
- Smiles and laughter
- A snack

At summer music camp, we spend a lot of time alone, to work on our skills as musicians, to create wonderful music together. As in any community, we need to show up physically, mentally, emotionally, and spiritually able to engage with others. To create together, we need to bring curiosity about what might happen as we learn together. Even with sheet music, musicians have ample room to create something unexpected and wonderful. And, of course, smiles and laughter get us through the tough times when we don't see eye to eye and have conflicting ideas about what we are to create together. And regardless of what happens, we put it all aside and enjoy snacks together.

In my dream job, many band camp components were in place. Employees were working feverishly and diligently, intent on serving the public well. We worked on our own and came together as a collective. We smiled and laughed and shared snacks. People in the organization were open and respectful; they were willing to learn and try new things. We were loyal to the community. But, still, in the fever and scramble of rapid population growth, the "band" was not in good working condition.

Somehow we were working against ourselves, our own worst enemies. Employee sick leaves were excessive; employee turnover was high. Human resource statistics revealed an organization under stress. Internally, we knew the reality without the statistics; we could feel the organization struggling. The result: a municipal government focused on trade-offs instead of possibility, on problems instead of the way through problems to a desired end. And that vicious circle gave us more of what we paid most of our attention to—problems. Unfortunately, our life in the vicious circle ended up harming loyal people who worked hard for their employer and their community.

We caused harm because we worked in a mode that author Timothy Gallwey calls performance momentum:[99] work done without conscious intent or awareness of purpose. While this may move the organization along, it does not make the organization nimble—able to effectively handle the challenges it faces. It stays in a rut. As an old-timer told my dad years ago about driving on bad roads, "Choose your rut carefully—you'll be in it for a long time."

We chose, for the most part, to work harder, not smarter, when things got tough. We talked about setting ourselves up to learn constantly while working so we could adjust and readily take new courses of action when needed. Pockets of the organization could do this, but not enough for the whole organization to learn to adjust as a whole.

The municipal government was the band, and with most instruments in poor working condition, it didn't perform well. There were moments of brilliance when the melody could be heard, but mostly we just created noise. We did not create a culture where strong relationships ensured our ability to work and learn together so we could make beautiful music. All of this took place because we did not attach to a clear and compelling purpose for the musical score. We just did our work, playing the notes vacantly—without adequate relationships among ourselves, with others, or with the community we served. The social habitat of our camp, and the band as a whole, was no longer conducive to learning and exploring. For me, my heart was no longer in it. It was time to walk away.

So, was the dream job a dream job after all? Yes, it was. I learned about the forces that create cities and about how our work, and our approach to our work, affects how well we create cities and how well they serve us in return. Can a city, like an organization, choose to look after itself and its people? If my employer had chosen to support me—and all of us—to be in good working condition, I was prepared to serve. I see now that my personal purpose—as a citizen and as a planner—is to create the conditions for new possibilities to emerge in our cities. We can only do this when we weave together our passion with our work. When we create the conditions to learn together and be in relationship with each other in ways that support our purpose and passion, we end up with good work, good organizations, and, potentially, good cities—a spectacular composition beautifully performed.

When people ask me what I do, I find myself saying that "by profession" I am a city planner and as a "citizen" I am also a city planner. It turns out that as a volunteer with my neighbourhood community league, I am also a city planner. Even as a small business owner, I am a city planner. My version of city planning is not just to figure out where streets and buildings go or what kind of land use bylaw applies in a neighbourhood. To me, city planning captures all of the choices we make as citizens, whether we reside in the city or rural areas, in between, or in the North or other remote areas. We make choices everywhere as elected officials, lawyers, coaches, parents, janitors, children, activists, religious leaders, secretaries, artists, and volunteers. In all walks of life, our choices influence the place we live, economically, socially, and physically: how we shape our cities and how our cities in turn shape us.

I see a new possibility where—as citizens and cities—we make choices that have a clear purpose, are clear about what we will learn together as we work toward that purpose, and are clear that we wish to be in relationship with one another in order to sustain what we build. This is the ultimate commitment we make to each other—to sustain life in a way that allows us to look after ourselves, each other, and the places we live. Without a place to live and fully be ourselves, with others, we do not live, let alone thrive.

City planning involves far more than city hall. When we are self-aware and engage with others to make decisions, we affect our city's well-being and directly impact what we get in return from our city. The summer camp checklist evokes a distinct setting: a band camp, where we gather to learn and grow with others. In the case of a city, we are musicians creating our city. We do not cooperate well with each other if we are not in good working condition; if we are not open and respectful; if we are not willing to try new things; if we rarely bring smiles and laughter; or if we do not take the initiative to provide the snacks that we need to nourish self and others. Our band camp—our nest—is only as good as we choose to make it.

1. Today's challenge is recalibrating the purpose of planning and planners; it is not up to planners alone to make the improvements we desire in our cities.

2. Cities behave in complex ways, an idea that is inconsistent with the plans that imagine them as linear and complicated. We can't **plan** many aspects of our cities, but we can **guide** them. As citizens, this requires us to have different expectations of our cities and planning professionals.

3. The purpose of city plans is to document our shared understanding of where we want to go and what it will take to get there. They outline our shared intentions and intended actions for reaching our goals.

4. Planning is an activity that supports a city's efforts to notice, adjust, and organize so that the city is able to fulfill its purpose as a habitat serving its inhabitants.

5. There are two kinds of planning support to our cities, both of which have their time and place: one, where planners provide answers to citizens in a traditional, linear form of technical planning expertise; and two, where planners support the creation of a social habitat in which the whole city becomes more aware of itself, through exploration, so it can respond purposefully and appropriately to life conditions.

6. Professional planners in our cities—and their plans— are not in control. Planning today is about a shared, clear sense of direction, allowing for learning and adjustment along the way and recognizing that we do not know exactly where we will end up.

7. As we all actively engage ourselves in city life, the many purposes of the city come to life, as do the many modes of organizing to meet those purposes. Planning is only one mode of organizing.

8. This is the ultimate commitment we make to each other, as citizens in cities—to sustain life in ways that allow us to look after ourselves, each other, and the places we live. This involves making choices that have a clear purpose, being clear about what we learn together as we work toward that purpose, and being clear that we wish to be in relationship with one another in order to sustain what we build.

9. Notice what it takes to organize cities that serve all inhabitants well. Our nest is only as good as we choose to make it.

NEST-MAKING PRACTICE
Choosing The City Nest

Over the years, I have talked with many people about how to create cities that serve citizens more fully. Five recurring messages have emerged for people who choose to make the city their nest:

1. Get to know yourself. The more you know about how you work and what drives you, the better you can serve others. I entertain regular conversations between my ego-self (who is afraid of what people think, judges others, and can get overly competitive) and my highest Self (who, when I choose to listen, always knows what to do and how to best do it). I entertain these two aspects of myself in a journal and they even talk to each other when I go for a walk. The more you know your Self, the more you show up for others and your city.

2. Notice what is life affirming (for you). When you work in ways and places that are life affirming, you make your city and your world a better place. What we put our attention to is what we get more of, so when you focus on things that don't work or things that don't fill you with joy, you get more of what doesn't work, more of what fills you with "ick". Choose work that feels good and don't be afraid to trust that your work, alongside the work of many others, meets the needs of the city.

3. Notice what you and others believe and understand—without judgment. If you feel that what you believe and understand is true, and it's not the same as others' beliefs, then can you find a way to accept that both views are true? Are you able to honour diversity? This is a great topic for your self and Self to talk about.

4. Learn to speak multiple languages, then speak theirs, not yours. When touring a brewery as part of a planning conference, the guide asked who we were and someone replied, "We are practitioners of the planning and orderly development of our urban and rural environments." That answer didn't cut it, so someone else said, "City planning," and our guide understood. It was just enough information. Figure out what you want to say, then translate it.

REFLECT

Take a moment with a journal or sketchbook and see where the following questions take you. There are no wrong or right answers.

Self—In what ways do I engage in the planning of the city? How do I see myself as a city planner?

Other—In what ways are others pulling the city in a different direction from where I'd like to see the city go? How are other ideas the same and different from mine?

City—What are the values embedded in the city's formal plans? Do they align with what I value? Do they align with what I sense citizens are looking for?

Care—In what ways do I make sure I am an "instrument in good working condition", to serve the city as my best "me"? How does the city support citizens to show up as their best selves?

Reminder: "city" means the city-habitat we make for ourselves, the community around us, not our municipal government (often referred to as "the City").

PART TWO
NESTING MATERIALS

We now know that cities are a result of our efforts to think, make, and do new things. But how do we wrap our heads, hearts, and intuition around ways to organize ourselves so that we make better cities? In the next three chapters, we focus on three ideas that need our attention: the destination we want to arrive at is both alive and adrift, we are meant to feel uneasy on our journey, and at every turn new thresholds lead to new possibilities—our emergence. These three elements—destination, journey, and emergence—form the Nestworks.

Humans not only have purposes, we have purposes for our purposes;
we have relative freedom of choice regarding the urges or impetuses we
want to act on and the appetites we want to resist. Moreover, humans
can have purposes that require a lifetime or more to fulfill; we can
have highly creative purposes, compassionate, loving purposes, and
world-changing purposes that improve conditions for everyone.

—Steve McIntosh[100]

5

DESTINATION: WE ARE ADRIFT AND ALIVE

SURVIVING AND IMPROVING

Whenever people work to improve conditions, they embark on a never-ending quest that allows them to perceive and pursue higher values and purposes. Writer and evolutionary thinker Steve McIntosh associates this quest with cultural evolution:

> [I]t is this emergent capacity to discern and make moral distinctions that gives us the ability to evolve our culture. Because of our sense of higher purpose—because we can feel the ever-widening potential of a better way—humans are continuously driven and drawn toward more complex forms of social organization.[101]

Our drive to improve pulls us forward, to create new and more complex ways of organizing ourselves. The cities that humanity has created serve two purposes: the survival of the human species and the improvement of life conditions.

When citizens work without a sense of purpose, their cities are directionless; they lose track of where they are going and why. Without purpose, in any situation and at any scale, we drift and flounder. That's why a destination—a purpose—is important. It provides a purpose that can be organized around. People experience two orders of purpose. For McIntosh, first-order purpose is evident in the inherent urge, which is shared by all forms of life, to survive and reproduce.[102] Instinctually, we know how to survive. A second-order purpose is "a self-reflective type of purpose that includes rational, moral, and aesthetic aspirations."[103] Through these aspirations we improve.

One way to look at increasingly complex forms of social organization is through the emerging levels of consciousness that we discussed in Chapter Three. As humans evolve, the purpose of our cities evolves along with us, as do our values. While we continuously organize ourselves to change and improve our living conditions, we move in a direction that is expansive and emergent—we grow. While the specific destination may be unknown, the general direction is clear: survive and improve. As we move toward our short-term destinations, we can trust that further destinations will emerge and that we will continue our journey to reach them.

Citizens Are Nest Makers

The city system has many systems within it, at many scales, and the purpose of each system can be different *and* complementary. Let's use the human body as an example. A cell in your body is a whole entity and a part of another whole, your liver for example. Your liver is a whole entity, but also a part of a larger entity, your body. At each scale, that whole entity—a "holon", as articulated by Arthur Koestler—has a distinct purpose. The purpose of a cell might be to break down old red blood cells, but the whole it is a part of, the liver, has a different purpose: cleansing the body of toxins. And the purpose of the liver is not the purpose of the human body, a whole new entity made up of smaller, complete wholes. Each holon—a cell, a liver, a human—is simultaneously a whole system and a part of another, larger whole. Smaller wholes are more numerous; the estimated 37.2 trillion cells make up your body[104] is much more than the one whole body that is you. Applying this model to cities, we see numerous citizens as the holons, making up the whole of the city.

The evolutionary pattern of holons, as articulated by Koestler, McIntosh, and Ken Wilber is helpful to understand purpose at scale. Here's the trick: when holons join to form a larger, new holon, that new holon is completely new. Twigs laying on the

ground are twigs, but together as a nest they are a whole
new thing, with a whole new purpose.

McIntosh and Wilber use the words "instrumental" and
"fundamental" to describe smaller holons because they have
a fundamental role to play as materials that make up the larger
holon (Figure K). In contrast, the larger holons are described
as having an "intrinsic" or "significant" purpose. The new entity
that has emerged from the combination of smaller holons is
of evolutionary significance.

In Figure K, the most numerous holons are the inhabitants of
a city (the birds). Just as the cells that make up your body are
fundamental to your existence, or twigs are fundamental to a
nest, citizens are fundamental to the existence of the city; without
citizens there is no city. Further, when we change our behaviours—
how we think, make, and do—we change our city. Cities, the
more recent and larger holons, in turn, play a significant role
in our lives. McIntosh tells us that as larger and larger holonic
entities appear (cities for example), with more and more whole

entities within them (citizens), the evolutionary significance of the larger entity increases.[105] From an evolutionary perspective, the city is more significant than citizens because it is the bigger whole. The citizens, however, as smaller wholes, are more fundamental. As the scale of our cities grows, and as cities become more and more connected to each other, pulling us into a potential new whole as "a planet of cities," as Marilyn Hamilton puts it, citizens become more fundamental.

There are two "pulls" in play here: one toward the smaller, fundamental role of encompassed parts and a second toward the increasing, significant role of emergent wholes where the smaller parts combine. While these pulls seem to be in opposition, they are complementary; they co-exist and are in relationship with each other. The wellness of the smaller wholes is impacted by the larger whole, and the larger whole depends on the smaller wholes that are its foundation. Recognizing a purposeful, evolutionary relationship between citizens and cities is vital to the creation of cities that serve citizens well. Citizens are becoming more numerous, which may lead to feeling inconsequential—yet city nest makers have an increasingly fundamental role to play. In taking on this role, we influence evolutionary progress. What kind of nest do we choose to make, and for what purpose? What materials will we choose?

For McIntosh, life is not static. Evolution is alive, thrilling, and always moving in the direction of goodness, beauty, and truth.[106] We do not know the precise significant, or intrinsic, purpose of larger holons. Evolutionary purpose is grand yet elusive, but not directionless. The same is true for cities. They are alive, free, thrilling, and always moving. They shift and adjust according to the choices citizens make, and they also cause citizens to make more choices. This city–citizen dance is where our evolution plays out.

To allow for our emergence, we need to consciously organize ourselves at the scale of the city and the citizen simultaneously. The city's destination becomes our own evolving purposes. If we drift from our purpose, then so too does the city drift. When we are aware of our relationship with the city, we serve our city better. Our cities are only as good as we make them.

City nest makers have an increasingly fundamental role to play. In taking on this role, we influence evolutionary progress. What kind of nest do we choose to make, and for what purpose? What materials will we choose?

Destination And Direction

As we organize cities and citizens for continuous improvement, the idea of destination is vital. Knowing our destination—what we want to accomplish—provides us with a sense of purpose, and just as there are two orders of purpose, there are two orders of destination: a specific, immediate destination and a general, less concrete destination further afield.

An immediate destination is a concrete goal or objective that holds our attention and focuses our actions. For example, my neighbour Michelle Hildebrand organized our neighbourhood to sponsor a refugee family. She merged two personal passions with this endeavour: connecting neighbours and supporting refugees. Michelle rallied her neighbours; she connected with the government agency responsible for private sponsorship of refugee families. Funds were raised, a house was donated, and the neighbourhood waited for a family to arrive. Despite desperate need, and the group's readiness, we knew we would wait six to twelve months for "our family" to arrive. With her eye on the destination—neighbourhood support of a refugee family— Michelle decided to change the plan. She knew of a government-sponsored refugee family already in Edmonton, living in a hotel. The family had seven children, with an eighth on the way within the month. After quickly checking in with her group of neighbours, Michelle offered the home that was sitting empty to the family.

Our cities are only as good as we make them.

Sharing her desire to help a refugee family, the group reorganized and aimed for a new destination: the family already in Edmonton. The funds we'd already raised were reserved for another family coming in six to twelve months and could not be used for this family, but the neighbourhood contributed in other ways: cleaning the house, finding and setting up furniture, organizing computers and the Internet, making sure the light bulbs worked. When the family arrived, other community members served as translators, played with the kids, took family members to doctor appointments, taught English, registered the kids for school and helped them get there each day. At the heart of all of this, Michelle lived her passion, making the neighbourhood and the world a better place. Her purpose—welcoming a refugee family into our neighbourhood—didn't change, but her path to accomplishing her purpose, her destination, did.

Specific, immediate destinations can be planned for because they follow a linear and rational path. When destinations are further away, it is more difficult to set a specific path for getting there. Deciding to set up a house for a refugee family is quite a specific destination; figuring out the processes for finding a family to live in the house is more complicated. When we imagine and plan for an expansive, evolutionary future, we may not know exactly where we are headed, but the general destination is known. The way we get there is best described as a direction.

In 2012, Edmonton, adopted a food and urban agriculture strategy, envisioning an agricultural system that would contribute to the local economy and the cultural, financial, social, and environmental sustainability of the city.[107] By adopting the strategy, the city chose the destination—be a resilient food and agriculture system that contributes to the local economy—and began to take action to move in that direction. In this case, the destination was further afield than Michelle's refugee work; it was bigger in scale and complexity. Her work was not less important, but it did take place at a smaller scale, so was more fundamental and had an immediate impact on citizens' lives.

Before arriving at more distant destinations, we pass through several specific and more immediate destinations. The food and urban agriculture strategy included several smaller steps, each connected to the larger purpose: establishing a food council, developing local food infrastructure capacity, growing local food supply and demand, treating food waste as a resource, and supporting urban farmers and ecological approaches to farming. Each of these strategies is made up of numerous, smaller destinations with specific purposes that contribute to the overall large purpose of the final destination.

The Edmonton Food Council (EFC) was established to advise and act on food and urban agriculture matters and actively support the implementation of the strategy.[108] Fifteen citizens, each passionate about food and urban agriculture systems, make up the Council, and they are changing the ways Edmontonians think about the food they eat and where it comes from. The diversity of their work as individuals is remarkable: they operate food businesses; they are formal experts (teachers and academics); communications professionals; community gardeners; supporters of the local food movement; master gardeners and urban farmers. To a person, they are outstanding Edmontonians. They care about their city, and they care about food security for the Edmonton region and beyond. Together, they act strategically, offering significant, intrinsic value to life in Edmonton as it relates to food. The EFC and the food and urban agriculture strategy have facilitated regulations to allow urban bees and hens, film screenings and community conversations, fruit tree mapping, food policy, and fundraising events to support local food initiatives. Their work is an example of how citizens, city government, business, and community organizations can play a fundamental role, together, in changing what food production in the city means to people in day-to-day life, for food producers or consumers.

In a city, the most immediate purposes, the most specific destinations, come from citizens like Michelle, who followed her passion and mobilized her neighbourhood to welcome a refugee family. She is a small holon that is fundamental to the larger holon of the city. The Edmonton Food Council is a larger holon, bringing together the work of many to serve more complex, longer-term purposes through the food and urban agriculture strategy—an evolutionarily significant destination. Small purposes are nested within the larger, serving as the foundation for larger, more expansive purposes. The smaller purposes are more about survival, while the larger purposes are about improvement. In each of us, our values inform our destinations as individuals as well as the larger wholes of which we are a part.

In Edmonton's 2013 municipal election, after being declared the winning mayoral candidate, Don Iveson noted that his team's approach to the campaign was to give the city an opportunity to see itself. In Iveson's case, his campaign told citizens that the election provided a moment to "live into" the dreams we have for our city. His goal for civic government is to give citizens the tools, the encouragement, the vision, the story, and the framework to create something even more extraordinary on the banks of the North Saskatchewan River.[109] He knows the city is moving in a direction and he values creating the conditions for self-organizing citizens to make the city we need. Iveson articulates the values and purpose of the city that we chose in 273 out of 279 polls on election day. (Iveson was re-elected with 74.5% of the popular vote in 2017.) And under the guidance of elected officials, city administration will prepare plans to reach in the direction of these values, and these plans will have both short-term destinations and reach for a vision that is further afield. Election results reflect voters' values. We see ourselves in the stories our chosen candidates tell.

Different groups of citizens work toward different destinations. Through their efforts, they purposefully respond to the variety of life conditions in the city. As I write this, a handful of destinations are alive in my city: city government and community organizations have opened a community recreation centre to serve as an emergency shelter for the city's homeless as temperatures drop to -35 C. Community organizations are supporting Edmonton's Iranian community as it mourns the death of 176 people, and 27 Edmontonians, who were killed when the Ukranian International Airline Flight 572 was shot down by two Iranian missiles. School systems are adjusting their budgets to accommodate a drop in funding while trying to maintain quality education. City government is looking for feedback on a draft city plan that will guide infrastructure investments before a public hearing in a few months. A utility company is working to install a solar farm. The result: we are collectively able to respond to the diverse needs of the city. Vast numbers of citizens, paid and unpaid, pitch in and help, ensuring that all of these activities take place in healthy ways, so we have a city that serves citizens well. These citizens are serving a variety of purposes, all alive at every scale, all reaching—as interested and able—into expanded purposes.

Each of us has this choice—to participate in the improvement of the city, and in doing do improve how well the city serves its citizens.

The City Is Alive When We Are Alive

Just as we feel adrift in our work from time to time, so too do our cities drift. Teasing out the direction we wish to go is as important as having a specific destination, because our understanding of the improvement we want to make points us in a specific direction. As we move in that direction, our purpose becomes more clear and our destinations materialize, providing us with tangible goals.

Feeling adrift is natural—particularly on larger scale endeavours or when working to achieve broad, expansive purposes. Feeling adrift is part of being alive. It is also an indicator of maturation, of moving from Blue purposes, full of structure and authority, to Orange, Green, and Yellow purposes in which we have less control.

At the scale of the individual and the larger scale of the collective, we are capable of striving for increasingly far-reaching purposes. At all scales, we have the potential for a range of purposes that we cannot yet contemplate or image, are waiting to be achieved. Each purpose responds to particular circumstances and is therefore always in flux. As life conditions change, we may be pulled down the Spiral to ensure survival, and up the Spiral, to improve our situation. The impulse to improve is not just for self—it is also for other. At the same time that we pursue self-improvement, we also give to the larger community.[110] McIntosh says, to "grow and thrive as individuals over the long term, we not only have to take care of ourselves, we also have to provide service to something larger than ourselves."[111] The work we do to improve our conditions for self and others is the evolutionary force that generates cities.

McIntosh argues that our evolution is co-created by the agency of humanity. The self–other relationships, embedded in our drive to improve, are also citizen–city relationships. McIntosh says:

> [A]s we are moved by evolution, as we grow in our ability to experience and create intrinsic value, we come to see how the purpose of evolution itself is still evolving—**it cannot be discerned with finality because it is still in the process of being determined by the beings whose choices are required for its creation.**[112]

The work we do to improve our conditions for self and others is the evolutionary force that generates cities.

We may not know exactly where we are going, but the choices we make determine our path. We choose the direction.

Destination and direction are of equal importance for both cities and citizens. As McIntosh tells us, every whole (holon) has two purposes, grounded in evolution's essential organizing structure of wholes and parts, because every whole is a part and vice versa.[113] Both specific destinations and a general direction are needed. We plan for the specific, and we organize to move in a direction, not knowing precisely where it will take us.

The linear, simple story of a city, with a beginning, middle, and end is a familiar tale. We latch onto a destination and plan how we will get there. A non-linear and more complex story of the city, however, does not have a predictable destination. Inspired by novelist Lynn Coady, I see city life as a frontier,[114] a place that generates new conditions and challenges that require us to notice a choice: innovate and adjust, or not. Noticing possibilities and making choices are the skills we need to fortify.

City life is a story without a defined ending. It consists of multiple lives and wills that, as Coady says, "shift and change and occasionally assert themselves in force."[115] The city belongs to us and is created by us—the collective; not by any individual. No matter how hard I work as an individual, the city moves forward because of the work we do together. We create it and we can shape it.

I have control over whether I make myself available for, or prevent myself from, a full life in my city. This is crucial: I choose, with every interaction I have, to allow the full potential for cities and citizens to emerge. I can help my city and its citizens be fully alive, if they so choose. There will be no trophy on the wall to mark my accomplishment, but I'll know that I contributed to my city's aliveness. Each of us has this choice—to participate in the improvement of the city, and in doing do improve how well the city serves its citizens.

Noticing possibilities and making choices are the skills we need to fortify.

In the citizens' story, the city is the antagonist, creating the challenges and tensions we need to grow. In the city's story, citizens are the antagonists, seeking ways to better serve the needs of self, others, and the city, yet always adding to the tension of city life. This is our fundamental role as citizens in the city: to create the conditions for self and others to grow. If we choose to not fulfill this role, we keep others from reaching their full potential. City life puts us on the edge, on the frontier of learning how to serve self, fellow citizens, and our cities. The more we step into the journey of discerning the work we are called to do, the more we contribute to fundamental shifts in the city's overall well-being.

Cities are alive with purpose, with a larger-than-our-life sense of direction. They are not precisely planned, but we are able to shape them, by pursuing our purposes—our passions—as citizens. Our work is the evolutionary force that generates cities.

1. City life puts us on the edge, asking us to learn about ourselves and others, and discern the work we are called to do. The more we step into the work we are called to do, the more we contribute to fundamental shifts in the city's overall well-being.

2. Citizens are becoming more numerous and have an increasingly fundamental role to play as city-nest makers. What kind of nest do we choose to make and for what purpose? What materials will we choose? Who will our city-nest serve?

3. There are two orders of destination in the city of equal importance: short-term, specific destinations, and general, less-concrete destinations that are further afield.

4. Teasing out the direction we want to move is as important as a specific destination because understanding what constitutes improvement points us in a direction. As we move in a direction, the purposes that show up as specific destinations along the way evolve, giving us clarity and specific tangible purposes.

5. When citizens lose their sense of purpose in their work, cities lose their sense of purpose. If we lose track of where we are going and why, then the cities we build to support us on our journey have lost track too. Cities are only as good as we make them.

6. We need to consciously organize ourselves at the scale of citizens and city, and destinations and direction, simultaneously.

7. Feeling adrift is an indicator of maturation, a sign that we are reaching for more expansive purposes. We choose, with every interaction we have with self and others, to allow the potential for cities and citizens to emerge. We create the conditions for self and others to grow, or not. We choose to support others to reach higher potentials or keep them from it.

NEST-MAKING PRACTICE
Knowing Who You Are And Where You Are Going

Cities are alive with purpose, with a larger-than-our-life sense of direction. They are not precisely planned, but we are able to shape them, by pursuing our purposes—our passions—as citizens. We give constantly to self, other, and our places, yet as McIntosh indicates, evolution cannot be seen from its conclusion because we who are evolving are making choices in the process.[116] The highest order purpose, the direction we are moving in, cannot be defined because it is alive, constantly changing; it is as universal as the citizen holons.

Our work as citizens, as the smaller holons, is to create possibility. The city, as the larger holon, creates probability. We are learning together about who we want to be. The more our work aligns with the improvement we want to see, the more our cities meet our needs, and, ironically, the more our cities challenge us to improve again. Our destination is simultaneously alive and adrift. It is most alive when we work from our passion, our inner drive to improve. When we catch glimpses of bigger destinations, for both self and the city, our direction is discerned for fleeting moments. Between these fleeting moments, we feel adrift, which is to feel alive.

Rabbi Shmuley asks, "Who, not what, do you want to be?" A question that speaks to character, not career.[117] There is a choice to be made about how we as citizens participate in community.

REFLECT

Take a moment with a journal or sketchbook and see where the following questions take you. There are no wrong or right answers.

Self—What is my significant, or intrinsic, purpose? How am I fundamental, or instrumental, to the city?

Other—What exciting work do I see in others? How are they—as people and their work—building blocks for the city?

City—What purposes are alive in me and my city? Into what new purposes am I and my city expanding?

Care—What support do I need to be honest with myself? What do others need? What does my city need?

Reminder: "city" means the city-habitat we make for ourselves, the community around us, not our municipal government (often referred to as "the City").

*[T]here is a constant unease under the skies.... We are on a ship that re-
quires us to navigate through channels whose depth we can never judge
in advance. For even the sea floor is constantly shifting: there are threats
to our existence and our future that cannot be seen.*
       —Henning Mankell[118]

*Our shoelaces have to come undone, said Avery, before we ever
think to kneel.*
       —Anne Michaels[119]

6

JOURNEY: MESSY AND UNEASY

CITIES ARE MEANT TO FEEL UNEASY

Cities are complex, hard to figure out, and far from perfect. Consciously or not, we choose to live in cities and the tension they create for us pulls us along to improve both them and ourselves. And, of course, once we make those improvements, new challenges surface—which lead to a whole new range of improvements. That is the essence of our evolutionary relationship with cities: endless unease.

The essence of our evolutionary relationship with cities: endless unease.

Progress and Three Kinds of Trouble
Cities are delicate; they can fail at any time and take their citizens down with them. As Ronald Wright points out, the myth of progress has sometimes served us well, but it is also dangerous: "Progress has an internal logic that can lead beyond reason to catastrophe. A seductive trail of successes may end up in a trap."[120] For Wright, civilization—and cities—is an experiment and a recent way of life for humans, one that we seem to struggle with, as we've seen human civilizations rise and fall. He says, a "small village on good land beside a river is a good idea, but when the village grows into a city and paves over the land, it becomes a bad idea."[121] At minimum, the city loses its ability to feed itself. When

we are caught in the progress trap, we do not have the foresight to consider the long-range consequences of our actions. The reasons, says Wright:

> ...may be inherent to our kind, shaped by the
> millions of years when we lived from hand to mouth
> by hunting and gathering. It may also be little
> more than a mix of inertia, greed, and foolishness
> encouraged by the shape of the social pyramid.
> The concentration of power at the top of large-scale
> societies gives the elite a vested interest in the
> status quo; they continue to prosper in the darken-
> ing times long after the environment and general
> populace begin to suffer.[122]

As we continue to experiment with civilization (and cities), Wright encourages us to heed the work of his contemporary, Joseph Tainter, who identified three types of trouble that can lead to the collapse of a civilization: the runaway train, the dinosaur, and the house of cards.

More than 125 years before Tainter proposed his theories about the collapse of civilized societies, these three phenomena appear in Charles Dickens's Little Dorrit,[123] a wonderful story of city life that has parallels in today's world. First, the runaway train symbolizes a problem that, when not dealt with right away, gets bigger and faster and more challenging, or even impossible, to address. Dickens illustrates the runaway train in Merdle's bank, where debt is allowed to pay off debt, to finance extraordinary returns on investments. Mr. Merdle alone, as the conductor of the train, allows the train to gather speed as he sees the inevitable financial crash. After his suicide, his financial schemes become apparent to his investors whose money is gone.

Next up—the dinosaur, which represents the belief that nothing can go wrong, that nothing can threaten life as we know it. Meet Dickens's dinosaurs: the people of position, privilege and prestige who have complete faith in themselves, hence Merdle, and seek his favour to invest at his bank. Although he despises them, Merdle welcomes them on board his train. They continue to believe in his wisdom and prowess to deliver the promised financial returns because this financial status is taken for granted. Merdle's success compels people to invest with him, because questioning his ability would mean questioning their own status and privilege. In the world of the dinosaur, nothing can go wrong. But it does: Merdle's bank falls and takes its investors' savings with it.

The house of cards, Tainter's third kind of trouble, denotes a structure or logic that is built on a shaky foundation—when a piece of foundation is removed, the entire structure collapses. In *Little Dorrit*, when Merdle's bank collapses, the savings of the story's families evaporate. Rich households lose the financial privilege to which they are accustomed. For those with newfound wealth, the joy of wealth is gone. "I might go back to dancing," says Fanny Dorrit. Her brother, Tip, "But what about me?" All in which they found meaning is gone. Some, like Arthur Clenham, are sentenced to debtors' prison because they couldn't pay creditors after having lost their fortune on Merdle's runaway train. Dickens's message: If you build a foundation based only on riches and material goods, the house will eventually crumble.

In today's world, Bernie Madoff's Ponzi scheme, that came to light with the Wall Street crisis in 2008, exemplified a financial house of cards. The dinosaur-like thinking of bankers, regulators and investors refused to acknowledge that the promised returns were unrealistic. The economic runaway train became apparent when Madoff was unable to maintain the fraud. The consequences were serious: 37,011 victimized investors defrauded of tens of billions of dollars.[124]

Another runaway train with dire consequences is underway. In 2019, ahead of the United Nations Climate Action Summit, the world's leading climate science organizations produced the *United in Science* report,[125] documenting the warmest five-year period on record, continued decrease of sea ice and ice mass, acceleration of sea-level rise, and record greenhouse gas concentrations in our atmosphere. The report documents the stunning and growing gap between agreed upon targets to address global warming and the reality we make for ourselves.

Whether we look at economic conditions, or environmental and health stresses, our privilege in the West can be seen as a house of cards and a runaway train. Let us be wary of dinosaur-like thinking that stops us from noticing the reality we are facing. We should strive to be the opposite of Tainter's dinosaur—the anti-dinosaur—alive, awake, conscious, in tune with our surroundings, in relationship with the world. The anti-dinosaur seeks understanding and solutions and is driven by a sense of happiness. In *Little Dorrit*, the happy folk have relationships that cross (yet keep) many boundaries—jailed and jailor, poor and rich, female and male, servant and master, harassed and harasser, young and old, unloved and loved. Perhaps the antidote to the dinosaur is a way of being that brings out the best in people so they can meet the challenges ahead: cultivate collective ingenuity.

Lessons from Dale the Dinosaur

When I first started working as a development officer in 1995, I had to learn the ropes. I was fresh out of school so I didn't know how urban development came about, how approvals took place, how a community's planning documents worked, or how people fit into these processes. So I asked questions, lots of questions. I wanted to understand the system so that I knew how to move forward. One colleague—let's call him Dale—always answered my questions the same way: "Because that's the way we've always done it."

I understand now that Dale didn't actually understand why things happened the way they did. He did not know the purpose of the rules and protocols. As a result, he didn't see the value in a different way of doing things, even if a different way would respond more effectively to the community's needs. Dale was a dinosaur; he had a hard time understanding that when the context changed, the purpose for our rules changed as well. Our rules needed to shift and adjust so our city could grow and progress.

And herein lies the planning trap. We so often rely on what has worked before, or we conduct research to see what has worked in other places. We look for trends and then assume that what has worked for years will continue to work. At the heart of this trap is standardization—predetermined courses of action that are detached from context and circumstances. There are times when life conditions require standardization. But we must also be open to diversity—which will spark our imagination. Moreover, we learn little when applying anything blindly, with no regard to circumstances. We do learn if we explore, notice patterns, reflect on what is happening in our milieu, then find a way forward that meets the life conditions of our own specific context.

Being aware of patterns can help us find a way through the trap. There is a distinction between standardization and patterns. Standardization is about having a recipe to create more of what has already happened, but this works only in simple and complicated systems, as we saw in Chapter Four (Table 5). Where standardization works when actions and consequences are predictable, pattern-thinking is about discerning consequences as best we can in complex systems. The latter requires us to be sensitive to what has previously happened with the knowledge that the pattern may change. We may be required to act differently depending on the feedback we receive. Planning, as an activity, is a dinosaur move only when standardization is disconnected from what we wish to achieve or when we mistakenly apply linear logic to a complex system.

A Learning Journey

Consider these two meanings of the word "journey:"[126]

- An occasion when you travel from one place to another, especially when there is a long distance between the places (synonyms: circuit, commute, crossing, excursion, expedition, exploration, peregrination, pilgrimage).
- A process of changing and developing over a period of time (synonyms: transition, conversion, transformation, revision, change, adaptation, modification, flux).

A journey is both an act of travelling and an act of learning. We sense where we are going (destination) even while we are unsure of where, exactly, we will end up (emergence). We embark on a journey to get "there" that involves learning along the way, and that learning takes place in our habitats—economic, social, and physical.

When it comes to cities, the direction we are moving creates city habitats that serve citizens well. And to do this, citizens learn to serve their cities well. Because of this reciprocity, the more explicit our relationship with cities the better they serve us. Today, city planning is about having a sense of where we are going, figuring out how to maintain that direction (correcting our course when warranted), and trusting that where we end up is where we ought to be.

This path involves living with a great deal of uncertainty and unease. As we organize ourselves in this habitat, we need to support self, others, whole cities and our planet of cities. Cities are the vehicles that propel the human evolutionary journey, and they need to be as worthy as we can make them. Both cities and our experience of cities is non-linear and complex. To get what we need from cities, we must accept them, and our experience of them, as imperfect, messy, and confusing and often at odds with our well-planned, rational, and linear ways of understanding the world. Our learning journey is at the heart of what makes us feel uneasy at every scale, from self to city to planet.

ITCHING FOR IMPROVEMENT

At the heart of our impulse to thrive is the itch to make our world a better place, to improve our quality of life, at every scale. When we see room for improvement, we are compelled to take action, to create new work. For McIntosh, "[T]he evolutionary perspective recognizes that the progressive improvement of the human condition is occurring simultaneously on many levels, with each level of evolution experiencing continuous growth and development within the confines of its worldview structure."[127]

As we experience and move through each level of development (the Spiral) noted in Chapter Three, we see challenges, we tackle them, and we make improvements. In the more recent levels of development (Yellow and Turquoise), we seek the well-being of all previous levels to support our evolution. We see there is a time and place for rules in our cities (Blue), for example, when we agree to pay taxes and have expectations for what that tax money will be used for. We see there is a time and place to cultivate our collective story so we each find a place where we feel we belong (Purple). Or we make sure that we take advantage of our entrepreneurial spirit (Orange). All these perspectives have a legitimate place in the city. They live together in the city, sometimes in conflict: not everyone will like the rules, the story, or the role of business all the time. This dynamic tension is in our nature, just as it is in our nature to work to improve as a result of this tension.

In every corner of every city, people work to improve their surroundings. Sometimes we know exactly what we are being called to do; other times we only have a sense of what we are called to do. We can be conscious or unconscious of the work that calls. The better we know self and other, the more likely we can identify what makes us uneasy. Then we can choose to seek deeper knowing by inviting and exploring our uneasiness. The insight gained allows us to move forward in wise ways.

As we work to organize ourselves, in cities, we learn to recognize when we are feeling uneasy and develop practices and processes that help us figure out why those feelings of uneasiness surface. By accepting those feelings and allowing them to inhabit us for a while, new ways of knowing and being emerge and thrive. As individuals and collectives, it takes a lot of practice to welcome this learning and the journey that ensues.

Tension Is an Evolutionary Driver

Cities are perpetually unfinished because evolution is ongoing. We are always learning; we are always improving our lives around us, and this changes our cities, leaving us with more improvements to realize. The tension we feel between what we have and what we could have—improvement—is hard to live with, yet essential to our evolution.

My whole being knows when I am uneasy, whether or not I am conscious of it. If I am unconscious of what bothers me, I avoid the natural itch to do what I know I ought to do or to be the way I want to be. I may be able to avoid my discomfort forever, or an event may jolt me to fully see the tension I am experiencing. This feeling is a clue that I am experiencing *akrasia*[128]—the tension I experience when what I choose to do is not what I know I ought to do—and I have a choice about how much attention to give the tension.

Keep in mind these seven important qualities about *akrasia*:

1. Living with the akratic gulf is unavoidable. We live in a world where we regularly grapple with what we know we ought to do and what we actually do.

2. Living with akrasia is hard because it means living with knowing, always, that there is room for improvement.

3. Akrasia can paralyze or serve us. We can choose to beat ourselves up about what we don't do or explore the change that wants to emerge as a result of discomfort. The choice is ours.

4. Living with akrasia means accepting vulnerability. When we choose to explore what makes us uncomfortable because the status quo may be threatened. Trust that discomfort signals that we want something different-- improvement.

5. Living with akrasia means scratching the itch from time to time. Getting rid of the itch is not the goal. Some itches are best left alone, other itches need a scratch to bring relief. Considering how much itch is helpful is a decision to be taken seriously.

6. Akrasia is about questions, not answers. Exploring the gulf between what I know I ought to do and what I actually do is not a linear exploration where questions have immediate or easy answers. An answer, whether given to me or provided by me, is really a way for me to avoid the deeper questions that will lead to more itch and deeper exploration.

7. Living with akrasia is a way of being that puts questions first. The tension of akrasia pulls us along an evolutionary path. This seventh quality is the essence of our evolutionary journey; as we constantly strive for improvement in self and in our collective endeavours, we are stepping individually and collectively into the future we create for ourselves.

When we purposefully explore the tension in our world, we are aware of and awake to what is happening with and around the self. This exploration may be difficult at the individual level, but is infinitely more challenging at larger scales, where the gap spans our collective consciousness. Imagine a canyon, with a city's action on one side and our knowledge of what we ought to do on the other. On the "ought to" side, however, there are many different perspectives on the correct action to take. The gulf is small for some and massive for others. Through discussion and debate we decide what should be done. The span of the collective gulf is as wide as the perspectives within the collective.

As individuals, it is imperative to explore the gulfs in our lives constructively and supportively, or they will paralyze us. For cities to explore their gulfs effectively, there need to be enough individuals who are capable to explore the gulf for themselves— the fundamental city nest-makers we identified in Chapter Five. This is a learning journey for cities with no simple solution. We have to figure out how to span the gulf in spite of our varied perspectives that make navigating our crossing, as a collective, a messy task.

As we navigate our lives as individuals, families, organizations, neighbourhoods, cities, and civilization, we need to consciously choose to accept each other and our tensions. The gulfs between us and within us do not have to be a hindrance. They can serve us, for the tension we experience moves our economic life—how we think, make, and do new things—and the very creation and evolution of our selves and our cities.

The Direction: Changing Versus Change

Cindy Wigglesworth, creator of the SQ21 spiritual intelligence self-assessment, reminds us to think of the self as a verb: "[R]efer to yourself in dynamic terms. See how it changes your sense of identity and possibility: I am learning and growing; I am considering the pros and cons of the choices in front of me; I am feeling many things at the same time—sad and happy, tired yet excited."[129] Citizens, as fundamental holons, are learning and growing; so too are our cities. For cities to serve citizens better, we citizens need to learn and grow. We are forever in the process of changing and Wigglesworth asks an essential question: Who is driving your life? Is it the calmer, wiser "Higher Self," the more self-centred ego, and/or the beliefs and ideals of others?[130]

Who is in charge of our city's learning and growing? The answer is "me" and "we," and the choice is ours.

Imagine city decision-making that is not driven by ego. Generative debates replace nasty debates. Exploration replaces confrontation. Imagine city decision-making that taps into our spirituality, our innate human need to be connected to something larger than ourselves. Imagine a social habitat that invites each of us to reach our full potential. Wigglesworth asks another vital question, one that applies at any scale: Who is in charge of this self-process in all its multi-layered and ever changing complexity?[131] Put more simply, who is in charge of our learning and growing? Who is in charge of our city's learning and growing? The answer is "me" and "we," and the choice is ours.

We move in the direction of learning and growing: changing not change. We learn and grow into what it means to be egocentric when the circumstances require and stretch into a bigger view of ourselves when required. For Wigglesworth, our spiritual intelligence matures from "me" to "we," from ego to the Higher Self. Making this shift invites the best part of ourselves to be in charge, and the destination suddenly becomes clearer, allowing us to develop at maximum speed.[132] When the ego is not in control, we are more available to the learning on offer.

How we engage with self and other has a profound effect on our social habitat. From a place of ego, I have little tolerance for others and their learning journey. From my Higher Self, I can respect others' learning journeys and better see my own. We all struggle with change—citizens, neighbourhoods, organizations, cities, nations, the planet. We are all developing our spiritual intelligence, the skills that come with time and practice, as we integrate our experiences with the ways we understand the world around us.

QUALITY OF SOCIAL HABITAT MATTERS

> *We are living in a culture of extreme advocacy, of confrontation, of judgment, and of verdict. Discussion has given way to debate. Communication has become a contest of wills. Public talking has become obnoxious and insincere. Why? Maybe it's because deep down under the chatter we have come to a place where we know that we don't know...anything. But nobody's willing to say that.*
> —John Patrick Stanley[133]

Practise Social Habitat
We need to practise what it means to live, work, and serve our cities. We need to practise active citizenship, rather than passive downloads of information, as we sit and listen, unwilling to notice that the quality of our communication with each other does little to foster deeper understanding. Here's my itch: for over twenty-five years I have had difficulty giving my full attention to speakers at conferences—I squirm in my seat.

When first working as a professional city planner at 25 years old, I would sit and listen with a notebook, using the time to explore the issues I was tackling on the job. While it may have looked like I was not paying attention, I was allowing the words of the presenters to negotiate with my real-life experience, emerging as concrete ideas for me to improve my work. My time was well spent. With some experience, my purpose at a conference adjusted to be about connecting with people; yet many conferences are not set up for this—they are set up for people to sit and listen, to take in what we find of value for personal, individual work but to reach no further. City planners are a collective performing the same work, but we are not the kind of collective that meets in ways that truly allow us to share what we know and to grow.

As professional planners, we are not creating social habitats that align with the complexity of the world in which we work. This is not an itch directed only at professional planners—this is a phenomenon in any profession. I've seen standing ovations for speakers who go overtime, cutting off any opportunity for a post-presentation Q and A. I've listened to experts brought in from near and far tell me how to make my work or my city better, but I am not given the opportunity to ask questions about my specific situation. We want to improve, but the social habitat we create to nurture that improvement maintains the status quo of our shared frustration, our slowly paced change. It is risky to create places for our minds, hearts, and souls to interact, to seek out what is not working and identify the needed improvements. If we only sit and listen—without engaging—we keep ourselves from taking action. We say we want to scratch the itch but we apply anti-itch cream.

A group wishing to take conscious, joint action, at any scale, relies on feedback. We need to share insights. We need to hear each others' stories and discover what resonates with individuals and the collective. We need to explore the issues and seek clarity on issues we struggle to understand. We need to be willing to say what is not working, individually and collectively, and then discern appropriate courses of action.

Conscious action does not come from simply talking about our practice. I've moderated many conference sessions where presenters speak about engaging the public and stakeholders in new ways; however, they choose to not engage the audience in those new ways. The audience hears about something new, but they do not experience something new, or practise something new.

I itch for balance, to hear what others have to say and to figure out the implications of what are hearing, and what we ought to do about our new understanding. This means processes that invite the chaos that comes with new understanding, with just enough order for self-organizing to take place. We need places where we can explicitly embark on a learning journey, alone and together, with great care for self, other and the cities we are making. And in this balance, we choose when to use the anti-itch cream.

A Redundant Habitat for Awareness

I live a privileged life: I have a safe home, a pretty consistent income, reliable supplies of food and goods, dependable transportation, and ample time for recreation. I am white, which means I also enjoy unearned privilege that black, Indigenous and people of colour do not experience. In this "magic bubble," my way of life is comfortable and stable. From time to time, though, something in my world changes, endangering my sanctuary, and I have to choose how to act: I can pretend the change is not happening, fight the change and defend my magic bubble, or welcome the change and adjust to new reality. If I feel particularly brave, I invite myself to live change as a verb; I seek out challenging points of view, causing my bubble to re-shape itself around a new understanding and compelling me to face challenges I would otherwise ignore.

As citizens and cities, we need to face situations we don't want to. In *Dark Age Ahead*, Jane Jacobs names five pillars of city culture that are in jeopardy:

1. Cities are not providing the public infrastructure to serve families in what are now unprecedented circumstances.
2. The credentialing of education has meant we have lost learning.
3. Partial scientific understanding combined with an overconfidence that "emboldens us to accept mistakes we would not otherwise accept."
4. Taxation and government powers are too far from the needs and possibilities of citizens.
5. Self-policing is a danger in the learned professions (foxes are not reliable guards of hen houses).

Her aim in defining these pillars is "to do the small bit [she] can to give stabilizing corrections a push."[134]

The value of *Dark Age Ahead*, as any cautionary work does, is that it encourages us to look at our cities and the world as they currently exist, instilling a need to consciously reach for a future

> *[where] each improvement and strengthening*
> *leads to other improvements and strengthening*
> *in the culture, in turn further strengthening the*
> *initial improvement… Responsive and responsible*
> *government encourages the corrective practices*
> *exerted by democracy, which in their turn strength-*
> *en good government and responsible citizenship.*
> *And so it goes. Beneficent spirals, operating by*
> *benign feedback, mean that everything needful is*
> *not required at once: each individual improvement*
> *is beneficial for the whole.* [135]

Dark Age Ahead describes the awareness we need to choose the beneficial spiral. Empires that rise and fall "seldom seem to retain sufficient cultural awareness to prevent them from overreaching and overgrasping… [T]he true power of a successful culture resides in its patient and grown-up attitude… [It] must be self-aware." [136]

In addition to awareness, Jacobs explains the importance of redundancy. We live in an era of highly complex cultural demands, and we need many mentors and examples to support us to learn and nurture new social habitats: "A culture, just to keep itself going, makes voracious demands on the energies of many people for hands-on mentoring." [137] We don't need one kind of social habitat, but many. We don't need one size of social habitat, but many. In fact, we are in the mess of learning the kinds of social habitats that we need because we don't know exactly what we need now or will need in the future.

Jacobs warns about the cultural genocide that might occur "when a culture is rich enough and inherently complex enough to afford redundancy of nurturers, but eliminates them as an extravagance or loses their cultural services through heedlessness." [138] This can be avoided by creating social habitats that support our city journey: "Helping individuals become acceptable and fulfilled members of a culture takes generous individual attention to each one, usually from numerous people." [139] We are as rich as the social habitat we create; the work needed to choose the beneficial spiral is ours to do, and this work takes place in the social habitat, as we learn together. As Jacobs says, "We can't rely on surprise rescues; mostly we must lie in the beds we make on the mattresses our culture provides." [140]

We need a social habitat that supports us to say what we need to say, encourages the lines of communication and feedback to remain open, prioritizes our relationships. Living in cities, and the process of creating and recreating them, is a learning journey that serves our own evolution. As we endlessly think, make, and do new things in response to our habitat, we scratch what itches at every scale (self, family, neighbourhood, organization, city, region, nation, planet). However, this learning journey only succeeds when we are receptive to feedback from our surroundings. Our ability to seek and receive feedback is a survival skill that depends on the health of the social habitat we create.

Now is the time to embark on a journey to create social habitats that bring out the best in people, that support individuals and the collective. Support is needed when we experience the discomfort that comes with listening to the call to do the work we long to do—both the discomfort within self as I figure out what is calling me, and as I react to the work others are called to do. We need to organize ourselves to physically build cities that work for us, and to support each other in the uneasiness of city building. This tough and critical work never ends because we are forever recreating our world and our cities and it hinges on the social habitats that encourage feedback to flow in all directions. While there will be many unanswered questions along the way, we do know that we will undertake this journey together.

When you get right down to it, it always comes back to desire, a willingness to learn, and the ability to really see. Many of us have the desire; it's the learning and seeing that's the hard part.
        —Garr Reynolds[141]

Doubt requires more courage than conviction does, and more energy; because conviction is a resting place and doubt is infinite—it is a passionate exercise. You may come out of my play uncertain. You may want to be sure. Look on that feeling. We've got to learn to live life with a full measure of uncertainty. There is no last word. That's the silence under the chatter of our time.
        —John Patrick Stanley[142]

1. Unease is a catalyst in our evolutionary relationship with cities. Our cities improve when we respond to the universal tension between what is and what could be: akrasia. And, of course, every improvement we make gives rise to new challenges which in turn lead to further improvements.

2. Choosing to be in relationship with our city builds resilience that allows us to adapt to our changing world.

3. Exploring the tensions that come with living in the city is a purposeful act that leads to self-awareness.

4. City planning is about having an idea of where we want to go, figuring out how to maintain that direction (with course corrections as warranted), and trusting that where we end up will not be perfect; it will require further improvement. To do so, we must avoid the trap of linear logic and learn to accept uncertainty and unease.

5. Embracing the messiness of city life as part of our personal and collective learning journey requires practice. This relationship work between self, other and the city is difficult; quality social habitats support us in navigating these relationships.

6. Our city habitats thrive when we embrace the process of changing, in the present, rather than aiming for change that takes place in the future.

7. To create cities that serve us better, we need to willingly look at situations that make us feel uncomfortable. The awareness that comes from discomfort enables us to be more self-aware and consciously reach for the future we want.

The development of cities depends on their citizens, so explicitly acknowledging our learning journeys as citizens is a survival skill that enables us to adapt and evolve. Cities are a launching point for our never-ending learning journey—and they are only as resilient and adaptable as we are. As we seek to understand our relationship with cities more deeply, we invite uneasiness into our lives. And, as we work to organize ourselves, in cities or at any scale, we must develop practices to explore this uneasiness.

NEST-MAKING PRACTICE
Practising Social Habitats

The following practices allow us to see, acknowledge, and respond to our cities' social habitats.

1. **Notice our response to the unknown.** No matter how hard and smart we work, we cannot shake the unknown. The more conscious we are of our inner worlds, the better we are able to serve ourselves, others, and our cities.

2. **Use "not knowing" purposefully.** Curiosity can deepen our understanding of our self and our city habitats. David Whyte says, "[N]ot knowing what to do is just as real and just as useful as knowing what to do. Not knowing stops us from taking false directions…If you think you know where you are, you stop looking."[143]

3. **Recognize if it's time for change.** Changes resolve tension in our cities and come when conditions are right. If the right conditions are not present, be patient. If they are present, seek ways to enact the change.

4. **Perform with purpose.** We benefit when we choose to work with purpose—and with feedback loops that reveal when we are on or off track. When are the wheels spinning and when is there traction? Take a risk and ask for feedback.

5. **Stop and listen—to self and city.** Breaking the performance momentum of busyness, we learn to stop and listen to our selves. Check in to see if our work moves us, if it's aligned with our changing habitat.

6. **Organize for emergence.** At every scale, from self to planet, we can choose to organize well by choosing our destination, embracing our learning journey, and allowing the city we need to emerge.

7. **Choose where to place attention.** When we pay attention to problems, we get more problems. When we put our attention on where we want to go, we move in a new direction.

8. **Create feedback loops.** City infrastructure is slow to change, but we can be wonderfully adaptable within that infrastructure. The customized feedback loops emerging with social media open opportunities to see cities more fully.

9. **Adjust rules as purposes change.** Rules are most useful when aligned with the purpose they are meant to serve. As purposes shift in response to our changing world, rules should shift, too.

Cities are the habitats we create for ourselves on a journey that takes us to unknown places and realizes unknown potentials. Our cities are platforms for future growth. The better we tend ourselves, the better we tend our cities. The better we tend our cities, the better we tend ourselves.

REFLECT

Take a moment with a journal or sketchbook and see where the following questions take you. There are no wrong or right answers.

Self—What do I notice in myself right now? What am I itching to improve? What tensions do I experience in the city and how do they cause me to grow?

Other—What do I know about how others experience the city around me? How is my experience the same as and different from theirs?

City—How does my city create social habitats that allow us to explore the diversity of tensions in the city? Do we ignore tension? Do we rely on others to fix what needs improvement? How do we pay attention to what is not working, and needs our attention?

Care—What support do I need to notice tensions in myself? What does my city need to embrace tensions in healthy ways?

Reminder: "city" means the city-habitat we make for ourselves, the community around us, not our municipal government (often referred to as "the City").

CHAPTER 7

We fear the disruption of our lives.
                    —Terry Patten[144]

Never again will we stand
On the threshold of a new age.
We that are here now are touched
In some mysterious way
With the ability to change
And make the future.
                    —Ben Okri[145]

EMERGENCE: THRESHOLDS OF (UN)KNOWN POSSIBILITY

AT THE THRESHOLD OF A NEW AGE

Social technology writer Peggy Holman defines *emergence* as the order arising out of chaos, the new and novel understandings we reach as more complex systems form.[146] Making the transition from one way of understanding the world to another, we encounter thresholds that, once crossed, allow us to see the world with fresh eyes. On the other side, we step into new worlds that work differently, are organized differently, and value different things for different purposes. The only way to see and experience these new worlds is to cross a threshold; without crossing, we are only imagining a new experience.

Standing at the threshold of a new city, we are called to offer more of ourselves, to bring our professional and leadership skills, our energy and passion to contribute to the always emerging, improving city. When individuals bring their higher selves to personal thresholds, the city as a collective can cross each threshold with increased confidence and courage. Together, we emerge, personally and collectively, emboldened into the next new age.

Our cities, and our future, unfold as we create and re-create them and ourselves. With each re-creation, large or small, we experience the necessary uneasiness of a changing world, an uneasiness that sparks our drive to improve our conditions, compelling us to name where we want to go and strive to get to those destinations. By doing so, we move with purpose, in a **direction**. What **emerges** on the way depends on our destination and on what we learn along that **journey**, which in turn changes our destination and journey. These three elements are in a continual dance with each other. We never make the city we think we will because our understanding shifts along the way. When we get "there," a new destination emerges to challenge us to improve, again. In this movement we find our direction.

We never make the city we think we will because our understanding shifts along the way. When we get "there," a new destination emerges to challenge us to improve, again. In this movement we find our direction.

As we organize our cities and the intelligence embedded within them, considering where we wish to go and how we'll get there is essential. Equally important, we must ensure that we create habitats conducive to learning, so that as obstacles emerge to thwart or aid our efforts we can skillfully navigate our way, creating new patterns of order that guide us through the chaos. We learn to handle new life conditions, get comfortable with those life conditions until we reach another chasm, which leads to another journey across another threshold and a new order again.

Being in relationship with the thresholds we encounter is a learning journey. We do not know what we will find after crossing a threshold nor do we know how the crossing will change us. Because we cannot see beyond the threshold, we don't know— and can't imagine—what we'll find on the other side. We can choose to stay where we are or we can journey into the unknown; this choice is part of the journey. Three elements affect our relationship with new ways of thinking, making and doing. First, we are asked to pause and notice our desire to reach what is on the other side—the impetus that pulls us across. Second, we are asked to make a choice, testing our resolve and questioning if we are going in the right direction. Third, we are reminded that to reach our desired destination, we must step into a whole new world, knowing that when we reach our destination it may not be what we expected. We will be changed by the act of crossing.

When we journey into the unknown, we move in a direction that feels ill-defined, but we trust that at each threshold there are good choices to be made. To arrive at the "new age" at the end of our journey, we first arrive at many short-term destinations that we can see clearly. We can only sense the farther destination, we can't define or know it because it is too far down our path. Margaret Wheatley and Deborah Frieze, in their exploration of the transition from an existing system to a new system, note that emergent occurrences share these characteristics: "They exert much more power than the sum of their parts; they always possess new capacities different from the local actions that engendered them; they always surprise us by their appearance."[147] The capacities of the more complex systems that emerge cannot be known, but they will have intelligence. That is our new age: trusting the intelligence of the unknown. Moreover, as Terry Patten says, our own "cultural evolution is moving quickly enough now to be directly perceptible during a human lifetime—even as it is happening. This is radical, and new."[148] Our world is changing before our eyes, at our hands.

Business and management experts Ian Goldin and Chris Kutarna say humanity is at a historic and decisive moment, on the brink of a new Renaissance and the first generation of the urban epoch.[149] The conditions that sparked the European Renaissance of the 15th and 16th centuries are present again, a similar sense of the cultural evolution that Patten highlights—a jump in collective genius, an increase in collective effort and a sense that the risks are higher. The volume and velocity of rich ideas is palpable. We are more educated and better fed than ever, another feature of a Renaissance. Yet Goldin and Kutarna highlight an essential feature of this new age: "A Renaissance age does not offer guarantees; it offers possibilities, and it's up to all of us to realize them."[150] There's a big catch in this new age: one of the conditions that nurtures our growth and development—complexity — brings risk. Goldin and Kutarna notice, "The more complex our interactions become, the harder it is for us to see relationships of cause and effect. We develop cognitive 'blind spots' in our vision of the events around us."[151] Our world is changing and we don't know how it is changing or how our interventions influence the world around us. In this new age, our standard, primarily linear, way of operating no longer works.

There is joy and grief in city life. In this new age, we steward change by nurturing sparks of innovation, but also by acknowledging the death of old ways that no longer serve us well. Imagine the lifecycle of a system that begins small, then grows and becomes full of life, then deteriorates and dies. While a system declines, it offers the nutrients for the green shoots of new systems to emerge. Our participation is necessary to support the new growth: if we do not let the dying die, we are putting our energy into fighting for its continued presence, which is no longer practical or healthy, rather than putting our energy into the new. While the new way grows, the systems in decay still require our attention; we are part of those systems and, consciously or not, we need to grieve the loss of what has served us well. Our cities count on us to do this well.

THRESHOLDS TELL US WE HAVE CHOICES

In 1969, Jane Jacobs noted that without new activities cities stagnate rather than develop:

> *Practical problems that persist and accumulate in cities are symptoms of arrested development. The point is seldom admitted. It has become conventional, for instance, to blame congested and excessive automobile traffic, air pollution and noise upon "rapid technological progress." But the automobiles, the fumes, the sewage and the noise are not new, and the persistently unsolved problems they afford only demonstrate lack of progress. Many evils conventionally blamed upon progress are, rather, evils of stagnation.[152]*

At that time, she made three significant points about new work that continue to apply in today's context. First of all, new work is essential to address current challenges. To tackle climate change, for example, new work is needed. We need to reorganize how we use energy in our households and businesses and industry. We need to create new technologies. We need to support the emergence of new ways of being in relationship with energy, and we need to move away from old ways that depend on the dying fossil fuel systems. Secondly, she states that new work replicates itself, as appropriate and as determined by us, across the city and between cities. New work in one city serves other cities too; a clever invention to better store solar power in cold climates will migrate to other cities. Thirdly, Jacobs reminds us that persistent practical problems in our cities indicate our unwillingness to change, our lack of emergence, our stagnation. Even with the technical advances made since 1969, the consequences of our actions have grown: climate change has become climate crisis.

Since 1969, Jacobs has been telling us that the well-being of our cities has everything to do with our willingness to grow and learn as individuals and as whole cities—and, I add, as a species. While en route to specific destinations, thresholds lead us to challenge our understanding of the world and our interactions with it. Each threshold is a crossroad on the learning journey, and as we explore each threshold we may even notice new destinations that better serve our needs, that better align with the direction we wish to travel. At each threshold, the action we, as citizens and as cities, choose to take (or not) matters.

Responding to Thresholds

Thresholds reveal themselves in a variety of ways. They can be a long, slow, and hidden presence in our lives or they can appear suddenly. A swift change of life conditions, in the form of a super typhoon or fire for example, are easy thresholds to identify and compel us to take immediate action. Thresholds that take time to notice are no less significant, for they equally power us up to be better citizens who create better cities.

I know I have reached a threshold, with a chasm in front of me, when I experience feelings of angst, uncertainty, discomfort, frustration, fear, unease, and even anger that signal something is awry. I don't need to see the chasm to know it is there; I can feel it. These feelings tell me that I have a decision to make, whether or not I recognize it as such.

While hiking the West Coast Trail, on Vancouver Island, Canada, with my brother, we encountered surge channels that had carved their way into an expansive flat shelf of sandstone where North America meets the Pacific Ocean. Rather than choose a path through the unruly wilds of forest beside us, we chose to walk where the ocean had eroded the sandstone and created channels perpendicular to the shore and our path of travel. These channels ranged from narrow to wide, and shallow to deep, and the ocean surged into them, thrusting back and forth.

Some of the crossings we made on that trip were simple—a matter of stepping over deep but narrow chasms or walking through wide but shallow channels. If too wide and deep, we found a route inland. Our most scary crossing was just wide enough to have us consider jumping over the boiling sea far below. We paused, recognizing we had a choice between difficult and more difficult; we chose to jump the channel instead of trekking a laborious inland route through the bush. It may have been wiser to go inland because the consequences of a mis-jump were significant. A fall into the cold water, gushing back and forth five metres below would have made for a difficult rescue. The trek inland meant certain hardship and time, but little risk to personal safety. Before making the leap, uncertainty washed over me, telling me that the risk was too great, that I was asking too much of myself. But we had made our choice carefully, though quickly. We chose to believe we could do it, found community and support in two other hikers, and made the leap.

Just because we stand at a threshold does not mean we are ready to cross it. We need to cultivate social habitats that help us discern when the time is right.

Choosing when to leap depends on context. If we had not had the physical ability to leap, if we had been tired at the end of a long day of hiking, if we'd lacked confidence, or if the sandstone was wet and slippery, the inland route would have been the better choice. It would have been an arduous leap of its own battling the wild bush, but our antennae were working well: we made the right choice.

Just because we stand at a threshold does not mean we are ready to cross it. We need to cultivate social habitats that help us discern when the time is right. To do so, we need to be willing to explore, to be curious. This can be a scary process because, as David Whyte recognizes, "The act of stopping can be the act of facing something we have kept hidden from ourselves for a very long time."[153] But to see thresholds, sometimes we need to invite them into our consciousness and choose to face challenges that, for some reason, we do not want to face. Despite what we think we see, the surge channels may be wide and shallow, enabling us to walk across with ease, or wide and deep, demanding a whole new route.

Intuition

During the writing process, I sometimes physically feel an intense, internal struggle, so I pause to explore what this angst is about.

I look at it, with curiosity, with the express purpose of exploring me. I go for a walk and talk to myself, write in my journal, or sit on a park bench and look at my city. Other times I draw and see where it takes me, or bang a drum, or meditate. I do this intentionally to find the intelligence within me and see what it has to teach me.

There is great intelligence in an inner struggle; it is instruction from a wiser self to the student ego-self. It is often inconvenient or painful to explore because it means acknowledging the status quo is not good enough. The inner struggle is a sign that improvement is needed, and sometimes it is hard to admit that what I have—or what I am doing or have done—is not good enough. Along the way, I make choices: fix what went wrong or grow into improvement. These are subtle but significant choices, for the former undermines improvement by remaining focused on what was and the latter seeks new understanding.

For Bruce Grierson, the struggle powers our way over a threshold into improvement and a new way of being. He conjures the image of significant change about to take place: standing over the proverbial frozen sea with an axe in hand, carrying the axe out onto the ice, and eventually using it. Action is powered by genuinely wanting something different and the internal struggle to bring on that something different. The moment the axe is used, the struggle dissipates because the old reality is gone and there is no going back.[154] In putting the axe to work, the world forever changes. Once a threshold is crossed the struggle ends.

Once a threshold is crossed the struggle ends.

Inner struggles can happen at any scale of time, over a few minutes, hours, years, a lifetime, or generations. They also take place in each of us as individuals and in the collectives of which we are a part. Families, neighbourhoods, organizations, cities, nations, and humanity struggle with how to deliver health care, organize economic systems, feed and shelter our citizens, and ensure the health of our planet. For our cities to be well, we need to explore our struggles deeply as individuals and collectives.

The struggle to improve our quality of life powers us to a point where the leap feels inevitable. It can be a chasm I have been walking alongside for years but choosing not to look over and see what's on my flank. It can be non-existent until something happens in life that makes it suddenly appear. It can sneak up on my consciousness or it can boldly jump out in front of me. Grierson says:

> Every day, in almost every field, individuals perceive themselves to be on the wrong side of a divide. The "second brain" in their gut—that ten-billion nerve knot—tells them their life must change. And, on moral, or at least deeply personal, grounds, they jump the gap. The apprehension can seem so sudden that it straightens them in their chair—and then seems inevitable.[155]

The divide shows up in a variety of ways.

Regardless of how they appear, suddenly or quietly, when I approach a threshold I look at it fully and recognize its inevitability. The persistent practical problems I face will not be resolved until I cross the divide. I am compelled to leap, yet I must choose the right time and the right approach. To do so, I must be aware that it is okay to step back from the edge from time to time. And since the choices of our cities are comprised of the choices of our citizens, individual intuition and courage is essential. Our collective ability to make the crossing comes from within each of us.

The tension we feel when standing at a threshold is an evolutionary slingshot—an opportunity to grow.

Struggle, conflict, and tension are unavoidable. They are a part of life and serve as opportunities to learn. Each time we face a struggle—small, large, or monstrous—we can choose to move forward or turn away, both of which could be right. It's the choice itself that offers the opportunity to learn about our struggles and our path to reach our fullest potential. Alone and together, we leap in unimaginable, yet inevitable, ways, powered by improvement and curiosity.

POSSIBILITY KNOWN AND UNKNOWN

The tension we feel when standing at a threshold is an evolutionary slingshot—an opportunity to grow. We have a choice on how to handle the threshold, that feeling Otto Scharmer and Katrin Kaufer call "going to the edge of letting go." Letting go happens in two ways: "Sometimes it means that you have to take the leap, to jump off the cliff from the known into the unknown. Sometimes when you feel that something is beginning to emerge, it can also mean to not jump away, but to stay with what wants to emerge."[156] The chasms we encounter are not barriers; they are portals to new ways of doing things. In city life, the chasms we encounter are markers of possibility. Noticing thresholds and our relationship with them helps us create the conditions to see possibility, grow possibility, and perform possibility.

See Possibility

Creating the conditions that allow cities to see possibilities starts with us, as citizens, and the choices we make. Consider this excerpt from Ben Okri's Mental Fight:[157]

> Or might we choose to make
> This time a waking-up even
> A moment of world empowerment?
> To pledge, in private, to be more aware
> More playful, more tolerant, and more fair
> More responsible, more wild, more loving
> Awake to our unsuspected powers, more amazing.
>
> We rise and fall by the choice we make
> It all depends on the road we take
> And the choice and the road each depend
> On the light that we have, the light we bend,
> On the light we use
> Or refuse

Creating the conditions to see possibilities within ourselves, others, and our cities means awakening to the direction in which we wish to move. The "light we bend" is the essence of the passion alive within each of us. We choose where we direct our attention, where to shine the light, what Scharmer and Kaufer call "bending the beam of attention."

Scharmer and Kaufer describe social evolution as having four levels of awareness—a simpler version of the Spiral we explored in Chapter Three—that tell the story of how we have learned to listen, converse, and organize. Each of these levels is a way we behave in context. The first level of awareness is habitual listening, where we "download" habits of thought. In this mode, we speak to tell others what to do, or demonstrate how we conform to what we are supposed to do. This is a Red/Blue world organized hierarchically. The second level involves factual and open-minded listening that allows debate and acknowledges difference. In this mode of listening, we organize ourselves around differences, in divisions and departments, in a Blue/Orange world. When competition and strategy are particularly important, this is an Orange way of operating. The third level is defined by empathic and open-hearted listening, where we see the viewpoint of the other. It is an Orange/Green world, where we enter into dialogue with each other, inquiring of self and others. In this mode, we organize around interests, resulting in distributed and networked structures, and from time-to-time, we stretch into Yellow ways of operating. In the fourth level of awareness, generative and open listening leads to conversations that take the form of collective creativity in a Yellow world, where we speak from "what is moving through" and organize around what emerges.

From the first level to the fourth, the way we organize and listen to each other shifts from a command-and-control hierarchy to a competitive market, to negotiated, co-operative dialogues, to co-creative and awareness-based collective action. Each mode of listening and awareness reflects and tunes into different kinds of possibility. Seeing possibility does not mean jumping from the first level of awareness to the fourth, rather it's about seeing the threshold from where you stand. No matter where we are in our development along the Spiral, self-awareness matters. To see possibility, we need, at each level, to tune into the tools we, and others, use to listen to self, others, and our cities—and reach ahead for new ways to listen. This recognition of our diverse ways of listening and organizing will grow the possibilities we see. With others, we need to tune into their listening needs.

For example, when operating from Scharmer and Kaufer's first level of listening, we look for experts, yearning for linear learning; from the fourth we look for participatory experiences. In the city, there are diverse and simultaneous modes of listening that vary based on scale and levels of awareness. When we listen with intention, we begin to notice if what we hear is what we want to hear or what wants to be heard. A good listener—at any scale—notices the filters in use.

Grow Possibility
The work we undertake to see possibility creates a social habitat that invites possibility to grow, making stronger connections

between and among city habitats (economic, social, physical). And possibility also needs a social habitat in which to thrive. In 2010, I designed and hosted a conference to explore ways to improve the work of city planning practitioners to better serve communities, cities and citizens. The format of the conference was unusual because we had an unusual objective: to create an experience that invited participants to explore a daring topic— the purpose of our work and the consequences of not working to that purpose.

First, a team of nine assembled to learn how to design and create a safe and effective social habitat for this event. We ensured that we had the support of each other to do this work, and we explored our personal and collective destination (a conference), the direction of the profession, and our individual and collective learning journeys. The design team posed two questions to frame the conference: What if we're not planning to survive? And who's planning our future anyway?

We created a two-and-a-half day "unconference,"[158] with the agenda and all content generated on site, in the moment. Without predetermined topics, we were able as a group to be responsive to the needs of participants and allow them to grow into new possibilities. From this experience I named the elephants in the room when we gather to learn:[159]

1. The future is unknown
2. Our work is open, dynamic and interconnected
3. Linear learning serves the past, not the future
4. Learning is an open and dynamic process
5. We need a place to practice (and learn) unusual behaviour
6. Learning is maximized if customized
7. It is time to sort out what it all means
8. Warning: learning is exhilarating and risky
9. Risk makes us look for the silver bullet
10. Offer support rather than rescue
11. It takes time to take responsibility
12. We know more than we think we do
13. The conventional conference is both loved and unloved

With a few years' perspective, I can see now that those elephants brought to light four essential concepts for understanding social habitat in cities: **the future is unknown; we know more than we think we do; the whole city system is learning; and a social habitat is a learning habitat.** The hallmark of each of these concepts is that they bring discomfort. It is disruptive to admit that we have no idea what will happen and to let our need to be in control fall to the side. It is disruptive to acknowledge our own intelligence, to not defer to the experts "out there" by default. It is disruptive to know that the city is not—and cannot be—perfect because it is constantly learning and improving. It is disruptive to let go of control and expertise, to allow a different kind of social habitat to emerge that encourages discomfort, because discomfort is what we feel when we learn something new.

Four essential concepts for understanding social habitat in cities: the future is unknown; we know more than we think we do; the whole city system is learning; and a social habitat is a learning habitat.

The notion of an unknown future is embedded deeply in each of us and is connected to our sense of self and our work. Growing possibility means accepting that **the future is unknown**, and Whyte reminds us to take that uncertainty seriously:

> *Being smitten by a path, a direction, an intuited possibility, no matter the territory it crosses, we can feel it in youth or at any threshold, as if life has found us at last. Beginning a courtship with a work, like beginning a courtship with a love, demands a fierce attention to understand what it is we belong to in the world. But to start the difficult path to what we want, we also have to be serious about what we want.*[160]

We need to simultaneously be aware of our anxieties and desires. This awareness is necessary to see possibilities both imagined and undefinable. This reality is best understood if we see that human creativity takes a variety of forms and shapes. We do not know what we need to learn for a future we cannot grasp. A quality social habitat involves discomfort, for discomfort begets new understanding.

We know more than we think we do because our work—our economic life—is open, dynamic, and interconnected with others' work just as the universe is open, dynamic, and interconnected. According to *Synchronicity* author Joseph Jawarski,

[O]ur mental model of how the world works must shift from images of a clockwork, machinelike universe that is fixed and determined, to the model of a universe that is open, dynamic, interconnected, and full of living qualities... Once we see this funda-mental open quality of the universe, it immediately opens us up to the potential for change; we see that the future is not fixed, and we shift from resignation to a sense of possibility. We are creating the future every moment.[161]

The silver-bullet trap of linear learning coaxes us into ignoring—and more damaging yet, discounting—the knowledge and skill that exists in cities. We sabotage ourselves when we remain in Sharmer and Kaufer's first three levels of awareness. Our true challenge is not to find the next best thing, but to integrate the knowledge and skills at our disposal—from citizens, civic institutions, the business community, and civil society. When we do, our social habitat evolves to align with the complexity of the day. The result will be wiser action that uses what we know, addressing, at least in part, the gap between the complexity of the world and our understanding of it.

Three ideas are embedded within the concept that **the whole city system is learning:** learning is open and dynamic; learning is exhilarating and risky; and learning is about new understanding. First, learning as an open and dynamic experience stretches our mental models of learning to match the open, dynamic character of the world in which we work. Linear learning, in the "download form," is a mechanical and industrial mode of learning;[162] it keeps what we know separate, isolated, and clear. This assembly-line mode of learning used to be appropriate, but in our evolving world we need opportunities to integrate what we know. In linear mode, we put others in charge of what we learn, of what we think, and what our next steps ought to be. We are passive learners in this mode, letting experts think for us. There is a time and place for this kind of learning experience, but it is no longer an effective default mode.

The alternative model of learning responds to real, live conditions where we explore our talents and passions. What we learn and how we apply our knowledge responsive to the needs of the learner in context and at any scale—a citizen or a city. This alternative feels messy, but comes from the diversity our cities need to serve us well. In this mode, citizen-learners take charge of what they learn, think, and do. Our learning systems are grounded in standardization, yet we are ready to add a layer of customization, recognizing that individually and collectively, we think, make, and do in relation to more complex ways of listening and organizing.

The second idea is a warning: learning is exhilarating and risky. Learning something new is a thrill when it feels easy. When learning feels confusing and messy, we experience risk, fear, and frustration. When I try something new I often feel inadequate and vulnerable. I have a choice to make: try it or coast with the status quo. Sometimes choosing the status quo is the right thing to do. Other times, if uncomfortable enough with the status quo, I summon the courage to take the risk. I have a choice to make about how I view vulnerability: as a threat that exposes my weakness or as a strength that allows me to lean more deeply into learning. The accuracy of my self-awareness has an impact on how well I assess threats—an exaggerated vulnerability that causes me to experience threats that are not present, or an accurate vulnerability that allows me to see true and honest threats.

Learning habitats are places where we practise (and learn) unusual behaviour.

As the whole city system learns, it acquires content and adopts processes on the inside and the outside. The third idea is that the learning process, at any scale, is about new understanding. American physicist and philosopher David Bohm tells us that "the ability to perceive or think differently is more important than the knowledge gained."[163] Knowing how to go about gaining new insight, the process of learning on the "inside," is an essential addition to the value we place on the external knowledge—the content—we gain. Both need to happen simultaneously.

One of the ways to grow possibility is to create places where citizens can practise quality **social habitats as learning habitats.** Eight years ago, I co-created a community of practice with Integral City practitioners, a group of people whose work has an affinity with the work of Marilyn Hamilton, and her *Integral City* book series. We gather to learn both with and from each other, and practise the kind of work we want to do with cities. Environments like this are "learning habitats," social habitats that foster new understanding. Such a place and space resembles a laboratory, where participants are the subjects and the objects of the learning space. Learning habitats are consciously created to support a city's efforts to create the conditions for its citizens to choose to do things differently—individually and collectively. Learning habitats are characterized by four qualities.

First, learning habitats are places where we practise (and learn) unusual behaviour. For example, a group of professional city planners noticed, in an explicit learning habitat space, that both they and citizens were most happy with city planning projects when city planners behaved in unusual ways.[164] They noticed their approach to their work, when they were most happy with the results, was different because they were:

- Willing to both lead and be led
- Aware of what was going on around them
- Open to change and looked for opportunities for change
- Interested in others, cared about others, understood others, and noticed what was going on for others
- Adaptable, self aware in the moment, learning from mistakes, strengths, and weaknesses
- Able to establish purpose or direction
- Curious about what made a place work
- Honest when the answers were not known

Learning habitats are places where we consciously and responsibly create time and space for learning.

These planners found better results in their work when they connected self with their work, allowing them to connect with others and their city; they made their own learning habitat bubble. In addition, they found themselves and others motivated by the work. All citizens, all of us in all the ways we work, need to show up in unusual ways, allowing new understanding.

Secondly, learning habitats are places where we consciously and responsibly create time and space for learning. Just as I need to move out of the jet stream of life to make meaning of my work, so too does a city. In pausing, we illuminate both what we know and the choices needed to move together to create cities that serve us well. Where do we wish to go together and how will we get there? As individuals and as a collective, we pause to notice the thresholds in our lives. In simply noticing them and our reactions to them, we learn.

A third vital quality of learning habitats is that they employ processes that support emergence.[165] Vast information stores are readily available on any topic through social media, websites, blogs, videos, webinars and other sources. The number of speakers, conferences, and symposia seems to be at an all-time high in our communities, all of which makes the conventional conference—to hear from the best thinkers and speakers about the best things and practices—redundant. The expertise of others is sufficiently amplified; what is not as readily available is the opportunity for us to know and understand things differently *as a result of knowing this expertise*, as individuals and as cities. We can listen to experts any time. Learning habitats put the emphasis on what can be done when we are together, virtually or face-to-face; collective intelligence is hidden, yet available to be made explicit should we choose.

Emergent practices acknowledge the need for linear and non-linear processes and structures, choosing which one depends on need and purpose. For example, in emergency situations (Red), information must flow from top to bottom (Red, Blue). To begin integration and emergence (Orange, Green, Yellow), non-linear forms of organizing and communicating are needed. We have a choice: maintain the status quo or create the conditions for new ways of being to emerge. In this choice we experience tension in the transition from order (the status quo that we understand) to chaos (the unknown); exploring the tension allows us to find the right kind and amount of structure that will serve self-organizing cities—minimal critical structure. Too much structure can sabotage a city's efforts to serve citizens well, while too little structure leaves no foundation upon which self-organizing can take place.

Emergent practices rely on dynamic learning habitats. For Grierson, to flip-flop is human. "The ability to nimbly adjust your views as new information comes in is a necessary evolutionary adaptation. Because new information is always coming in, faster and faster laying siege to your well-considered opinions."[166] Holacracy founder Brian Robertson[167] compares reacting to the context around us to riding a bicycle. Steering with rigid arms, in predict-and-control mode, doesn't work well; instead the rider needs to point to a destination and adjust rapidly to feedback while moving. Robertson calls this *dynamic steering*, principles of which are well-suited to learning habitats:

- Focus on the next action to take, in light of your overall aim
- Experiment and adapt

- Focus on present tensions
- Get real data, steer continuously
- Aim for workable decisions, not the "best" decision
- Revisit decisions at any time
- Delay making decisions until the last responsible moment
- Allow for short cycles, incremental steps

When the world changes, we must adapt our decisions, the assumptions we make, and the processes we use to make decisions.

Finally, learning habitats are places where we are offered and receive support, not where we are rescued. "Who could we be together if I were to let go of who I think we should be?" asks Art of Hosting colleague Chris Corrigan,[168] noting how difficult it is to let go of what we feel must happen. This is a question that scales up to a group the size of a city or a planet of cities. The "we" can be neighbourhood, city, or even workplace or corporation. The "I" can be all of these things, too. It is a question of trust and whether I, and we, trust citizens and cities to carve out their own future.

Learning habitats are places where we are offered and receive support, not where we are rescued.

In rescue mode (Red), I swoop in with my own ideas, ostensibly to help, but really to control, rather than assist. (Rescue mode is only needed in situations that are life threatening, or morally threatening. A rescue is memetically sensitive too: the context matters.) Just because I am uncomfortable when my neighbour or my city struggles, it is my discomfort, not theirs, that compels me to insert myself. I look for a silver-bullet rescue (me) when I am uncomfortable because a more independently wrought solution will take too long or require too much effort. Often, the urge to rescue is simply my need to control a situation in order to avoid discomfort. True learning, however, often involves discomfort, so as we make our way through the morass of life, our individual and collective learning journey involves noticing the kind of support we need in a particular context, being willing to ask for it, being courageous enough to accept it. It is counter-intuitive, but support often is not the alleviation of, or rescue from, discomfort. (It might be companionship while being uncomfortable.)

The city-system cultivates connections to purpose, at scale, in learning habitats. We each do the work we do because we believe our actions improve our situations, that it is possible to survive and thrive. Our individual purposes shape the city in instrumental ways. In return, the city provides us with opportunities to commit further to our work, forever challenging us to develop. A learning habitat that serves possibility cultivates citizens' connections to individual purpose, the collective's connection to the city's purpose, and the purposes of all scales of organizing. The processes we use in our social habitat need to be sufficiently complex to allow connections between people and various purposes.

Growing possibility means creating social habitats in which possibilities thrive. These habitats often make us uncomfortable because we struggle with the primary ideas behind them: we have no idea what the future holds, we already have what it takes to meet challenges, the whole city system is learning along with us, and we need to consciously create places to grow possibility—learning habitats.

*To **perform possibility**, we need to be smitten with a destination to such a degree that it pulls us over thresholds that test our resolve.*

Perform Possibility

To step into possibility, both known and unknown, we need to be willing to take risks.

We rely on the indispensable creatively destructive forces of desire and longing to pull us into possibility. Without desire and longing, says Whyte, "our protected sense of self cannot be destabilized or subverted from our old way of being; we cannot be chaotically reorganized to accommodate ourselves to anything fresh. A certain state of blind ecstasy seems necessary for navigating the first crucial thresholds."[169] It is human nature to be smitten with an idea as much as we are designed to be smitten with a person; we become "blinded" in order to take the risk, so it appears to be not so risky after all. Whether in a relationship, trying out a new job, or renewing a commitment to self, work, family, or city, a leap of faith gets us across the threshold. To *perform possibility*, we need to be smitten with a destination to such a degree that it pulls us over thresholds that test our resolve.

Otto Scharmer describes this journey toward performing new possibilities in *Theory U*. He says that the journey develops seven leadership capacities that make the future we want possible:[170]

1. Listening to self, others, and the collective
2. Observing while suspending the voice of judgment

3. Sensing the openness of an open mind, open heart, and open will

4. Connecting to the deepest source of self and will in the present

5. Crystalizing the power of intention

6. Prototyping and learning by doing

7. Performing at a scale that allows co-creation of the new

The first three leadership skills travel down the left side of the U, preparing us for a deep personal connection to the work the future is asking of us. The fourth is the bottom of the U, where the new possibility presents itself. The last three, up the right side of the U, articulate how we, together, bring the new future into being, when we reach from simply *seeing* something new and improved to *doing* something new and improved.

The turning point in the U journey, the bottom, is the place where

> *...we have to let go of everything and offload all the baggage that isn't essential. Going through that gate means encountering the two root questions of our journey: "Who is my Self?" and "What is my Work?" The capital-S Self is our highest future possibility. The capital-W Work is our sense of purpose or calling. It's what we are here on this earth to do.*[171]

Who we are and what we contribute through our work matters. Our work may be volunteer or paid. It may be as a politician or a civic employee, as a software developer or a home builder, as a secretary for a not-for-profit board or a do-it-yourselfer building a new garage. Whatever we do, and how we behave to perform the task, shapes our cities. The more we work to nurture our capital-S Self, the more we pursue our capital-W Work, the better our city becomes.

American academic Douglas Hofstadter, who focuses on consciousness and creativity, writes: "It turns out that an eerie type of chaos can lurk just behind a façade of order—and yet, deep inside the chaos lurks an even eerier type of order."[172] In the messiness of city life, I sense an eerie order: that the possibilities for city life depend upon citizens' pursuits of what they see as possible. The city will perform possibility better if we each perform better, leaning into possibility. When we do so, the results for each of us—and all of us—are not known ahead of time.

The more consciously we explore the thresholds before us and their nature within us, the more wisely we will choose when to go forward or turn away, as appropriate. The inner struggle, in every moment, powers us up for bigger and more demanding challenges. It is in each of us to dream of and reach the places we wish to go. It is in each of us to look for and explore the edges in our economic, physical, and social lives, which will, with practice, allow us to serve possibility—known and unknown—in our lives.

1. Peggy Holman defines "emergence" as the new order that arises out of chaos, the new and novel understandings we reach as more complex systems form.

2. At each transition to new understanding, we encounter a threshold. The act of crossing this threshold calls us to offer more of ourselves, even when we do not know what we will find on the other side or how the crossing will change us.

3. We are at the threshold of a new age, a more complex world. We are simultaneously part of a world that is in decline, and part of a new possible world. Our cities are counting on us to give attention to, and care for, both endings and possibilities.

4. Jane Jacobs reminded us that the well-being of our cities has everything to do with our willingness to grow and learn as individuals and as whole cities—and, I would add, as a species.

5. Each time we face a struggle—small, large or monstrous—we have a choice to go forward or turn away, both of which could be right. The choice offers an opportunity to learn. Alone and together, we leap in unimaginable and inevitable ways, powered by improvement and curiosity.

6. The tension we feel when standing at a threshold is an evolutionary slingshot—an opportunity to grow. Noticing thresholds and our relationship with them helps us create the conditions to:

    • **See possibility:** We need to tune into the tools we, and others, use to listen to self, others, and our cities—and reach ahead for new ways to listen.

- **Grow possibility:** For possibilities to thrive, we need quality social habitats that involve four essential concepts: the future is unknown; we know more than we think we do; the whole city system is learning; and a social habitat is a learning habitat.

- **Perform possibility:** We explore the thresholds before us and their nature within us, making wiser choices about when to go forward or turn away. The inner struggle, in every moment, powers us up for bigger and more demanding challenges when we are ready.

7. It is in each of us to attune to and explore the edges in our economic, physical, and social lives, which will, with practice, allow us to serve the known and unknown possibilities in our lives.

NEST-MAKING PRACTICE
Discerning Possibility

In every moment, we stand at the threshold of a new age, with choices that shape our future destinations and directions. When ready, as individuals and collectives, we reach toward more complex systems and ways of organizing, and in each transition, there is a threshold that, once crossed, allows us to see with fresh eyes.

Creating cities that serve citizens well is a never-ending journey. The destinations we are focusing on, what we are learning, and what is emerging within and around us, are always revisited. This is the dance in cities: focus, learn, emerge. It is a dance of relationship with the habitat that is given to us, created by us. If we choose to join the dance, we create wonderful possibilities, both known and unknown. And, of course, how well we dance has an impact on what we create.

When we organize for emergence, we actively engage in our individual and collective learning journeys, stopping to notice where we wish to go, and trusting that the thresholds we encounter (and cross) along the way allow us to travel in that direction. We may not quite reach the destination in mind, but we will land at a place that suits us, that somehow makes more sense. Organizing for emergence means co-creating nests of possibility. This takes focus, openly learning along the way, and choosing the uncertainty of emergence.

REFLECT

Take a moment with a journal or sketchbook and see where the following questions take you. There are no wrong or right answers.

Self—What practices create the conditions for me to see possibility in my life? What are the possibilities that I see right now?

Other—What relationships do I have that fuel possibility in me and other(s)?

City—What prototypes are performing new possibilities in my city?

Care—What support do I need to be able to see possibility, rather than what's wrong? What do others need? What does my city need?

Reminder: "city" means the city-habitat we make for ourselves, the community around us, not our municipal government (often referred to as "the City").

Figure L
**Activating City
Nestworks**

PART THREE
NESTWORKS

A couple of years ago, after the ice started to melt in the spring, my mom watched two loons on the lake near her home. As the wind picked up, the ice blew toward the shore, leaving less and less water around the loons. As she watched, she soon learned that loons need open water for their runway, to allow for take-off. The slushy ice creeping toward them made take-off impossibly exhausting. They couldn't do it.

Like the loons, people interact with their habitat, but in our case, there is a significant difference. As the creators of our city habitat, we choose to build evolutionary runways—that give us energy rather than deplete us. We can choose to create cities that give us lift.

Part Three explores the intersection of the elements introduced in Part Two: the destination, learning journey, and emergence as they relate to the ways we organize our city habitats. Each chapter focuses on a key idea:

- As we journey toward our chosen destinations, we become city-makers—we enter explicitly into a relationship with our cities in ways that allow us to recreate cities and welcome how they recreate us (Chapter Eight).

- As we choose to embark on learning journeys we enter into unknown territory, deepening our civic practices as citizens and more fully engaging with the dance of the city (Chapter Nine).

- As we explore the unknown, we choose destinations and tap into the direction in which our cities naturally want to move (Chapter Ten).

The cities we live in are ours to make and remake. Everyone, everywhere, is creating city life, and in return the city is a place from which we explore our evolutionary potential. City making is, in fact, a survival skill. While the loons had to wait for open water, it's in our hands to regenerate and recreate our cities to serve us better.

CHAPTER 8

The truth about stories is that that's all we are.
        —Thomas King[173]

*Hazel realized wearily that Bigwig was probably going to be trouble-
some. He was certainly no coward, but he was likely to remain steady
only as long as he could see his way clear and be sure of what to do.
To him, perplexity was worse than danger; and when he was perplexed,
he usually grew angry.*
        —Richard Adams[174]

WE ARE CITY MAKERS

PASSION AND HAPPINESS

Let's make a clear distinction: city **building** involves civic managers, civic builders and developers; city **making** involves these folks **plus** civil society and citizens. City **building** focuses only on the physical habitat we create in our cities, the externalities, ignoring the aspect of care that comes from citizens and civil society. City **making** involves everyone and in so doing includes the social and economic life of our cities alongside the physical, integrating the inner workings of the city with the externalities, the care, and the building.

In Part Three, I invite you to imagine all aspects of your life being engaged in city making. You are, of course, a citizen. If you work in or with community organizations, you are a city maker as part of civil society. Maybe you work for a public institution—health organization, government, school board, university—and are a city maker as a civic manager, whether working politically or in administration, as a cashier or a professional engineer, you are a custodian of our public resources. Many work in the business community, as city makers in roles as civic builders and developers. Many of us are engaged in our city in two, three, or four of these perspectives. Each individual role, or two or more stitched together, makes every citizen a city maker. Even if you live outside the city, you interact with it and are, if only some of the time, a citizen of the city. Remember that all your work matters, whether paid or unpaid.

The City Regenerates Itself

Take a look at your local media and you'll see many examples of the ways people are reshaping your city. Here are some stories that reflect my city's direction, all from within a few days of each other in May 2018:[175] My city council committed to cut greenhouse gas emissions in half by 2030 and reach carbon neutrality for city operations by 2050. They are choosing to buy green energy. Just outside my city, Sephra Buffalo, a Samson Cree First Nation member planned on taking her ideas for sustainable housing for First Nations people to national elected officials and policy-makers. The 17-year-old was responding to a need for improved housing for her community of Maskwacis, and her work would help shape housing for Aboriginal people across her province and country. Maarten and Amy Verstoep's restaurant was the first in my city to achieve Gluten-Free Food Program certification, an effort endorsed by the Canadian Celiac Association. The Verstoeps have made their entire menu available to people on a strict gluten-free diet.

That's the beauty of the city—among us all, we can choose to look after us all.

In their own ways, each of these individuals or collectives is reshaping my city and how it is organized. My city government is taking responsibility for its energy use. Buffalo wants to improve the physical habitat for her people and others. The Verstoeps are responding to and leading a dietary culture shift. This work might not be of interest to everyone, but it still changes the city around us. Even if you're not interested in how local governments source their energy needs, others are looking after that for you. That's the beauty of the city—among us all, we can choose to look after us all.

A Happiness Project (with Tension)

The second chapter of Charles Montgomery's book, *Happy City* is called "The city has always been a happiness project." In the chapter, Montgomery identifies two significant ideas about our relationship with cities. First, embodied in every citizen is the tension between selfishness and altruism:

> [E]ach of us benefits when some of us subsume
> private goals for the sake of the community, and
> everyone benefits when everyone cooperates…
> At the same time, the drive by each of us to promote
> our own interests creates a dynamism and wealth
> that can overflow through the city.[176]

We are "in it" for ourselves and for some kind of collective good. For Montgomery, this means that cities are a shared project that invites us to thrive together. This notion is linked to his second big idea—that the city challenges us to do more than simply live together: "[W]e are hard-wired to trust one another,"[177] says Montgomery. In our cities, we are challenged to cooperate, to negotiate the tension when personal goals and community goals diverge, trusting that tension and conflict are purposeful. The tension, which derives from our desire to reach our personal goals, our personal destinations, stimulates us to improve—and thrive.

We cannot build a city on our own; it is a shared project that creates a common good.[178] Drawing on Aristotle's notion of *eudaimonia* (contentment)[179] and developmental physiologist Carol Ryff's work on happiness and psychological well-being, Montgomery associates the following characteristics with city happiness or the good life:[180] self awareness and acceptance, the ability to navigate and thrive in the world, positive relations with others, personal growth throughout life, a sense of meaning and purpose, and feelings of autonomy and independence. Citizens are never separate from their cities; they are always in relationship with each other and with the creative tension that benefits the individual and the collective. The way we navigate this tension matters; when we look tension in the eye, and engage, we improve our experience of the city and, of course, change others' experience of the city as well.

CITY MAKING IS STORY MAKING

The Story of the City is in the Village

For Christina Baldwin and Ann Linnea, the circle, as a form of conversation, started around the cook-fires of humanity's ancestors and has been with us ever since.[181] In contrast to the "sage on the stage," expert-oriented conversations we are familiar with in our cities, Baldwin and Linnea see conversation circles as creating the conditions for "villageness," where more diverse ways of seeing the world are encouraged and welcomed. The work in a village is diverse, all connected to story and the heart of a place. For Baldwin and Linnea, the village habitat:

- **Builds webs of identity and relationship** that nurture belonging, supporting couples, families, generations, friendships, clans, and other alliances within the whole.

- **Educates and initiates**; it provides each generation with tools for contributing to the common good, leading successful lives, and developing social intelligence for village life.

- **Supports work, crafts, and arts** by offering ways for citizens to live and contribute in meaningful ways, to express their gifts and be compensated so they may participate in community commerce.

- **Feeds and trades**; it develops a food system, both the growth of food and its delivery, and ensures the goods and services that sustain the people are in place within the village and with other villages.

- **Grows the spirit of the place** by developing a tradition of meaning—a relationship with the divine—and places people in the order of things. It organizes ritual, ceremony, and offerings.

- **Protects its people** from aggression, when attacked by enemies, and also organizes recovery. It **tends** to its vulnerable members and develops a social safety net.

- **Governs** by providing social structure, articulating shared mores and values, establishing consequences, setting limits and controls, and envisioning the future.

City making is story making. Story making is city making.

In the village habitat, we look after individual and collective needs at a small scale. When I look at Baldwin and Linnea's model, I see the first four levels of Beck and Cowan's Spiral[182], the initial progression of values that we explored in Chapter Three. The basic survival needs of villagers, individually and collectively, are

Figure M
*What a Village
Is and What it
Does*

met (Beige and Purple). The village articulates the relationship
of people to the world and marks rites of passage with ceremony
and ritual (Purple). The village offers protection and a sense of
identity (Red) and provides structure in rules and protocols and
a sense of future (Blue). These four levels are found in a village
of any scale—in a neighbourhood or in a whole city—
to varying degrees. In simple ways, they are found in the story
of St. John's, Newfoundland and in the simple Spirals in Figures
C and D, showing city purposes and how we organize for them.
"Villageness" is a quality of gathering that ensures our collective
survival; we are better together than we are alone. Baldwin and
Linnea's village model invites us to consider the first four levels
of the Spiral in a new light (Figure N[183]) with a deeper view of the
purpose of the city in our lives.

The foundational story of the city is in the story of the village.
Together we can best ensure our individual needs are met (Beige).
The city then serves our needs for a shared sense of belonging
and identity (Purple and Red). A city has an intangible hold on us,
and we feel pride in our place, whether in a sports team that has
a good showing, a filmmaker we all get behind, or the story of

a local hero. The story of a city is also found in how we organize ourselves formally to meet each others' needs (Blue) in the form of tax regimes, food banks, not-for-profits, and the roles that public institutions play in our collective life.

To reach beyond Baldwin and Linnea's village-specific model, we have the guidance of Beck and Cowan and Hamilton as well as the blurred lines between the silos that come with the transition from Blue to Orange. As my city government made the move to establish design standards for new neighbourhoods, it decided to move out of its traditional role. As a government, it kept its legislated responsibility to set rules, but it changed how it wrote those rules. Instead of writing the new document and asking for feedback, champions Kalen Anderson, Lisa Larson, and Barnali Bannerjee brought stakeholders into the room and provided them with support to write the document themselves. The stories told by citizens, community organizations, the business and development community, and public institutions were woven together to describe how—in the Edmonton context— a neighbourhood nest best creates the conditions for prosperity, growth, and development of all (Orange). To do this work, Anderson, Larson, and Bannerjee recognized that they needed a different social habitat in which to work, one where they could share individual knowledge and expand shared knowledge (Green).

From Yellow, we created, together with the stakeholders, a social habitat in our meetings that provided opportunities for them to find a shared sense of identity and purpose (Red and Blue) from a wider knowledge base (Green). We were able to see strategic opportunities and act on them (Orange) with a high level of trust because we made room for all perspectives (Purple). In very simple ways, because it was an emerging capacity, we were able to figure out how the neighbourhoods we made for ourselves contributed to an overall healthier habitat and planet. Because our social habitat was strong, we constructed a good product in a timely fashion. After only twelve months of work, the document was in front of City Council with unanimous and vociferous support. Normally, it would have taken years of work and there would have been vociferous objections to the end result. The conflict wasn't absent in our approach; it had been acknowledged and integrated.

In a city, as in a village, diverse work takes place simultaneously. As life conditions change, our attention shifts to meet the demands of each moment, and the city shifts too. The story that binds a village together provides the foundation on which we build cities with great diversity of work. When our basic needs are met, when we feel we belong and have a shared identity, and we organize further to meet each others' needs, we are able to reach further, to grow and expand together. As we figure out how to make our way in a world of conflicting truths, we discern how to live more harmoniously with our planetary habitat.

Who Does Your City Want to Be?

Who do you want to be?
—Rabbi Shmuley Boteach[184]

Be careful what stories you tell: they become true and they
become you.
—Trevor Anderson[185]

While hiking the West Coast Trail of Vancouver Island, my brother and I came upon an abandoned donkey engine. We stopped to marvel at the rusted hulk at the edge of North America in the traditional territory of the Huu-ay-aht, Ditidaht, and Pacheedaht Nations for thousands of years.[186] Sailing ships from faraway European lands had reached this coast two hundred years ago, many of which met a tragic fate navigating unfamiliar and hazardous waters. Sailors referred to this coastline as the "Graveyard of the Pacific." The derelict engine is a reminder of how humanity works; when we need something to improve life for self and others, we organize for it, and in the process, we change the shape of the places that are involved. In this case, lighthouses were built and a telegraph line, which became a trail for shipwreck victims and their rescuers. (Yes, this was about colonial needs, not Indigenous needs.) The donkey engine's job was to pull the telegraph line through the forest, and once its job was done, was left where it stood, a symbol of a story, a marker of an earlier purpose of the trail.

Decades later, the users of the trail are explorers of a different kind—not shipwreck victims and their rescuers now, but hikers exploring the beauty and challenge of the terrain (and, occasionally, rescuers of hikers). A structure's purpose changes over time. This is the city's story, too; only we see it in many more layers. Stories give shape to our worlds, at every scale of time and geography in our communities, for ourselves, our families, neighbourhoods, city, nation, and humanity. Are we telling the stories we want and need to tell as we recreate our cities?

My fellow citizen, Lewis Cardinal, works to create and maintain relationships across cross-cultural divides, particularly between his Indigenous heritage and our current city. Cardinal's vision is to tell the story of Edmonton as a waiting place, a centre of trade, celebration, and ceremony. On a bend in the river, Indigenous peoples gathered here for eight to ten thousand years before Europeans settled this part of North America. He speaks of the need to reclaim Edmonton's *monto*,[187] a word he uses to connect what is now Edmonton to the spirit and great mystery of this place. The river valley, where people first settled, is "rich in history, stories, and spirit waiting to be brought into being." For Cardinal, "sacred is the only word to describe the full depth of this land."[188] The "spirit waiting to be brought into being" here is no different than in other places and cities. What is the *monto* of your city?

Every city has a story that weaves through collective self-awareness, the result of an exchange that takes place between three elements—self, other, and place—at any scale. Just as I need to have a sense of purpose, so, too, does my city. As I work toward my purpose, I am in relationship with others and the places around me. Place is the habitat I find myself in, and that, too, is at scale, from the office I work in, to my home, my block and neighbourhood, and city, as well as my country and my planet. At every turn, an exchange takes place between me, others, and place. Rabbi Shmuley Boteach's simple question leads us to consider purpose and destination, whether asked of a citizen or a city: "Who do you want to be?"

Novelist Richard Adams, in *Watership Down*, articulates the struggle of the human condition when we are unsure and the emotional charge embedded in uncertainty. Cities are no different—when they lack a sense of purpose, we certainly feel the emotional charges. It shows in our exchanges with others and the quality of the habitats we build for ourselves. Filmmaker Trevor Anderson advises that the stories we tell become us. What we tell ourselves about our purpose, or don't tell ourselves, is our story.

When we ask ourselves who we want to be, *as citizens*, we contribute to and benefit the whole city. So, let's take that question a step further and ask ourselves who we want to be *as a city*. This isn't about figuring out a vision of what we want to do, but an articulation of the kind of people we are in a given city. The answer becomes a source of identity and knowing it helps our city find itself and helps us find ourselves.

Edmonton author Todd Babiak thought about this question deeply and shared his ideas in his blog, *Magpie Town*. He said,

> I had worked on the City Vision for 2040, and I had noticed — in community halls all over the city — that citizens were obsessed with the Edmonton story. What makes this place different from other places? Where did we come from? How does it feel unique? What does Edmonton want and what is stopping us from getting it? What are we most proud of? They spoke in anecdotes and shouted at each other: yes, yes, that's it![189]

Babiak realized that the people working on the vision were working on the essence of Edmonton's story. As an author and journalist, Babiak tells stories of Edmonton. As part of his City Vision work, he explored how story could shape his city, searching for what he calls a master story, which

> …can't be borrowed by any other place or corporation or person. We support the story with key anecdotes, mini-stories that every ambassador and evangelist can use: plumbers, CEOs and ballet dancers. [It's] an anecdote generator, a way to honour the past and the culture, and it's a provocation, an incitement to further action.[190]

He was looking for the essential Edmonton story, the key ingredient that tells us who we are and what we are about.

By listening to its citizens' stories, Babiak discovered that Edmonton is an unusually good place to make something, from the ground up: "The festivals, events, institutions, businesses, and initiatives Edmontonians love grew from idea to reality here. …If you have the courage to make something, Edmonton is your city."[191] It's not something we aspire to; it's not a vision. This story is already true.

The story of Edmonton, as it has grown into the city it is today, is about making things. It's a place where people can contribute, make something, and see and feel the impact their creation has on the city. Babiak has tapped into the think, make, and do pattern explored in Part One, and asked his fellow citizens to actively step into shaping their city. He launched a project called

Make Something Edmonton and invited Edmontonians to draw on this history of making things to improve their city. He invited citizens to make something and tell others about it. He invited citizens to "make Edmonton a verb"[192]—we are what we make. He's on a quest to create the conditions for Edmonton to see and claim its spirit, its great mystery, its *monto*.

Babiak realized that citizens want to feel they are on a journey with their cities: "If there's no journey, it's just infrastructure."[193] We can change Edmonton in any way we like, right now. We can come up with a new idea for improvement (thinking); we can make something and then do it. And Babiak gave Edmontonians an explicit invitation, and support, to do just this. In May 2016, over six hundred projects were registered on the *Make Something Edmonton* website.[194] The projects are Edmonton's *monto* in the making.

We have a hand in the city we make. We choose who and what our city will be with every decision we make. We choose to engage in its improvement, and in return we make ourselves happy by doing the work we love and improving the city for others. Our cities are what we make them.

We have a hand in the city we make. We choose who and what our city will be with every decision we make.

Choose Stories of Possibility

Is the story we tell ourselves about our city a healthy story? Has the story changed over time, or has it stayed the same, even as the world—and our city—is changing? As it changes, do we resist or find ways to improve our city?

Thinking of the village in the city has allowed me to think about how citizens can be more connected to each other. Not in nostalgic ways that take us back in time, but in ways that encourage a new story to be told. These days, my city is testing out a new story: In a vast area of mature neighbourhoods created over forty years ago, my city is asking if the entrenched belief that owning a piece of land with one home on it is the best use of the land. City Council has made a series of decisions that confront that belief. A fifty-foot lot can be subdivided into two lots, allowing the construction of a "skinny home" on each of the new twenty-five-foot lots or a duplex where each unit shares a property line. On fifty-foot lots on the corner of a block, it is possible to build a three-unit building. As well, homeowners can now build a suite in the basement, over a garage, or in the backyard. Because the new construction will change the look and feel of neighbourhoods, as will the improvements to or replacement of older homes, Council is looking to update the rules that guide development in these mature neighbourhoods. The changes have caused great controversy, and this is where story comes in—because there are many stories we tell ourselves about our relationship with the city around us.

Here are some of the stories I've heard from citizens:

- I've lived in this neighbourhood for sixty years. The two skinny homes across the street are bringing down my property value. I don't like it. I don't like that Council is jamming this down our throats.

- I've lived in this neighbourhood for forty years. The two skinny homes next to me are driving my property value up, which means I have to pay more taxes. I want to stay in my home for twenty more years but I'm on a fixed income, so this is a problem.

- I like that I have been able to build a suite and get some income to help pay for my mortgage.

- The additional units in my neighbourhood will bring kids into the neighbourhood. There aren't as many kids in our families any more, which means that more homes are needed to have enough kids to keep the schools open in older neighbourhoods.

- The city needs to make better use of our infrastructure, which means we need more housing on our streets. I don't necessarily like it, but I recognize it needs to happen.

- I like the idea of other options for housing in the neighbourhood. I don't want to own a home anymore and have to look after the yard all year. But I don't want to have to move out of the neighbourhood.

- There are many homes coming down and being replaced with huge buildings, even for one family. They are too big and too ugly and this is destroying the character of our neighbourhood.

The stories vary. Some like what is happening and others do not. Perhaps these are the growing pains of leaving an old story behind and finding a way into a new story, where we move people into existing neighbourhoods instead of only moving people into new neighbourhoods. My city is now asking the question: How do we welcome more people and homes in our older neighbourhoods? All of the views expressed are true, even when they are in conflict, because they reflect the truth of the person living that story. How we meet each other to talk about the city we make together matters. A quality social habitat enables us to see, explore, and revisit the work we do to shape our physical habitat. A quality social habitat enables our economic life to improve our physical habitat.

Just as we demonstrate evolutionary intelligence in our city–habitats, we also have evolutionary intelligence about how we live with each other, what I call our civic practice. The Spiral we explored in Part One provides insight into how we, as citizens, engage with our city (Figure O). After our basic survival needs are met, we engage in story, which feeds everything in the city, at every scale. In the city, as in a village, we share stories to ensure our collective survival, stories about how the mysterious world works, where to find food, what rituals mark the seasons, and how we organize ourselves socially. Our stories are full of passion and they feed our pride and identity; we are even willing to do battle when our stories are threatened. In a city, we are called to be clear about our agreements with each other and hold ourselves accountable to each other, to be fair and just. As a city develops, we are compelled to take action, and be creative and entrepreneurial, allowing our drive-to-thrive to fuel us. When we are able to see, learn, and benefit from everyone's contributions and gifts, the city becomes a place where we learn to live with conflicting truths and uncertainties. It is a place where we can integrate feeling and knowing and simply be in awe of how the world works.

A city's stories are everywhere. Everything a city does or does not do is a result of our actions as citizens, community organizations, the business community, and our public institutions. How each of us shows up in the city affects how the city serves us in return, and at the heart of this city-making relationship is the story that shapes what we think, make, and do. As we grow and evolve with our cities, the relationship we have with the world around us also grows and evolves.

In every story, we choose what we tell ourselves. Our stories are the soundtrack we play in our heads and they can be negative and destructive or positive and generative. They can be grounded in scarcity and deprivation or appreciative of the wonder of abundance. Noticing what our stories are telling us is a useful

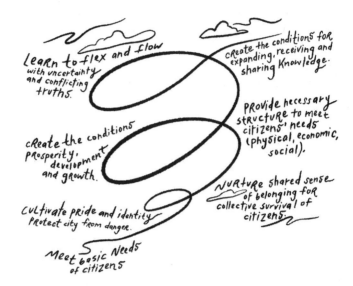

Inside the figure (handwritten):

learn to flex and flow with uncertainty and conflicting truths.

create the conditions for expanding, receiving and sharing knowledge.

create the conditions prosperity, development and growth.

provide necessary structure to meet citizens' needs (physical, economic, social).

nurture shared sense of belonging for collective survival of citizens.

cultivate pride and identity Protect city from danger.

Meet basic needs of citizens

practice. Do we choose despair or possibility? What we choose shapes the world around us.

Do we choose despair or possibility? What we choose shapes the world around us.

Finding the essential story of a place means living into Lewis Cardinal's notion of *monto*—the spirit and great mystery of a place. Reclaiming *monto* in Edmonton is as much about living with the uncertainty of the mystery of the city as it is in finding answers. The effort we make to truly see ourselves, at whatever scale, is a choice to move in a direction of deeper understanding, embarking on a learning journey, and emergence, all at once. We find our story one story at a time, one citizen at a time, and trust that the stories add up to a larger story and that "story catchers" like Todd Babiak will help us see the bigger stories of how think–make–do show up at city-scale today. Make the story; we make the city.

CITY MAKING IS A PATHLESS PATH

Our destination and our learning journey are integrated, inseparable. They serve different purposes, but both are critical to our growth and evolution, and the interrelationship between the two propels us forward as people, as individuals, as communities, and as a species.

Years ago, as my son and I watched an episode of *Mayday*, a TV series that chronicles events leading to and resulting in airplane disasters or near disasters, I was reminded of the connectedness of destination and journey. In the episode "Panic Over the Pacific,"[195] China Airlines Flight 006 is bound for San Francisco. One of the Boeing 747's four engines fails, which should have caused no significant issues. But the plane plunges, losing ten kilometres of elevation in just two minutes. The force of the plunge rips the undercarriage doors and horizontal stabilizers off the plane; somehow, miraculously, the crew manages to land the plane safely. Two stunning parts to this story: 1) with the damage, they should not have been able to land the plane safely, and 2) the plunge need not have happened in the first place. The pilot made what should have been a deadly error but then performed a superhuman feat to save the day.

Before the plunge occurred, the pilot consulted the one instrument that told him the plunge was imminent, but he chose not to believe it. Because he was experiencing incredible fatigue and jet lag, he was spatially disoriented and unable to accommodate the engine failure. Investigators confirmed that all instruments were in working order. All that the pilot needed to do was look at the other instruments to see that the plunge was indeed beginning, disengage autopilot, and put his foot on a pedal. The corroborating evidence was on hand—as well as a simple solution.

Investigators offered two significant observations relating to survival on an airplane. First, focus on the entire dashboard, not one instrument. Paying attention to only one instrument—whether we believe it is right or wrong—provides only a sliver of information. A dashboard of instruments delivers more complete information and lets us know if we are on the right track. One instrument cannot tell the whole story. Second, there is a reason for the human at the front of the plane. Autopilot is designed to solve familiar problems, but a creative mind is needed when new problems arise. In the flight over the Pacific Ocean, the pilot needed to intervene—by putting a foot on a pedal. He didn't, and the plane plunged to earth.

Compared to a human community, an airplane is a simple system. There is a chain of command, and it is clear who is in charge. When we consider a town, city, region, province, country, continent, or even the planet, it is less clear who is in charge and where we are going. The many destinations and modes of travel become a collective direction in a city, but the lessons learned by the investigators of China Airlines Flight 006 invite the following questions for a community of any scale in any setting:

1. What brings us together? Who are we? What is important to us?
2. What direction are we moving in?
3. Who has the power to move us in the direction we wish to go?
4. What agreements and structures do we need in order to move in our chosen direction?
5. What are the wise ways to move in our chosen direction?
6. What diversity of skills and gifts do we bring to get us there?
7. How do we weave all of the above together through the messy process of community?
8. How do we behave when things don't go as planned?

When we imagine the kinds of cities we long for, we inevitably contemplate the well-being of varied aspects of the city: housing, economic development, transportation, health care, ecology, food security, and so on.

In our cities, we use various services, and a handful of us measure how each one improves or declines. In small collectives, like the education system or an environmental watchdog, indicators tell us how we are doing. Each system follows its own measures, which is akin to our pilot paying attention to just one instrument. We need to find ways and places for watching all the instruments. Monitoring the whole dashboard is crucial to our survival.

We are city makers when we create times and places to connect the systems that look after the well-being of the entire city. We are city makers when we allow information to come alive and become something to act on, in a way that allows citizens to consider new understanding and deepen their work. At every scale, we are on a learning journey, where we dive into the work we love and cities show up better for the citizens they serve. Even when a sense of direction is hard to grasp, we are on a learning journey that may feel like David Whyte's "pathless path:"

> [W]hen we first come across the idea of a pathless path, by definition, we are not meant to understand

*what it means. We are meant to pay a different
kind of attention—the kind of attention we might
pay if we thought our life was at stake at high alti-
tude—one that starts to change us from the inside
out.*[196]

The pilot of China Airlines Flight 006 was able to redeem
himself. He, alone, had the ability to correct his mistakes in the
complicated work of flying a plane. Being a city maker is a form
of piloting that is unfamiliar because it is shared; "piloting" a
city does not involve an individual on a linear path with a clear
destination. Rather, the pilot's role in city making is diffused, with
no familiar clear roles and responsibilities. An unusual form of
leadership emerges on a pathless path. Parker J. Palmer shares
these wise words on the pursuit of community:

> *Leadership is a concept we often resist. It seems
> immodest, even self-aggrandizing, to think of our-
> selves as leaders. But if it is true that we are made
> for community, then leadership is everyone's voca-
> tion, and it is evasion to insist that it is not. When we
> live in the close-knit ecosystem called community,
> everyone follows and everyone leads.*
>
> *Even I…have come to understand that for better
> or worse, I lead by word and deed simply because
> I am here doing what I do. If you are also here,
> doing what you do, then you also exercise leader-
> ship of some sort.*[197]

*We are city makers
when we allow
information to come
alive and become
something to act on,
in a way that allows
citizens to consider
new understanding
and deepen their work.*

When we engage in individual and collective learning journeys
to figure out the work we long to do (direction), we step into our
roles as city makers. We shape the city, and the city shapes us.

AWAKEN TO WHAT WE WANT

I moderate many election forums across my city and use a
process that allows a range of underground audience questions
to emerge. Over the years, one question in particular has stood
out: "We often speak of what rights are owed to citizens by the
city. But I think we should be asking: What responsibilities do
citizens owe to the city as a whole?" This citizen did not direct her
question to only the political candidates in the room. She was also
asking her fellow citizens to contemplate what they could do for

the city habitat we share and for the city government that serves us. This big question invites us to consider what we contribute to our cities, while suggesting it is not just up to city hall. We need to be the best citizens we can be, and being the best citizens means being evolutionary agents.

For me, a number of trade-offs (between the larger city and my neighbourhood within it) immediately came to mind in the context of this citizen's question: welcome the LRT through my neighbourhood to allow the larger transportation network to work better; embrace higher density housing in my neighbourhood to make better use of city infrastructure; embrace a variety of housing densities in my neighbourhood to accommodate a variety of citizens; encourage expenditures for neighbourhood infrastructure renewal first in neighbourhoods that need it. To truly serve the whole city in these (and many other) ways, we need to create, together, a social habitat that allows ideas like these to be raised, then acted upon. I need to be open to co-creating the space that the city needs versus what my immediate community needs. To put the city's needs first, we must put our egos aside, removing their ability to sabotage our desire and responding to the cosmic call to let out our creative impulse.

We choose the city we want by naming it, and describing it.

Citizens are city makers. We build the physical city in which we live; we build the economic systems within which we work; and we make the social habitats that help us navigate our complex world in cities. We choose the city we want by naming it, and describing it. When we speak only of what's wrong, we get more of what's wrong. It's time to speak about—and create—the social habitat that we want, that delivers on the improvements we seek. This is important work because at every scale (self, family, neighbourhood or organization, city, nation, planet) what we build lasts: it reverberates for a long time to come. Everything we do shapes our city.

When it comes to the physical habitat we make for ourselves, being an evolutionary agent means being awake. As citizens we spend a lot of time talking about what we don't like about our cities: "We are causing great environmental damage;" "Our economic systems are collapsing;" "There is too much traffic;" "We pay too many taxes;" "The potholes aren't fixed." If we focus on what's wrong, we get more of what's wrong. Paying attention to what we want gives us the city we want.

1. City **building** involves civic managers and civic builders and developers. City **caring** involves citizens and civil society. City **making** involves everyone.

2. The city regenerates itself with the new work we do to improve the city. This requires trusting that the new work serves citizens.

3. For Charles Montgomery, the city is a happiness project, a shared endeavour that challenges us to engage with the tension between personal and community goals. When we do so, we improve our experience, and change others' experiences, of the city.

4. When we are able to see, learn, and benefit from everyone's contributions and gifts, the city becomes a place where we learn to live with conflicting truths and uncertainties. It is a place where we can integrate feeling and knowing and simply be in awe of how the city does many things at once.

5. We choose the city we want by naming it, describing it. Are our stories grounded in scarcity and deprivation, or are they appreciative of the wonder of abundance? Do we choose stories of despair or possibility? City making is story making. Story making is city making.

6. We are city makers when we create spaces and places to connect the systems that look after the overall well-being of the city. We are city makers when we allow information to come alive and become something to act on, in a way that allows citizens to consider new understanding and deepen their work.

7. Being a city maker is a form of piloting without clear roles and responsibilities.

8. Citizens are city makers. We build the physical city in which we live, we build the economic systems in which we work; and we build the social habitat that helps us navigate our complex world in cities.

9. When we engage in individual and collective learning journeys to figure out the work we long to do (direction), we step into our roles as city makers.

NEST-MAKING PRACTICE
Hearing The Call To Make Cities For Ourselves

The very attempt to continually find out what people might want for themselves is a generous and beneficial act that can often heal.
—David Whyte[198]

Looking after self, others, and place applies at any scale: with spouses and partners, with children and family, in neighbourhoods and in organizations, in cities. When you find yourself in a position where you make decisions on behalf of others, ask when it is appropriate **not** to decide, choosing instead to create the conditions for them to decide. Inspire social habitats that put decisions in the right places. This feels pathless, but it is an essential ingredient in creating cities that serve citizens well.

What are citizens called to make? What are businesses called to make? What are community organizations called to make? What are public institutions called to make? The answers to these questions are found partially in you and me. The answers to these questions are entirely in all of us. We find the answers when we seek to understand what we truly want in and from our cities.

REFLECT

Take a moment with a journal or sketchbook and see where the following questions take you. There are no wrong or right answers.

Self—What am I courageously smitten with? Is it an idea, a project, something tangible or intangible? What has got its hooks in me?

Other—What are others courageously stepping into? What am I courageously stepping into with others? Where am I serving my city with others? In what ways?

City—Who does my city want to be? What ideas keep popping up? What are the new ideas looking for attention?

Care—What support do I need to be courageously smitten, to allow something to get its hooks into me? What support do others need from me? What do I need from my city?

Reminder: *"city" means the city-habitat we make for ourselves, the community around us, not our municipal government (often referred to as "the City").*

CHAPTER 9

To be an effective agent of change does not mean we have to know everything. But it does require opening to another level of transformation and creativity . . . openness to growth and to creative responses that we didn't know were possible. We give ourselves over to something that feels true. . . . Our souls are positively stirred, and conscripted. This process of growth is clearly never-ending.
        —*Terry Patten*[199]

As human beings, we are on a journey of becoming who we really are. This journey to ourselves—to our Selves—is open-ended and full of disruptions, confusion, and breakdowns, but also breakthroughs. It is a journey that essentially is about accessing the deep sources of the Self.
        —*Otto Scharmer and Katrin Kaufer*[200]

When we say yes to the evolutionary impulse within, when our own egoic, local selves become transparent to our Essential Selves, this impulse is rapidly coming into new form through us.
        —*Barbara Marx Hubbard*[201]

EVOLUTIONARY AGENTS FOR THE CITY

LEARN TO BE THE MEANS

As evolutionary agents, we connect our learning journey with emergence. We accept the messiness of city life, and we explore the thresholds that challenge us to improve ourselves, our work, and our city. When we embrace the role of emergence in our learning journey, we choose possibility. Each time we choose to respond to the creative evolutionary impulse within, we collectively respond to the evolutionary impulse at every scale.

Humanity is the living embodiment of "crossing over," say Otto Scharmer and Katrin Kaufer as they consider Nietzsche's reflection of man as a rope or a bridge, not an end in itself:

> At the beginning of the 21st century, probably for the first time in human history, the living presence of the abyss—that is, the simultaneous existence of one world that is dying and another that is being born—is a widely shared experience for millions of people across cultures, sectors and generations.[202]

At the edge of the abyss we approach a threshold, where we can choose to ignore what lies before us, turn away from it, or leap ahead. Each choice—whether we are deciding to switch jobs, build a community garden, or invest in an underground train system—is appropriate depending on the circumstances. At every scale, the **choice** needs to be discerned, which means listening to the inside voice that pulls us to first notice the tension, then make a choice, and then take action.

Scharmer and Kaufer identify four levels of listening that allow access to increasingly deeper sources of self by connecting our exterior and interior worlds.

- **Habitual listening**—projects old judgments.
- **Factual listening**—directs the beam of observation onto the world around us.
- **Empathic listening**—adopts another person's perspective, thereby allows us to see ourselves through the eyes of the other.
- **Generative listening**—listens from the whole and the emerging new, which further turns the beam of observation onto the deep sources of Self.

Listening deeply to ourselves invites profound shifts on individual and collective levels.

Listening deeply to ourselves invites profound shifts on individual and collective levels. Scharmer and Kaufer describe three conditions that make the shifts possible.[203] First, we need to "bend the beam of observation" back on its source. Factual listening to the world around us remains separate from self. Bending the beam of observation back to ourselves means listening to ourselves through the ears of another (empathic) or through the whole (generative). Second, a profound shift occurs when we open our minds and hearts, creating a quality of space where deep, unsaid thoughts and feelings are not only spoken, but welcomed and received. Finally, we need to be willing to step up "to the edge of the abyss, to let go, to lean into the unknown—and take the leap."[204]

As we learn to listen to ourselves and others, and to create the conditions for profound shifts in learning about the world around and within us, we are learning to **be the means** through which what is on the other side of the abyss comes to pass. We enact the title of Scharmer and Kaufer's book: *Leading from the Emerging Future*. Our inner and outer work matters because we are the bridge connecting the present we have to the future we want. Being a vehicle for the future is a civic practice, within and without, that invites us to shift how we think, make, and do.

EMBRACE VOCATION AS CONSCIOUS CITIZENSHIP

Embrace Perpetual Development

> *I invite you to begin now. Begin beautifully.*
> *Begin riding the waves of your joy and interest.*
> —Risa F. Kaparo[205]

When we choose to be the best citizens we can be, by seeking out and embracing the shifting world around us, we act as evolutionary agents for the city. When we open ourselves to the interior creative evolutionary impulse that calls us to pursue our passions in our work, we contribute continuously to our personal and collective habitats—cities.

Making continuous contributions to our city habitats requires faith, trusting that our efforts will make a difference even if we don't immediately—or ever—see the results. Andrew Cohen sees an evolutionary perspective as a new path to spiritual awakening. He identifies five tenets that we can *think* about, *make* our practice, and *do* in our daily life, allowing infinite possibilities within each of us to come into being. They serve as challenges for citizens, as evolutionary agents, to:

1. **Make a bold, foundational commitment** to be a vehicle for the evolutionary impulse in the world. Craft a clear intention to live into your potential. Own your own potential to serve the future.

2. **Take unconditional and conscious responsibility** for all of yourself. Make yourself available to participate in the present and the future with positivity, without the burden of negativity. You can choose to enable evolution in and through yourself.

3. **Face everything and avoid nothing.** You stand tall with a new emotional strength when you don't hide anything from yourself. This means tolerating a higher degree of reality about yourself and the world around you. The walls of self-protection and denial erode, allowing you to experience the complexity of being human.

4. **Cultivate a bigger perspective.** The drama of your personal experiences feels less overwhelming when you look at it from a larger context. The larger context is our creative impulse, the evolutionary impulse that eclipses personal concerns.

5. **Cast a circle of care wider than the world as you know it.** Notice the moral imperative to ensure that the evolutionary process evolves through you. Imagine a kind of cosmocentric care, not related to your ego, well beyond your sense of self. Extraordinary things happen when you emotionally respond to life from this stance.[206]

The goal of life is perpetual development, involving both a path (a direction) and a goal (destination). When we choose to fully engage with the world and to respond to our creative impulses, we serve the evolutionary process. In the city, this means we build economic, social, and physical habitats that serve evolution.

VOCATION IS A JOURNEY OF CONSCIOUS CITIZENSHIP

*Cities are not supposed to work perfectly—their imperfections compel us to contribute. There is showing up, and then there is **consciously** showing up.*

We serve self, others, and our places better when we follow our work impulse. As an evolutionary agent, we take passionate vocational leaps as a form of conscious citizenship. In *The Nature of Economies*, Jacobs articulates ways to think of work:[207]

- **Encourage initiative and resourcefulness in yourself.** When not discouraged or suppressed, the qualities of taking initiative and being resourceful are abundant. Genius and extraordinary talent are not necessary preconditions.

- **Look for and support endangered species of work** in both yourself and others; different kinds of work are our economic gene pools.

- **Work with passion** for self and others, doing work you love to do. When you do, your hunger for learning and exploring generates what the city needs of us all.

- **Recognize that a healthy work life contributes to the city's healthy economic life.** Individual actions and perspectives are connected to the overall health of the city and vice versa.

Consider David Whyte's proposal:

> *To glimpse our vocation, we must learn how to be sought out and found by our work as much as we strive to identify it ourselves. We must make ourselves findable by being seen and to do that we must hazard ourselves and make ourselves available to the world we want to enter.*[208]

A vocation is a journey of finding yourself. In the context of the city, our collective vocation is a journey of the city finding itself. That is conscious citizenship—a passionate vocational leap.

A few years ago, a friend said to me, "The world is run by those who show up." These words made me realize that cities, too, are run by those who show up, but for a city habitat to thrive, it takes more than just showing up. Cultural anthropologist Angeles Arrien identifies stepping stones for conscious citizenship: show up and be present; pay attention to what has heart and meaning; tell the truth without blame or judgment; and be open, not attached, to outcome.[209]

When we live in cities, and/or interact with our cities, we are "showing up." As we build homes, choose apartments, and work to make our communities better places, we are making and re-making our cities. When I am present, I notice—and tune into—the city around me. I pay attention to what has heart and meaning in the city, acknowledging the attitudes and actions that nourish my sense of self and the world around me. Telling the truth without blame or judgment means sharing my observations about my city and my relationship with it. It means articulating an authentic vision for me and my city that is not superficial, but comes from deep within. Being open to outcome enables me to tap into the wisdom within me and my city and to see and realize new possibilities.

In the context of the city, our collective vocation is a journey of the city finding itself.

Conscious citizens have the courage to be more than just physically present; they have the mental courage to be present, the full-hearted courage to pay attention to what has meaning, the visionary courage to name what they see, and the emotional courage to be open to outcome. Conscious citizens respond to the world with work that matters, further changing the city, then choosing to show up and be present again for a new reality.

At times, we don't participate fully or consciously in city life. We "show up" but we are not engaged. Perhaps this happens because we feel we don't have a say in what happens, but we need to realize that cities are not supposed to work perfectly—their imperfections compel us to contribute. There is showing up, and then there is **consciously showing up.** The city is run by those who consciously show up, throwing their body, mind, and soul into city life. The city is run by conscious citizens who pursue their passions in their work, organizing for it, and inviting and receiving feedback. Doing the work they love serves their—and our—evolutionary purpose.

Do people who are unhappy in their work drag us down? Not really. Even with the status quo, humanity is growing and our knowledge and understanding of the world are expanding. Many indicators, such as life expectancy, reveal that humanity is healthier now than ever before. In contrast, other indicators demonstrate that humanity has caused unprecedented damage to Earth, our ultimate physical habitat. Remember this from Chapter One: our work, or economic life, responds to our physical and social habitats. That means we will work to resolve the matters that cause harm. By digging into what really matters, the work that is calling to us from our very core **will cause improvement**. I choose to put the emphasis on what "will cause improvement." Being true to your Self serves community.

Parker J. Palmer makes a connection between Self and service.

> *If we are unfaithful to true self, we will extract a price from others. We will make promises we cannot keep, we will make houses from flimsy stuff, conjure dreams that devolve into nightmares, and other people will suffer—if we are unfaithful to true self.*[210]

Your work—your vocation—is a journey of conscious citizenship.

Embedded in this thought is a big idea: if you are unhappy in your work, you are causing harm. You owe it to yourself to be happy in your work—when you do, you help others, even others you do not know. Civic practice is getting to know your Self and the gifts you have to offer your city, as well as what you need from your city. If you are looking to find your place in the world and serve it well, you need to find your Self first. The magic in this is that collectively we have our bases covered. Your work—your vocation—is a journey of conscious citizenship.

ACTIVATE THE UNDERGROUND SUPERHERO

Inhabit the Social
A new form of leadership is emerging that cultivates collective ingenuity at any scale (self, family, neighbourhood, organization,

city, nation, species). When we create social habitats, or simply participate well in them, we give ourselves space to figure out how to serve ourselves well, so we can serve our cities well. We become evolutionary agents.

Creating social habitats that allow citizens and cities to thrive is critical prototype work. Quality social habitats require us to create spaces that "help people co-sense, co-develop, and co-create their entrepreneurial capacities by serving the real needs in their communities."[211] Our understanding of our development makes a significant shift; instead of developing in isolation, we develop with others. Instead of "me" or "you," "we" create our world together; we co-sense, co-develop, co-create *and co-evolve* our world. Leadership in this context means taking the initiative to create these spaces and places, and also shared leadership that invites co-initiation, to jump in on the learning journey together. Parallel learning journeys are not good enough. The "leaders" are all those who choose to join in. The work to create social habitats that allow us to expand our awareness and consciousness belongs to all of us. We are asked to consider ourselves not subject to change, but to **changing.**

Creating social habitats that allow citizens and cities to thrive is critical prototype work.

Emerging social habitats are more easily felt than articulated. We can discern the qualities of a sense of direction, but not a tangible destination. Tension is found in this emerging habitat, which is full of diverse knowledge and opinions, positions that are at cross-purposes, conflict and uncertainty. When we hold the intention to see more fully what we know collectively, in our massive diversity, a quality of integration is involved. To allow this integration, we need distributed leadership, that co-exists with hierarchy, that seeks to meet the needs of many and trusts that the work we each do is meaningful. Two shifts need to be made: from avoiding conflict to welcoming tension, from separating people (and their ideas and values) to embracing integration.

We are embarking on what Terry Patten calls "our great shared work:" transforming human culture. This involves a new kind of political activism, with no more "boring public meetings and venting your anger after having waited a long time for your turn" that most people don't want to be involved in, rather "a spirit of celebration, care and intimacy", a "heartfelt fellowship, and a transformative opening into a new possibility."[212] We have been invited to come together to take personal and collective responsibility for how we care for self and other, and the city we make for ourselves. The emerging social habitats for our cities are not public meetings, or vicious online discussions; they are something else, something we don't quite yet know and will need practise.

Do it All; All at Once

As humanity evolves, so, too, do the social structures we create to organize ourselves. Scharmer and Kaufer note that the state of consciousness of the social field (their term for social habitat), or the quality of our awareness, shape our social systems, resulting in different social structures and behaviours. They compare the natural laws of a physical system with those of our social systems, noting this significant difference: humans in social systems are able to initiate change.[213]

Scharmer and Kaufer describe four levels of social structures that have emerged as humanity has grown and developed (Structures 1-4 in Table 6). Drawing on the Spiral, I propose two more levels (Structures 5 and 6 in Table 6[214]). To make the connection between Scharmer and Kaufer's structures and the Spiral outlined in Chapter Three, let's consider the first structure Red and Blue, where power is centralized at the top. In the second structure, Blue and Orange, power is still at the top, but decentralized. The third structure, Orange, involves relational and networked power. The fourth structure, one we are growing into, is Green with a hint of Yellow; power is in the social structure.

In this fourth structure, Scharmer and Kaufer identify how to create habitats that allow access to knowledge and intelligence that was not available within previous structures. I propose a fifth and sixth that imagine the social habitat when Yellow and Turquoise are activated. The fifth is more than the expansion of the social habitat; it encompasses all preceding structures and enables each of them as context requires; power is in all structures. The sixth expands further to be in explicit relationship with the habitat itself, where power is in both the structures and the field.

When firefighters respond to an emergency, Structure 1 works perfectly. When there is no emergency, Structure 2 may be more appropriate. The fire chief and his personnel retain their hierarchical expectations and organize themselves to make sure the resources are in place for the next emergency; their power is

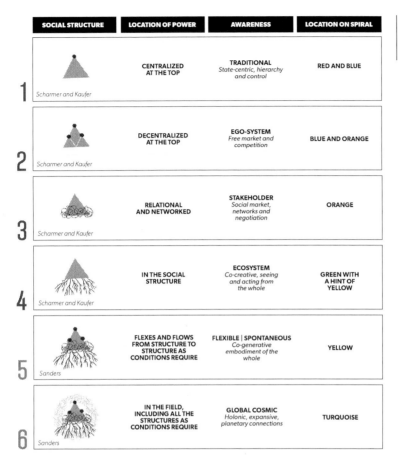

SOCIAL STRUCTURE	LOCATION OF POWER	AWARENESS	LOCATION ON SPIRAL
1 Scharmer and Kaufer	CENTRALIZED AT THE TOP	**TRADITIONAL** *State-centric, hierarchy and control*	RED AND BLUE
2 Scharmer and Kaufer	DECENTRALIZED AT THE TOP	**EGO-SYSTEM** *Free market and competition*	BLUE AND ORANGE
3 Scharmer and Kaufer	RELATIONAL AND NETWORKED	**STAKEHOLDER** *Social market, networks and negotiation*	ORANGE
4 Scharmer and Kaufer	IN THE SOCIAL STRUCTURE	**ECOSYSTEM** *Co-creative, seeing and acting from the whole*	GREEN WITH A HINT OF YELLOW
5 Sanders	FLEXES AND FLOWS FROM STRUCTURE TO STRUCTURE AS CONDITIONS REQUIRE	**FLEXIBLE | SPONTANEOUS** *Co-generative embodiment of the whole*	YELLOW
6 Sanders	IN THE FIELD, INCLUDING ALL THE STRUCTURES AS CONDITIONS REQUIRE	**GLOBAL COSMIC** *Holonic, expansive, planetary connections*	TURQUOISE

Table 6
Social
Structures

decentralized. Even further behind the scenes, fire department personnel work collaboratively within a network of city builders to make sure that the design of new neighbourhoods meets the needs of citizens' day to day life, as well as their own emergency response needs. Their "turf" gets mixed in with that of many other stakeholders in Structure 3.

Structure 4 is appropriate when the context allows the firefighters to sit back and contemplate what they are doing and why. It might be a strategic planning session at the fire hall that involves a diverse range of expertise and experience to make wise choices. From Structure 5, fire department personnel see that the time and place varies for each approach—that they all happen naturally.

From Structure 6, they more fully understand their role in the co-evolutionary development of the city.

The social structures at play in the city, how we organize ourselves, are transforming; they reflect our evolving awareness. The traditional awareness of Structure 1 is state-centric, relying on traditional hierarchy and control to organize ourselves. Structure 2 shifts to an ego-system awareness, relying on markets and competition to organize ourselves. We shift to stakeholder awareness in Structure 3, where networks and negotiation are our organizing principles. A larger ecosystem emerges with Structure 4, organizing in a co-creative fashion, seeing and sensing from the whole. A flexible, spontaneous awareness emerges with Structure 5, where we embody the wholeness of the four previous structures. The awareness of Structure 6 expands again, to contemplate the wholeness of the planet and beyond. In these last two structures, we find ourselves organizing in co-creative, co-generative ways.[215]

In our work as citizens, civic institutions, civic builders and developers, and community organizations, we need to engage the systems in which we live and work. We do not automatically operate with all six of these structures; we each grow into them, with fewer people having grown into the latter structures at this time. It does not matter which structure we operate from when we are healthy and responding appropriately to our context. Each social structure has valuable contributions to make—from Structures 5 and 6 we see that the first four, like the first six levels of the Spiral, have a role in the systems of the city. So all social structures need to be activated, all at once, as conditions require. They are all necessary in the right time and place. Activating all social structures all at once allows us to effectively engage our entire social habitat—in all these ways and at every scale.

Be Your Own Superhero

In practical terms, what does it mean to live into our social habitat and be evolutionary agents? Let me introduce you to three people who helped me understand the answer to that question: Pam Moody, Jim Mustard, and Paul McNeil.

When Pam Moody was elected mayor of Yarmouth, Nova Scotia, she was inundated with demands: "The town should do this; you should do that," her citizens clamoured. She could see the difference between a pity party in a struggling town and a town that stood up to look after what needed to be done. Her response? You are the town! Instead of taking ownership for all the problems of the town, she transferred ownership to everyone in the town. She invited co-creation of the town.

Jim Mustard, deputy warden of the County of Inverness, Nova Scotia, believes in the value of nurturing children, the next generation of adult citizens, to reach their full potential. In his exploration of early childhood development, he learned that brain development relies on people spending time together. Linking this idea to his community, he saw lost opportunities for us to grow and develop when we place experts at the front of the room. When we sit and listen, rather than talk about what binds us, we are not creating the new structures in our brains that encourage us to build connections with each other. Such connections allow us to be more resilient, to create communities that serve us in the best ways possible.

Paul McNeil, publisher of Island Press Ltd., has created a place for Atlantic Canada's rural communities to find local solutions to community economic, social and environmental challenges. He brought people like Pam and Jim from across Atlantic Canada to Georgetown, Prince Edward Island, to tell stories and notice what enables communities to find—and implement—solutions to the challenges they are facing. Paul did not ask participants to sit and listen to a few experts and then go home; he asked them to tell stories, explore the stories, and then to go home and change the face of rural communities.

I met Pam, Jim, and Paul when I moderated a session at the Federation of Canadian Municipalities' Sustainable Communities Conference in Charlottetown, PEI. To replicate the Georgetown Experience, which was all about connecting people and supporting the development of new relationships, we began with their stories of Georgetown. Then we invited participants to dig into the panelists' stories, teasing out deeper meaning in a series of small conversations that allowed our little conference community to make connections between their ideas and themselves. We created the conditions to foster relationships that would not have been possible if we had used the traditional "sage on the stage" conference format. We also learned that there was significant expertise everywhere in the room—in the community.

This little conference community found that when citizens are engaged, they:

- Bring their best selves, leaving the negative at the door
- Tell stories
- Pursue unusual partnerships
- Take action—not worrying about the specifics
- Trust that people want to contribute
- Trust that people want to take responsibility
- Offer minimal structure
- Practice working with each other—commit to meeting more than once
- Get together—bursting the silos
- Pause to look at the bigger picture issues at play

As Pam, Jim, and Paul reflected on the session, they noticed that their citizens were starved for leadership, but it wasn't leadership from elected officials that was missing. It was the leadership of people standing up to say: **I can. We can.**

So what holds us back from fully contributing to our cities? Perhaps it is our own inability to choose to contribute, because we sabotage ourselves. In *Positive Intelligence*, Shirzad Chamine argues that our mind is both a friend and an enemy. Positive intelligence "measures the relative strength of those two modes in your mind. High Positive Intelligence means your mind acts as your friend far more than as your enemy. Low Positive Intelligence is the reverse."[216] How we choose to use our brains shapes the social habitats we make for ourselves and our cities.

Within each of us, according to Chamine, lives a master saboteur of happiness—the Judge—and nine accomplices. The Judge compels us to find fault with everything, and powered by the fight-or-flight parts of our brain (brainstem and limbic system), the accomplices aim for survival and power. They do whatever it takes to convince us that our survival depends on them:

1. The Stickler takes perfection, order, and organization too far.

2. The Pleaser compels us to gain acceptance and affection by helping, pleasing, rescuing, or flattering others constantly.

3. The Hyper-Achiever makes us dependent on constant performance and achievement for self-respect and self-validation.

4. The Victim wants us to feel emotional and temperamental to gain attention and affection.

5. The Hyper-Rational involves intense and exclusive focus on the rational, causing us to regard emotions as unworthy for consideration.

6. The Hyper-Vigilant makes us feel intense and continuous anxiety about everything that could go wrong.

7. The Restless is constantly in search of greater excitement and is perpetually busy.

8. The Controller runs on an anxiety-based need to take charge, control situations, and bend others' actions to its will.

9. The Avoider focuses on the positive and the unpleasant in an extreme way.

Do you recognize any of these bandits sabotaging your way of thinking? These saboteurs keep us from reaching our fullest potential. They keep us—and our brains—focused on short-term threats to our short-term survival. But if you are aware of their presence, you can choose a different path.

In contrast to the short-term thinking of the saboteurs, Chamine identifies the Sage—what I call our Higher Self. This is a "deeper and wiser part of you. It is the part that can rise above the fray and resist getting carried away by the drama and tension of the moment or falling victim to the lies of the saboteurs." Our Higher Self uses entirely different areas of the brain for entirely different purposes. The middle prefrontal cortex contains what Chamine calls the "empathic circuitry;" the right brain gives us the ability to see the bigger picture, empathize, and detect the invisible, such as energy and mood. When our lives are not threatened, we and our brain can choose how we are going to show up—in defensive survival mode or as our Higher Self.

Five powers enable the Higher Self to move ahead "one positive step at a time, regardless of what life throws at [us]."[217] I call these our Citizen Superpowers, and they are alive in Pam, Jim and Paul's stories:

1. **Explore** with curiosity and an open mind
2. **Empathize** with yourself and others in any situation
3. **Create** outside-the-box solutions with new perspectives
4. **Choose** a path that best aligns with your deeper underlying values and mission
5. **Act** without the distress, interference, or distractions of the saboteurs[218]

Citizen Superpowers value acceptance over denial, rejection, or resentment. They consider every situation a gift and opportunity. The Higher Self acts out of empathy, inspiration, the joy of exploration, a longing to create, a desire to contribute, and an urge to find meaning in the midst of even the greatest crises. There are no bad circumstances or outcomes, only opportunities. The stronger our relationship is with our Higher Self, the stronger our Citizen Superpowers—and our cities—become.

The more we exercise our Citizen Superpower muscles, the more comfortable we are with them. Through practice, we learn to handle the "flight" parts of our brain that try to sabotage deeper knowing when flight is not necessary. We grow our abilities, becoming skillful and wise with their application. Our actions may be large or small. Never mind the size—using our powers is what's important.

Understand the Underground
I refer to the implicit, internal inner workings of the city as "the underground." I don't mean the traditional, physical underground network of pipes and culverts and drains that serve the city, but the connections and conduits within, among, and between citizens in our social habitat. We don't always see "the underground" when we look at the city nest we've made for ourselves, but it is there. If we want our cities to evolve , then we must evolve; we can do this by exploring the underground, the invisible in the city, that connects our work and our souls. That's where our Citizen Superpowers lie, and when we choose to use them we become evolutionary agents for the city.

Cities are about connecting people and the ways we think, make, and do together. This is how cities are formed, how they energize us—by giving us opportunities to follow our passions. In turn we energize our cities. The quality of how we relate to self, each other, and our cities is essential. Everywhere, at all times, we need to listen—to notice—all that forms, in the air and underground. This is a citizenship practice, of stopping to notice what and how we each show up to dance and our relationship with the dancers and the changing dance floor itself.

NOTICE THE PHYSICAL NATURE OF YOUR CITY

Happiness is slippery, it slithers away between your fingers, but problems are something you can hold on to, they've got handles, they're rough and hard.
        —Isabel Allende[219]

Partly because sprawl has forced Americans to drive automobiles farther and farther in the course of every day, per capita road death rates in the United States hover around forty thousand per year. That's a third more people than are killed by guns. It's more than 10 times the number of people killed in the terrorist attacks of September 11, 2001. Here's an image that sticks: imagine a loaded Boeing 747 crashing every three days, killing everyone on board. That's how many people die on U.S. highways every year... A rational policy maker would wage war, not on other nations, but on traffic deaths.
        —Charles Montgomery[220]

We Design Our Cities
A simple syllogism for you:

1. The design of our cities affects our social networks, and

2. The quality of our social networks affects the quality of our lives, therefore

3. The design of our cities affects the quality of our lives.

As evolutionary agents we shape the physical nature of our cities, and design the quality of our lives—our personal, individual lives, and the lives of others. The cities we make matter. Charles Montgomery observes:

> *[It is] audacious to believe that the city might build happiness just by changing its shape. But it is foolish not to chase the thought, because around the world, and especially amid the sprawlscapes*

of modern North America, the evidence shows that cities do indeed design our lives. [221]

A healthy social network is like the roots of a tree, and, as Montgomery points out, a tree with a small root ball is more likely to fall over when the wind blows. In our cities, "people's root networks are contracting, closing in on themselves, circling more and more tightly around spouses, partners, parents, and kids." [222] People are living increasingly solitary lives, which increases our risk of falling—individually and collectively—when the wind blows. When we build our nests in trees with shallow roots, we put ourselves at risk. Montgomery argues that our changing social habitat (marriages do not last as long; people work longer hours; people move more frequently) as well as our physical habitat (increased commute times; less trust in mono-functional, car-dependent neighbourhoods than in walkable neighbourhoods with diverse housing, shops, and places to work) are contributing to these shallow root systems. Research shows that our social habitats struggle when our cities are dispersed. We like to tell ourselves that we want space from each other, but in reality we want and need to be close to one another.

Our social habitats struggle when our cities are dispersed. We like to tell ourselves that we want space from each other, but in reality we want and need to be close to one another.

We create our city nests, the high and dense, and the now-common dispersed and sprawling city in North America. For Montgomery, two simple actions occurred for these nests to be built: first, by putting everything in its place with zoning laws—the rules that tell us what we can and cannot do on our land; and second, by discarding the shared street. Zoning laws emerged in the 1880s to ban Chinese public laundries from San Francisco's city's core in the United States (a racist law that was invalidated by a 1886 Supreme Court Case). Their purpose was to separate the ways we use land and the people who use and live on the land. As a result, first-generation suburbs closer to downtowns are not diverse and dense and do not grow more diverse and dense. They resist change and adaptations. Further, the rules push new development to the edges of the city and ensure that they too are resistant to change and adaptation. We lost shared streets not because of the advent of cars, but because of the way we handled them. When the first Model T car rolled out onto the streets of Detroit in 1907, our streets were shared by everyone. Montgomery describes them as a reigning "messy kind of freedom," chaotic with horse dung and cars, which served as a market, playground, park, and thoroughfare all at once.[223]

As more cars and trucks arrived in American cities in the 1920s, road culture was transformed. "More than two hundred thousand people were killed in motor accidents in the United States that decade. Most were killed in cities. Most of the dead were pedestrians. Half were children and youth,"[224] says Montogmery. The subsequent design and financing of city streets put motorists first. We separated what we use land for, which means we need to get in our cars more, and we made rules for streets that put cars first. In thinking we were designing cities for ourselves, we were designing for our retreat from one another.

The conundrum of the city is found in two words: proximity and retreat. Our current design to resolve this tension is the dispersed city. We retreat from each other, and we demand and create expanses of space between us. At the same time, we recognize that the most exciting places in the city are alive with people and activity. As evolutionary agents for the city, we have a choice, on a continuum: retreat or community. The rules that guide the development of our streets and buildings can keep us apart or they can draw us toward messy, vibrant places that we need to thrive—including places for retreat.

The conundrum of the city is found in two words: proximity and retreat.

Notice the Patterns Around You

As you can see, this book is not a set of instructions about how to design the city; there are plenty of those available. You may also realize that city work is not about "fixing" the city, because "fixing" implies that problems and their solutions are simple. A city is far more complex than that. The real way to get the city you want is to be in relationship with it.

When you explore other cities, you learn to look at your own city with fresh eyes. A few years ago, my family went on an unusual winter holiday. Rather than travel somewhere warm, we visited five winter cities. In December and January, we explored the capital cities of Earth's Nordic nations: Reykjavik, Iceland; Oslo, Norway; Copenhagen, Denmark; Stockholm, Sweden; and Helsinki, Finland. We chose to stay in apartments in neighbourhoods, experiencing the city in a more intimate way than if we'd stayed in downtown hotels. In some ways, these five cities were entirely different from cities on the Canadian Prairies; in other ways, they were much the same.

The most startling difference was in the ways we moved around the cities. At home, we walk and bicycle quite a bit, take the bus occasionally, and most certainly use a car. In the Nordic cities, we found groceries and services within a couple minutes' walk from our apartments and public transportation was only a minute or two away. We noticed schools everywhere. The streets were alive with people and business. Bicycle infrastructure lined busy streets, along with cars and buses and trams and trolleys. In Edmonton, these kinds of amenities are found in tiny pockets; in these Nordic cities, they are expansive networks. Two city patterns were at work: one to serve the movement of cars; a second to serve the movement of people.

Let's look at these cities by the numbers. First, consider the five Nordic cities and the three largest cities on the Canadian Prairies: Edmonton, Calgary, and Winnipeg. Table 7 reflects each city's population, area and density numbers by municipal boundary.[225] Reykjavik is the smallest in population. Winnipeg, Oslo, Copenhagen, and Helsinki all sit at about the same level. Stockholm approaches the size of Edmonton and Calgary is the largest. By geographic area, Edmonton covers the most land, with Calgary second. Winnipeg and Oslo are about the same, while Stockholm and Helsinki are about one-quarter the area of Edmonton, and Copenhagen covers about half the area of the two larger Nordic cities. Tiny Reykjavik is less than half the size again. The real story is in population density. The Canadian prairie cities are the least dense. Once again, Oslo is somewhat comparable, but Reykjavik and Helsinki are significantly more

Table 7
Nordic and Western Canadian Cities— Population, Area, Density Municipal Boundary)

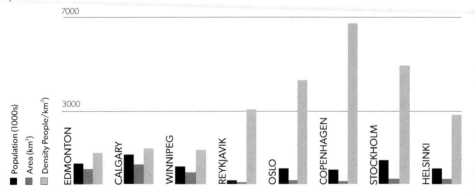

NEST CITY

dense in population than the Canadian cities, and Stockholm and Copenhagen make greater leaps—Copenhagen being more than five times the density of Edmonton.

Our home city and the cities we visited are very different. In Copenhagen, we stayed in an apartment in Frederiksberg, a good example of a neighbourhood that accommodates density without high-rise buildings. For the most part, six-storey buildings are located around the edges of a block with a courtyard in the center. Every apartment has access to daylight. Every apartment has access to outdoor yard space that is semi-private. All services are stitched into the fabric of the neighbourhood. Businesses, schools, and shopping centres are all close at hand. So, too, are transportation systems to move people in various ways—by car, by bike, on foot, or by bus. Nearby is a Metro station, their underground subway.

In contrast, my neighbourhood in Edmonton contains mostly single-family dwellings. Occasionally, spurts of uproar arise about new rules that allow duplexes and secondary suites in the neighbourhood as a strategy to increase density in the city. The one tall building in the neighbourhood raises the overall density, but the overall pattern is simple: ten homes per block. This low-density pattern means that I have a twenty-minute walk, one way, for groceries and some services. Adequate bus service is nearby. The streets are lined with wonderful trees. In the short daylight hours of winter, the sun shines into our homes. When I moved in thirteen years ago, my neighbourhood was fighting a proposed second tall building in the neighbourhood, reinforcing the pattern of low density and the inevitable use of cars (though we are active and fit enough to walk or ride our bikes most often and to take the bus).

By official municipal boundary, Copenhagen is five times more densely populated than Edmonton. By urban agglomeration—the continuous built-up area into neighbouring municipalities—it is four times more densely populated than Edmonton. These two cities exemplify two different cultural patterns of city building. The Copenhagen pattern compels us to live in close proximity to each other. The Edmonton pattern compels us to live physically apart from each other, creating space for us to be alone, both on our properties and in our cars. In Edmonton, we live mostly in single-family homes or duplexes (76%)[226] and the result is few places where we live "on top" of each other. Both patterns have merits. I put this question to an urban planning group on LinkedIn: "Which habitat feels more comfortable—four- to six-storey buildings with courtyards or single family dwellings?" The responses were numerous and varied. A few threads in the conversation flagged the idea that density does not necessarily mean a better urban environment.

Three decades ago, Copenhagen's streets were full of cars, not bicycles, as they are today. We choose the infrastructure we build in our cities—and how we will use it, too. We can change how we use these "bones"—our streets and tunnels for example—and put new muscles and tendons around them so they serve us better.

In observing the complexity of cities and their spirit of experimentation, Montgomery noticed five simple design principles that generate happiness, and I spotted the same principles at play in the more densely populated areas of the Nordic cities I visited. Happiness happens when we design for:[227]

- Connectivity—we design for more walking (more intersections), rather than for more driving (more cul-de-sacs).

- Destinations—we design for destinations within easy reach by multiple modes of transportation, rather than one.

- Choice—people have choices about how to move around the city (walk, car, bike, bus, or train). A test: Is it possible to get to the doctor or a restaurant without a car?

- Multiple modes of transportation—every person making a trip has different needs, abilities, weaknesses, and desires.

- Universal freedom of movement—we design for everyone to freely move around the city. Making active transportation and transit systems practical options improves citizens' ability to move around the city and meet their needs. The brave and able-bodied are not the only citizens who move in the city.

Vibrant parts of the Nordic cities had additional qualities as well; they were accessible, social, and active. The parts of the city that feel most alive are the places with many ways to move around; where people gather and bump into each other, stop and enjoy each other's company at a sidewalk cafe. They offer wonderful places for people to walk, play, dance, ski, skate, or build snow castles. They offer, quite simply, delightful city experiences.

The Happy City Grows Us

Open yourself to the new understanding that emerges when you notice the patterns around you in the city. When you observe your city, you reshape how you relate to our city—and how it relates to its citizens. We don't need to be city planners to do this—just citizens.

We can change the city by thinking about it differently. Rethink how we consider it, our relationship with others, and our relationship with the city itself. When we do, the rest of the city will recalibrate itself. And recognize that in this dynamic, when we make improvements, other calls for improvement present themselves. The calls for improvements—emergence—will not stop. Don't be frustrated; rather, accept that the challenges before us are the challenges we need at this time. The city we want is not delayed, or off track—it is right on schedule.

Our work is to discern our personal role in the city. If you are unhappy, that's the first clue. Notice what is making you unhappy and start with that. The reason may be big or small. Trust that all efforts towards improvement are part of a shared project to build a habitat that sustains all of us. Citizenship means we pitch in and make the city work.

The current design of our cities is, in some significant ways, working against us, but we have the power to reshape the city to meet our needs. Montgomery's key message is that social habitats struggle when physical habitats are dispersed. Citizens feel less trusting in mono-functional, car-dependent neighbourhoods than in walkable neighbourhoods with diverse housing, shops, and places to work. Building on this, he notes that a city is not happy when the only way to move around is by car. Happy mobility is multi-modal, when we have choices about how we move around and more destinations are within reach. Multiple modes of transportation, rather than focus on the car, invite us to tap into the abundance of the city. The interconnections in city life are our resilience strategy, and this understanding inspires a new story of the city, one where the city gives so much in return.

City design can resolve the proximity–retreat conundrum. When we change the rules that guide the physical development of the city, we change the physical shape of the city. This requires thinking of the city and our roles in it differently. The physical ideas are not separate from the social habitat, and our social habitat includes every one of us, everywhere. Everyone, everywhere, can actively make a city that is economically, socially, and physically healthier—collectively and individually. We do have to recognize that we make bad decisions all the time. We have to recognize that happiness is hard to grab on to. Every time we reach for what makes us happy, it just might move on, rendering us dissatisfied. Life is a journey that requires us at every turn to be present to the changes demanded of us. This never-ending journey is the force that invites us to improve our cities—and ourselves.

Being an evolutionary agent means inhabiting territory that often feels uncomfortable: the uneasy feeling of a learning journey and the emerging thresholds of the unknown. It means crossing thresholds without fully comprehending the consequences.

The calls for improrove-ments—emer-gence—will not stop. Don't be frustrated; rath-er, accept that the challenges before us are the challenges we need at this time.

When we inhabit territory like this, it means putting our sense of self at risk. It means digging into our Higher Selves, the more authentic selves, and figuring out how we are in relationship with others and the places we find ourselves. It means taking risks to feel good about self, life, and work. David Whyte shares wise words, "We know we have the right vocation and are happily married to a work when we get a song in our hearts simply from doing the work itself."[228] The song pulls us through the confusion and the terror of stepping into unimaginable consequences.

At heart, being an evolutionary agent is a continuous journey of finding identity in work. Whyte calls this "pilgrimage," where we are sustained by a connection to something bigger than ourselves. Bigger than our Higher Selves, too. Simultaneously, we ask for something bigger, and the work asks us to be bigger.

> *Following this path . . . we reach a certain threshold where our freedom to choose seems to disappear and is replaced by an understanding that we were made for the world in a very particular way and that this way of being is at bottom nonnegotiable. Like the mountain or the sky, it just is. It is as if we choose and choose until there is actually no choice at all.*[229]

NOTICE HOW YOU
THINK ABOUT THE CITY

When each of us, in our small and **significant** ways, shifts our energy from fixing to improving, we engage differently in the systems of the city. We become instrumental agents for the city everywhere: in city hall, in living rooms, in board rooms, on street corners, and in skateboard parks, at swimming pools, on walking paths, behind cash registers, in community centres, and in the streets. Everyone's work on the margin, promoting and trying out new ideas, lets us see what else is possible for our cities.

While Montgomery argues that it is time for citizens to fight city hall, this is not the real fight; the real fight is within ourselves, in how we think about our cities and our relationships with each other and our cities. The real fight is that the voices of municipal governments, the business community, citizens, and civil society need to be brought together, to physically inhabit their cities in ways that generate a robust social habitat and allow the economic lives of all to prosper. It is time for civic managers and civic developers to be open to the influence of the people who do not "build" the city. It is time for citizens and civil society to connect to the physical world around them in thoughtful ways. How could a city best serve all of these voices? And within each of these voices, how could a city best serve the varied and conflicting values? It is time for the superheroes everywhere to spend some time figuring this out.

We can change the city by thinking about it differently.

In changing how we think, we will change what we get. Here are concrete ways we can think differently about city life.

Think engagement and curiosity, rather than retreat. Today's city is a design problem (in the realm of civic managers and builders), but also a psychological, cultural problem (citizens and civil society). Montgomery says, "We have translated the uncertainty of city life into retreat instead of curiosity and engagement."[230]

Think trust and cooperation. There are parts of ourselves that are more inclined toward curiosity, trust, and cooperation, and these qualities of behaviour make us feel good. We are as equally hardwired for dissatisfaction and status anxiety as we are for trust and cooperation.

The real fight is within ourselves, in how we think about our cities and our relationships with each other and our cities.

Think relationships. Relationships are, of course, between people, but there is a key relationship to ponder—that of the city with its citizens, the village with its villagers. Does the city around you welcome the multiplicity of values and needs in the city? Does it work for the economic, social, and physical well-being of individuals and the collective? What do you do to make the city work for yourself and others?

Think of your place in the city. Confront your relationship with the city. Can you change your place in the city? Are your habits making you unhappy? Do you need to revisit what "the good life" looks like? Do you live where you can leave your car at home or does it have to go wherever you go?

Stand up with imagination. There is a struggle underway as citizens—and even some civic managers and civic builders—grapple with policies and practices that create unhappy cities. But there are lots of creative ways to create the changes we want. You can stand up in full-blown political ways or in simple choices about you to live in the city.

The city we want will emerge when we live it.

THE IDEAS TAKING F L I G H T

The city we want will emerge when we live it.

1. Thresholds are everywhere, flagging a choice to be made. This means listening to the inside voice that pulls us to first notice the tension, then the choice, then the action.

2. The quality of listening space we offer to self and others allows profound shifts in individuals and collectives.

3. We are the bridge connecting the present we have to the future we want. Our inner and outer work is a form of civic practice that enables us to be a vehicle for the future.

4. Being an evolutionary agent, according to Andrew Cohen, involves making bold commitments, taking unconditional and conscious responsibility, facing everything, cultivating bigger perspectives and casting wider circles of care than the world we know.

5. As evolutionary agents, we take passionate vocational leaps as a form of conscious citizenship. Collectively, we enable the city to improve.

6. Our social habitat is the social field and the social structures we find within and among ourselves. The creation of social habitats that allow citizens and cities to thrive is critical prototype work.

7. A variety of social structures are needed at the same time.

8. Our social habitats struggle when we are physically dispersed. We like to tell ourselves that we want space from each other, but we also want and need proximity.

9. We choose the rules we put in place to guide the physical development of our streets and buildings that shape the physical

experience of our cities. We design the quality of our lives. Do we want cities that keep us apart or bring us together?.

10. Happy cities are designed for connectivity, destinations within easy reach, choice about how to move around, and multiple modes of transportation.

11. The calls to improve the city will not stop. Accept that the challenges before us are the challenges we needed--at this time—to grow. There is nothing to "fight," rather a call to work to improve our shared project: the city.

12. The city we want will emerge when we live it.

13. Notice the work that asks you to grow.

NEST-MAKING PRACTICE
Becoming The Evolutionary Agent

[A]lmost all human endeavour needs a cradle to hold it and carry it along, particularly in its early stages.
        —David Whyte[231]

Find what is important to you and work on it. You are not the kind of superhero that swoops in and saves other people. You are the kind of superhero that looks after what you think needs to be worked on. Your passion is what drives you. It comes from inside, not from what others need of you. You are not alone; superheroes are everywhere in our cities. As an evolutionary agent for the city, you put your sense of self at risk to be more of your Self, trusting that this is how your superpowers are exercised.

I have a hunch you already know what kinds of social habitats are full of energy for you. Consider the questions below to help you decide where to spend your time. If a room, or a client, or a meeting feels like it is making you feel invisible, constrained and small, move on. If you feel open, like you can expand outwards, and you gain energy, then you will recognize it as a place where you belong.

Social habitats that feel good are needed, at every scale: with ourselves, our families, neighbourhoods, organizations we work in, our cities, and our planet. And all we need to do is step in and experiment. An easy place to start is simply to think of little things to try, to test.

REFLECT

Take a moment with a journal or sketchbook and see where the following questions take you. There are no wrong or right answers.

Self—What does the evolutionary agent in me long to do to shape my city? (Don't forget: The evolutionary agent might be looking for small things to do.)

Other—What are the qualities of physical places that encourage healthy interaction among us?

City—Where are new social and physical habitats emerging in my city?

Care—What makes me feel mentally, emotionally, physically, and spiritually amazing—my true Self?

Reminder: "city" means the city-habitat we make for ourselves, the community around us, not our municipal government (often referred to as "the City").

Whether or not we'll muff it isn't predictable, because we'll be making ourselves up as we go along—just as we've always done so far.
—Jane Jacobs[232]

[F]aith is not the belief in a received set of facts but the ability to keep one's star in sight, to pay attention to the horizon to which we belong while not betraying our present responsibilities.
—David Whyte[233]

10

WE RIDE THE WINDS OF CITY EMERGENCE

THE CITY EMERGES FROM THE ACTIONS AND INQUIRY

The future of our cities—and humanity—lies in our ability to intentionally "make ourselves up as we go along." Notice this distinction: we are not making it up, but rather making ourselves up. In 2016, Edmonton, along with five other Canadian cities, extended an invitation to citizens to transform the city with the 100In1Day project. The project centred on one question: What if hundreds of people, each taking one small action, united to improve their city all on the same day? The project guidelines are simple: An individual or group leads a single activity, project, or installation that makes the community a better place. The undertaking can be big or small, is practical or social or artistic in nature, and can challenge citizens or fix a problem. It has to be safe, legal, and inclusive.[234] The local organizers were not telling people what to do; they were inviting citizens to make the improvements they believed were needed and providing a bit of structure so they could undertake the improvements together.

This initiative started in 2012 with a group of design students in Bogatá, Columbia, who aimed to launch one hundred interventions in one day to improve their city. From there, as happens with good ideas, the initiative moved to other cities. On the Canadian "100In1Day" website, the words "citizen movement" are front and center,[235] and the site mentions that the movement has spread to over 31 cities around the world. The invitation asks participants to notice what the city asks of them and to improve the city around them. The projects take place in back alleys and on streets, as benches and art in front yards, as stories, music and play across the city.

Riding the winds of emergence means trusting that we know what to do and where we are going. This trust occurs when we use feedback loops—between our economic life and our social and physical habitats—to discern the direction in which we are moving and to create the conditions to thrive, even when we don't know our exact destination. The 100In1Day website provides a feedback loop that allows participants to see their collective efforts for improvement. Participants and others looking on can see how getting involved makes better cities. Amid all the projects—the destinations people have chosen—we can see the direction they are moving, their flight path. Our intentional choice to step in and improve the city shapes the direction in which we move. This is the dance between emergence and destination.

Riding the winds of emergence means trusting that we know what to do and where we are going.

Seek Wild Messages From the City

Most mornings, I visit the North Saskatchewan River valley near my home. One winter morning, instead of standing at the top edge of the ravine overlooking the wild and the city knit into each other, I descended toward the river. I peeled myself away from the infrastructure of the city, leaving the formal trail behind, stepping onto the unofficial path (closed by authorities) that runs beside the river. I walked for a few minutes, then responded to a wee path calling me down to the river herself. More specifically, the footprints I saw on the frozen river were calling me.

I realized that I have spent a lot of time in my river city, but I have never been on the river. So I stepped out for a new view. After a few cautious steps on to the river, I noticed that I did not have the courage to venture out as far on to the ice as others had. My comfort had rippled out far enough, so I trusted my instincts and stayed put for a while, curious about this perspective of my river city in winter.

Like most journeys, when I turned back I saw something new. When I looked back toward the bank, I realized my city is not simply up on the riverbank; it is in the river. Concrete construction waste, culverts and discarded beer cans have reached down to the river. Downstream, storm sewer outfalls whisk water away from city streets into the river. Upstream, I see a couple making their way down to the river and toward me. While the footprints on the river provided a clue that others had been here before me, the couple were evidence that others traveled with me. The footprints also indicated that others travel further than I do. While there are few situations when I am truly the first to do anything, there are endless situations when it is my first time.

It occurs to me that first times can be both daunting and exhilarating, scary and thrilling. First times, and how we handle them, play a critical role in our ability to see possibilities in all aspects of our lives, for seeing possibility often means seeing things from a different perspective. A fresh outlook might be a physical perspective or a mental one, or finding a way to look anew at an old perspective, generating a "first time" feeling that allows possibilities to emerge.

I wasn't the first person to look at the city from on the river, and I won't be the last, but that is not the point. The objective is to find the courage to step out on the ice and to see what I will see, and discover what I will do with my new perspective. When I walked on the river, I saw my city—and myself—differently.

Months later, in the autumn, as I again overlooked the river valley, a group of young adults walked along the path in the valley below. How odd to see a group of twenty people at 9 a.m. on a weekday morning, hiking down the path full of energy. I thought about waving, and resisted the urge, but then a young woman in the pack waved up at me. I waved back.

"Someone waved back at me," she shouted to her friends.

A series of waves followed, as I waved and paused, parts of the pack realized what was happening and they joined in. It went back and forth until they moved out of sight. And then I cried. I sobbed as I tried to figure out why this moved me, what cracked me open. And then it hit me—my city waved at me.

This group of young people moved my soul. I found myself wanting to thank them, but they were long gone, and just as I thought I missed the opportunity, I heard them behind me. They had circled up onto the road; I turned and I could see their faces, their smiles, their exuberance, and, of course, we started to wave at each other. I shouted to them, "Thank you! You made my day!"

"Thank you, River Valley Friend!" they called back, as they continued their hike.

It didn't matter who I was; it mattered that I waved. It doesn't matter who starts waving; it matters that someone starts. It doesn't matter if we know each other. It matters simply that we let ourselves interact with joy. When we do, we allow the city to come and find us.

In cities everywhere, the wave is underway. We are organizing for emergence at local and global scales. Edmonton high school teacher Dustin Bajer took the initiative one summer to work with his city government and invite citizens to reforest our river valley with edible native plants. Community builder Shelley Sabo experiments with multigenerational community building in her neighbourhood, children and seniors and everyone in between are rebuilding public places with love and meaning. Home designer and builder Chris Buyze is pushing boundaries with sustainable building practices in sustainable locations. Robin Mazumder is an occupational therapist by day, and by night he lights our winter city with colourful lights and organizes snowball fights. Chelsea deBoos and Carmen Douville brought an abandoned rail bridge back to life. It's alive with vegetables, fruit, and community members in the summer, a beautiful blend of people who rarely mix, from swanky new office tower employees to soup kitchen volunteers and clients. These are Edmonton examples, mirrored in cities around the world.

It doesn't matter if we know each other. It matters simply that we let ourselves interact with joy. When we do, we allow the city to come and find us.

These folks are reshaping their city on the ground, with ideas grown in the wild. They are driven to improve their own little piece of the city, and their efforts contribute far more than they could imagine. The city we have today emerges from their actions. They provide huge gifts to the city and its citizens, and in return they are rewarded with work that has heart and meaning. As citizens, we receive new ways to see and experience our cities.

Organize Feedback Loops

Our cities consist of a mass of feedback loops, of many sizes and scales, at many points in time. The city habitats in which we find ourselves shape us; they give us a context in which we create work to improve life around us. And as we work, we reshape our cities. This is an ancient and intricate feedback loop.

So, are we making the cities we want and need? Are we getting the cities we are seeking? These questions, of course, are for citizens to explore, but they are equally important for community organizations, the business community, and the folks who run our public institutions. It is time for the voices in the city to interact, to search for what they have to say together, rather than separately. Within each of these voices, and between them, is a new possibility that is rooted not in content, but in how we make meaning of what we know. We can be more conscious of what we already know, as individuals and collectives. This involves new feedback loops at much larger scales, always asking: What do we need from our cities? What do our cities need from us?

Some people's work and their drive to follow their passion offer us feedback loops. Patricia McCarney's decade of work with the University of Toronto's Global Cities Indicators Facility[236] brought the Global Cities Summit to Toronto in May 2014, where fifteen cities formed the World Council on City Data. McCarney's work involved the development of uniform indicators for cities, tested on 258 cities in 82 countries. The result? The first international standard for cities, created by cities. Called "ISO 37120: Sustainable Development of Communities—Indicators for City Services and Quality of Life,"[237] the data in the document is public, open for the use of citizens and researchers, for any purpose people feel compelled to explore. In 2017, the World Council on City Data made the Dubai Declaration, a commitment to city data as the universal language, with three agendas for 2030: inclusive cities, smart nations, and a sustainable planet.[238]

Neal Peirce, editor and founder of Citiscope, an online resource on all things city, notes the significance of this work: "The people of cities—civic, business organizations, ordinary citizens—will be able to access the same new global standards. This means they can ask city leaders tough questions, stoking debate about their own city's performance on the basis of verified measures ranging from education to public safety to water and sanitation."[239]

Two things are significant in this work: data on our cities is increasingly open and publicly available; and open data enables a host of creative ways for anyone in the city to improve our experience of the city. A handful of Citiscope's headlines say it all:

- Can an app for borrowing housewares make neighbourhoods stronger?
- Boston bus startup operates where demand is greatest
- How Helsinki mashed up "open data" with regionalism
- Can text messaging solve Karachi's incredible unpaid water bill problem?
- Vancouver re-imagines the library as part of a broader digital strategy
- Urban insights can be gleaned from how we walk and talk
- Indian city uses "smart cards" to assess health of police officers

We need a culture of curiosity to ask good questions, a culture of intention to focus on the questions that need to be asked, a culture of courage to look at the findings, a culture of vision to see the findings, and a culture of inquiry that welcomes the findings, whatever they bring.

Creativity thrives all over the planet. When ideas and data that have never before been connected are woven together, we have new nesting materials. Feedback loops are changing how we experience the city, but also changing how we see the city. In February 2014, in the heart of winter, Patricio Davilo and Dave Colangelo, graduate students at Ryerson University in Toronto, shone live weather and homelessness data in a display of coloured lights on the exterior of a building to the surrounding neighbourhood.[240] They helped their city see the city's homelessness numbers in a new light, potentially changing subsequent actions. How's that for a feedback loop?

Engage the Inquiring City

Feedback loops are more effective when used thoughtfully. If we measure without looking, we waste resources. If we measure and ignore the findings, or do not understand the findings, or do not care about the findings, we also waste resources. Thoughtful feedback loops provide us with the information we need to learn and adjust courses of action. Feedback loops invite us to know and understand the world around us differently. We need a culture of curiosity to ask good questions, a culture of intention to focus on the questions that need to be asked, a culture of courage to look at the findings, a culture of vision to see the findings, and a culture of inquiry that welcomes the findings, whatever they bring.

Inquiry starts with a willingness to notice the world around us, to generate the conditions for a sneeze—a reaction. Inquiry is our willingness to be open and curious and to explore in ways that lead to new work that reshapes the world. Scholar and consultant Bill Torbert explores the role of inquiry in organizational transformation through a body of work he calls "action inquiry." When we consider that all action is a form of inquiry, and all inquiry is a form of action, and explore the feedback loops between action and inquiry, we are able to transform our experiences and understanding. [241] Let's see how this can inform the way we think about cities.

Unlike ISO indicators, action inquiry works from the inside out. Let me use a personal example to explain what I mean. Generally speaking, I should weigh about 145 pounds; that weight makes sense for me. But from what I know about me, my body, and my relationship with my body, I am much happier and feel healthier with an extra ten to fifteen pounds. I know this from the inside; it is not an arbitrary number from the external world. It means I know myself and what works for me. Even when I ask myself about the conditions when I feel best about myself, I inquire. A trigger on the inside activates action inquiry, and it takes place when we experience—at any scale—a gap between what we wish to do and what we are able to do. For Torbert, this gap can lead to "the development of a clear intent to accomplish something beyond our own current capacity." [242] It sets us off, reaching for a destination.

Inquiry is our willingness to be open and curious and to explore in ways that lead to new work that reshapes the world.

Action inquiry has two essential elements: inquiry about what is necessary to learn how to do something new and inquiry about whether that new thing has been accomplished. [243] And, of course, behind the scenes lies an evolutionary thirst for finding gaps. When we actively engage in the relationship between curiosity and action, we transform ourselves and the world around us. We inquire for the purpose of transformation. Since the work we choose shapes our city habitat, entering into the action inquiry relationship transforms our cities.

Torbert works with people, teams, organizations, and institutions that wish to become increasingly capable of making future visions come true, of recognizing the dangers and opportunities of the present moment, and of performing in effective and transformational ways. [244] These are all objectives that apply to the city. In fact, they shed a new light on what it means to organize—not plan—for a city that serves citizens well. As evolutionary agents, we notice new ways to improve the city; this is an invitation to explore both what we want to do and to decide if we have accomplished our goals. Evolutionary agents undertake this work at the scale of self, at the scale of the city, and everything in between.

Torbert's action inquiry model involves single-loop, double-loop, and triple-loop feedback—each with a distinct purpose. Single-loop inquiry focuses on individual integrity, inquiring into the gaps within oneself. To the outside world, the results are revealed through changes in an individual's behaviour. Double-loop inquiry aims for mutuality between parties. This involves creative actions that lead to shared visions and strategies, as well as collaborative learning along the way. The results are agreed-upon strategies, structures, and goals between parties. With triple-loop inquiry, the organizing structures are sustainable, encouraging effectiveness, mutuality, and integrity. The organizations continuously transform. The outcomes pay attention to what matters, and are accompanied by clear intention and a vision that serves as a direction for the organization. While single-loop learning results in changes in behaviour (or operations), double-loop learning results in shared strategy, structure, and goals. Triple-loop learning moves the learning forward even further, focusing on directional intention and continual transformation.

When we actively engage in the relationship between curiosity and action, we transform ourselves and the world around us.

When people are self aware, at many scales, action inquiry takes flight. Let me tell you the story of Pat, which combines several stories to reveal the action-inquiry pattern (summarized in Table 8).

Pat used to drive everywhere. One day, reality hit and she realized she needed to find time to get some exercise and improve her health. All the time she spent in her car was having a harmful impact on her health. So, she chose to move to a neighbourhood where she could walk to do her errands. She realized this was better for both her and the planet. As she got healthier, Pat realized that her home was within cycling distance of work, but there was no safe route for her to do so. Driving to work, she watched cycle commuters on her route, but she didn't feel brave enough to join them. She started to talk to neighbours about all the commuting options available to her—car, bus, bicycle, walking. In conversation with others, she found a shared vision: the ability to choose how to get to work each day. Pat found similar people in other neighbourhoods, and they met to support each other in their learning journeys, discovering new gaps within self, and finding the need to continually transform themselves.

For most of us, single-loop feedback feels risky, as we explore, for example, if we are doing the work we want to be doing. At times, this personal inquiry can be unsettling. Double-loop learning is as strong as the single-loop feedback, of course, and it too can feel risky when leaning into mutuality. Sharing the risk with others is both good and precarious if someone else doesn't do what they've promised. Triple-loop feedback comes with risk again, because it means openly questioning self and other. The benefit

Table 8
*Three Aims Of
Action Inquiry
For City Making*

AIMS OF ACTION INQUIRY	INQUIRY INTO	OUTCOMES OUT IN THE CITY	AN EXAMPLE OF AWARENESS IN THE CITY
Integrity of Self (Single-loop feedback)	The gaps within self: What is happening in the outside world that requires me to change my behaviour?	I behave differently because I am making choices that are more aligned with who I want to be in the world.	"I used to drive my car everywhere, but I realized that it was costly-not just financially, but also to my health and to my planet. I moved to a place where I can do all my errands on foot. I feel a lot better."
Mutuality with Others (Double feedback)	The gaps between self and others: What creative action can we take to find shared visions and strategies? How can we learn together, collaboratively?	We find strategies to work together. We put structures in place to help us reach our shared goals.	"From my new neighbourhood, I don't feel comfortable riding my bike to work because there isn't a clear place on the street for bicycles. I've started working with my neighbours and city government to test out some paths that will work for less-confident riders like me."
Sustainability (Triple-loop feedback)	The structures that encourage effectiveness, integrity, and mutuality:How do we organize ourselves to ensure continual learning and transformation?	We need to support each other in sticking to our intention for a city with many transportation options. We pay attention to our vision.	"I have connected with transportation thinkers across the city with the aim of supporting each other in our personal learning. We want to learn about how we all need to move around the city."

often outweighs the risk. Triple-loop feedback comes with a choice: learn and grow or become stagnant.

For Torbert, patterns of speech reveal patterns of action. He identifies ways to notice if we have entered into a space of inquiry or if we have stopped short. Framing language explicitly states the purpose for an occasion, the dilemma to be resolved, and the assumptions shared and not shared. Advocating language explicitly asserts an option, perception, feeling, or strategy for action in relatively abstract terms. Illustrating language tells a tangible story, adding key details to the advocacy to orient and motivate others more clearly. Finally, inquiring language questions self and others for the purpose of learning.[245]

The quality of communication in these patterns shifts from "telling" to "embracing," with each method valuable and appropriate in different circumstances. Each pattern is effective only if we are aware of ourselves in action in the moment. Torbert advises that successfully framing, advocating, illustrating, and inquiring cannot happen until we sincerely want to be aware of ourselves in action in the present. In other words, we need to question the things we frame, advocate, and illustrate.[246]

The inquiring city sets out to continually learn, act, learn, act.

Deep inside, within self, with others, and as the city, we need to know what we want to accomplish together from a place far deeper than framing, advocating, or illustrating. The inquiring city embraces the continual transformation of self, others, and the city around us. The inquiring city sets out to continually learn, act, learn, act.

KNOW WHERE THE CITY WANTS TO GO

For a city, triple-loop inquiry means knowing where we want to go (both destination and direction) and embarking on a learning journey that explores and welcomes thresholds of emergence. To do this, we need to listen to our intelligence.

Remember that group of young people who travelled through the river valley and waved at me? They waved; I waved back. Then more waves, back and forth. What fed us grew. In contrast, they could have yelled something nasty at me, prompting me to do the same and feed a different, meaner part of ourselves. What we pay attention to and choose to feed changes the world around us.

Our choices have everything to do with how we organize for city emergence.

Feedback loops can be measurable targets (destinations), but they can also be directional indicators, letting us know if we are on track with the kind of city we want to be. At the scale of the city, we want to know how we are doing, what direction we are moving in. To do this, we need to know who we are and where we want to go. We need a dashboard that tells us how we are doing.

When thinking about the city as a system, I find it helpful to think of my physical body and how I use its feedback loops. In my body, many scales of "beings" are doing their work, fulfilling their "economic life." Cells, organs, and tissues all add up to me. They interact with each other in a complex social habitat, exchanging information and materials, as they work together. When I eat too much Halloween candy, for example, my system works less effectively. If I pay attention, my body has a lot to tell me: I feel jittery and ill at ease. When I ignore the signals telling me I have had enough candy, my relationship with the feedback loops deteriorates: I feel bad about eating too much candy so I eat more. I am unsatisfied with what I have eaten because I have lost track of what it tastes like; that feedback loop is closed, too. Then, believing that I will be depriving myself of candy, I continue to eat. I disconnect my information systems from each other. Out of fear of scarcity, I continue to consume, ignoring my body's signals that I have had enough. The joy I had with the first few bites is lost. Emotional circuitry and fear take hold. A city will do the same.

Triple-loop inquiry offers us a way to listen to our own intelligence.

If the social habitat of our city operates out of scarcity and fear, we lose contact with our feedback loops. Even if we have accurate and meaningful information, which is generated more and more readily with today's technology, if we are unwilling to truly see that information, we sabotage ourselves. How do we set ourselves up to listen to our own intelligence?

Triple-loop inquiry offers us a way to listen to our own intelligence. At the scale of the city, it is essential in single-loop inquiry to notice gaps and changes needed in behaviour—how citizens, civic managers, community organizations, and the business community show up. Double-loop inquiry invites these same perspectives to search for and act on shared goals and strategies. In triple-loop inquiry, they further organize themselves to support each other's effectiveness, mutuality, and integrity. They choose where to focus their attention and their flight path. Most importantly, they choose to learn and transform themselves along the way. They think, make, and do together; they focus, learn, and choose together; they inquire together at all scales. And then they are able to organize together to make cities that serve all well. In this realm of city organizing, "city planning" has a new function—to convene the city and help it be in conversation with itself. Yes, planning policy and bylaws put in place rules and regulations, enabling us to move in the direction we wish, but city planning is no longer about the plans and rules. It's about the actions we take as a result of the conversation we have with ourselves and each other.

Meeting Versus Learning

In order to see the patterns, connections, and relationships that come with the emerging city, the quality of our social habitat must be high. The quality of the civic practice must be high.

City planning is no longer about the plans and rules. It's about the actions we take as a result of the conversation we have with ourselves and each other.

Here's an easy way to reframe a gathering of people—instead of planning and organizing for a meeting or a series of meetings, organize for participants to know and understand things differently. What if the objective of every meeting we enter—at work, with our kid's teacher, with a client, or our doctor—is for us and others to learn something new?

Rather than meeting to simply exchange information, consider a meeting that compels those involved to feel connected to the work or themselves. Scharmer and Kaufer offer these characteristics of habitat that support and sustain learning:

- We are in charge of what we learn. We are in the driver's seat.
- We dive into what inspires us. We immerse ourselves in learning journeys that allow us to feel, empathize, and connect with multiple perspectives.
- We spend time with peers, deeply listening to each other. This allows deep learning to occur.
- We learn at many scales. We are connected to self, as well as others at many scales, from our families, work lives, or neighbourhood to our city and the planet.

- We work to be aware. As individuals and as the groups we are a part of, we seek to notice and be aware of our context and what it asks of us.

- We experiment. We collaborate with ourselves, our context, and others, to try solutions for the challenges we face. This part of our learning relationship, with the world around us, needs energy and attention.

- We are on a lifelong journey. We recognize that we are on a journey to awaken, activate, and strengthen our capacity to be ourselves.

- We need a place to practise. To do all the above, we need safe places to try new practices, explore ideas, or simply be ourselves for a time.

Imagine meetings where we bring our true selves to the table, where we learn about ourselves and our relationship to the work at hand. When we are able to be honest to others and true to ourselves, then as groups we undertake the learning that needs to be undertaken to improve our collective work. These habitats naturally form when we seek to know and understand things differently.

In order to see the patterns, connections, and relationships that come with the emerging city, the quality of our social habitat must be high.

A few years ago, I co-hosted two workshops with The Natural Step Canada, engaging multiple generations to declare what makes an awesome neighbourhood. We extended an invitation for folks from many walks of life to tease out what they know about their neighbourhoods and cities. Rather than follow a conventional format—with experts telling participants how to build awesome neighbourhoods—the participants collaborated in small groups to make models of their dream neighbourhoods using materials from the Re-Use Centre. When the model neighbourhoods were moved next to each other, like in a city, they noticed the characteristics of their awesome neighbourhoods. A room of citizens, civic managers, the business community, and community organizations simply named what makes a neighbourhood awesome. Here are the main ideas they came up with.[247]

- Integrate the neighbourhood, the city, and the region. The well-being of the rural areas, the city, and the neighbourhoods affect each other.

- Nurture community, nature, and design. We cultivate and spread wisdom through community. Natural areas and biodiversity contribute to our identity and sense of place, as does design (colour, art, and personality).

- Offer essential places to gather or to simply bump into each other, indoors and outdoors, in all seasons, private and public, programmed and flexible, formal and informal. The more ways there are for neighbours to connect, the better.

- Welcome and tap into multiple perspectives, interests, skills, knowledge, spirit, and culture. Living together connects us with a larger collective purpose that allows us to address our individual needs (housing, business, recreation, spirituality, and employment).

- Offer connected movement options. Multiple modes of transportation (walking, cycling, public transportation, and private vehicles) ensure connections and interconnections within and between neighbourhoods.

- Generate healthy citizens by providing an abundance of choices for active lifestyles, food sources, support networks, and health services. Neighbours help and support each other. We make a built environment that adds value to the whole region's ecosystem.

- Support multiple business models. Conventional business models, co-ops, and social enterprises all thrive. Local manufacturing and various employment opportunities allow diverse citizens to live near work.

- Organize for energy resilience. Renewable energy systems need to be front and centre: wind farms, active and passive solar, and district energy systems. Other forms of resilience include local food production, wastewater treatment, and natural storm water management.

- Organize for private and public lives in neighbourhoods. Our neighbourhoods become sustainable when we are able to see the value of living closer together, and they serve each other well when community and privacy thrive simultaneously.

- Organize for neighbourhood life cycles with long-term planning and annual city budgets that contemplate life cycle assessments of infrastructure. This is not simple, because everything is interconnected.

- Self-organize for wisdom. Neighbours listen to each other, look after each other, and explore how to grow and evolve our thinking to better meet our needs. Mentors, leaders, and champions all have roles to play in building social capital.

- Support neighbours' individual and collective dreams. The more we share our individual dreams, the more the collective helps us achieve them. The collective benefits when individual needs are met.

- Build trust to take risks. The more we interact with each other and explore different perspectives, the more we find in common. Listening to each other, looking for common goals, and finding time for what is important builds trust and community.

These citizen-participants were experts in city making. They understood perfectly the direction in which they wished to move. Their ideas reinforced the understanding that specialized forms of work help us reach our destinations, like the professional engineer who builds a pedestrian bridge to connect two neighbourhoods or the landscape architect who designs a park that serves as a public market, a concert venue and anything else that might be dreamed up. What matters is that we know the intention for the city (or a street, or a park, or a neighbourhood) so that the designers know the purpose of their design. We need to have a sense of intention or direction.

Movement

A sense of direction is essential because it helps us choose appropriate destinations. Without a clear sense of intention, we can easily be thrown off track.

A sense of direction is essential because it helps us choose appropriate destinations.

Let's zip back to Part One, where movement up and down the Spiral takes place in two directions. Movement upward is characterized by increased complexity and integration, while movement downward by fragmentation and silos, turf and territory. The stops along the way—destinations—respond to the context around us, our life conditions. These stops are not good or bad; they simply reflect where we are on our journey, our values and purposes. Our purpose may be basic survival, belonging and connection, pride and passion, rules and structures, the beginnings of integration and strategy, the use of the diversity of gifts available to us, or the flex and flow of all these values combined.

Our movement up and down the Spiral also responds to our context, so it's important to notice what makes most sense for the circumstances. For example, when economic conditions are good, and there are no environmental threats, aiming to move upward makes sense. When a flood, wildfire or pandemic threatens, movement down the Spiral toward survival priorities makes sense.

The Spiral helps us see our values and purposes. In the case of a city habitat, the purpose may be a military territory (Red), a structure in which we organize ourselves to live in large numbers (Blue), or a place to take advantage of opportunities for economic well-being (Orange). Every decision we make as a city responds to our context, our life conditions. We choose destinations that reflect our values and purposes, which are themselves a reflection of our life conditions. It's all connected.

When our survival needs are met, we can choose to move upward along the Spiral, to expand our understanding of the city and our relationship with it. We can choose this direction even if we do not know exactly what the results will be. The significant word here is choice; in what direction do we choose to move? As I'm working on the final edit of *Nest City*, the COVID-19 pandemic has moved me and my fellow citizens into self-isolation. Schools are closed, people have lost their jobs or are told to work at home. We have choices to make about how to share what we have. Toilet paper has become symbolic of the struggle: do we make sure there is enough for everyone (Blue, Green), or do we hoard and let people fend for themselves (Beige, Red)? In tackling these questions we choose from two distinct directions: to learn about how to improve how we live together (interdependence), or to reinforce protection of separate turf and territory (independence).

We choose from two distinct directions: to learn about how to improve how we live together (interdependence), or to reinforce protection of separate turf and territory (independence).

The key words of Part Two—destination, journey, and emergence—shift slightly, but significantly, to destination, journey, and emergence in service to a direction. We shift from having specific, tangible stops along the way to choosing to grow, expand, and integrate our understanding wherever that learning takes us. Thresholds open doors to unknown possibilities, and in choosing to move in a direction, we still won't know where we are going with precision. We shift from operating with goals and objectives to operating with goals and objectives and an explicit aim to inquire and learn along the way.

Feedback as vital signs

The reason we need feedback for our cities is simple. Overall, we want to know our values and the direction we are moving in. We also want to know the perspectives of different groups:

citizens, civic managers, the business community, and community organizations. Through consideration of our values and intended direction, we can start to see how a city perceives its economic, social, and physical habitat and where it wishes to move.

When we organize for feedback, we are able to better learn about and understand ourselves in ways that tell us if we are moving in the right direction. Like blood pressure, body temperature and heart rate, feedback provides basic, vital information. Depending on the purpose of the feedback, a city views itself in different ways. For example, if the overall purpose is to create healthy economic, social and physical habitats, the feedback may reflect the Global Cities Indicators described above (governance, shelter, etc.). It may also include aspects that are more specific to the city, such as the health of the river that runs through the city.

Identify what needs to be understood, then measure what matters. Find a simple way to help the city view itself, so we can choose actions that support the movement we desire. My city has a citizen dashboard[248] that measures a variety of indicators relating to transportation, livability, environment, urban form, economy, and finance. Twenty-eight community foundations across Canada released "Vital Signs" reports for their cities, a database with a robust set of indicators that tells the story of a city's quality of life.[249] While an important tool for community foundations to decide where to focus their attention and resources, these sets of data are also released to the wider community and the city. Feedback helps a city see where it needs improvement and helps citizens and organizations step into their work more meaningfully and responsibly. Feedback helps us raise the quality of our inquiry.

The work ahead for cities is challenging. The quality of our inquiry about how cities work needs to deepen, as does the quality of individual actions that allows us to respond to the changing world with integrity. We can start to achieve this ideal by examining the feedback provided by city government, as the City of Edmonton has done, and by the community, as community foundations have done. Next, this information needs to be developed with the perspectives of other civic managers, citizens, and the business community, followed by city-wide consultation to see what we can collectively learn. Imagine a set of indicators that looks at the entire city system—citizens, civic managers, business community, and community organizations—and is looked at by the whole city system. In this, we will inquire and act in ways that stimulate the fullness of what citizens have to offer the city, which in turn improves how the city serves its citizens.

The story of Edmonton's Evolving Infill project reveals the importance of looking at the entire city system, revealing how different voices don't see or value the same things. Edmonton's first Infill Roadmap was created in 2014, with 23 actions guiding demand for infill development in the city's older neighbourhoods. The Roadmap focused primarily on the development of small scale housing: homes on narrow lots; duplexes; and secondary, basement, and garden suites. In 2017, with these actions largely complete, the Evolving Infill team began to create a new Roadmap. My colleague Dnyanesh Deshpande and I assembled a team, made a successful proposal, and began the year-long process of working on the project with planners Hani Quan, Yvonne Pronovost, Daniel Boric, and Anne Huizinga. One of our first findings together was an inquiry to guide the entire project: how do we welcome more people and homes in our older neighbourhoods?

We reached out to the city with this question, with the intention of including a range of perspectives. Using the four Integral City voices—civic managers, citizens, community organizations, and the business community—we engaged with and listened closely to each voice in ways that allowed them to hear one another. They described the challenges and benefits of infill development, as well as the actions needed to address the challenges and support the benefits. We presented the data we collected to the city, clearly articulating each voice—the city could see what each of its four integral voices said, and see itself and others in the documentation.

Behind the scenes, the Evolving Infill team drafted a set of outcomes:

1. Infill development responds to context and addresses emerging needs
2. The costs of doing infill development are reduced
3. We have a diverse mix of housing options in our neighbourhoods that support social and community inclusion
4. Laneway housing opportunities are expanded

5. City infrastructure investment is aligned with infill development

6. Everyone involved is clear about the development process and what to expect

These outcomes guided our next steps: the development and evaluation of proposed actions that would welcome more people and homes into older neighbourhoods.

The outcomes and ideas generated by citizens, community organizations, the business community and civic managers were given to city administration to discern possible actions that civic managers could take. City administration drafted forty actions and the four voices were invited to work together to get to know the actions, as well as to evaluate and improve them. We played some simple games (mixing up the four voices) to identify actions that made no sense or perfect sense, and the ones that were confusing or unclear. Some of the participants committed extra time, providing detailed feedback on each of the forty actions. They identified duplications and contradictions, and proposals for new actions emerged, all of which landed back with a group of city administrators who had to decide which ones they were prepared to commit to. From the original 40, the group developed 26 clear, concise actions. The four voices came together again to review and refine what became known as Infill Roadmap 2018. Now, with inquiry complete, they have moved into implementation, with each step involving further inquiries always aligned with the overarching question: How do we welcome more people and homes in our older neighbourhoods?

By starting with a single, clear question, the Evolving Infill team could reach out to the city with a named direction and with the time and space for the four voices to explore the question separately and together. The separate explorations (citizens together, builders together, for example) allowed the voices to be more clearly heard, both by the specific groups and each other. In the project's later stages, when the voices came together, each group could more easily see their shared desire to create a better city. Most importantly, they noticed the benefits of different perspectives; together they saw the city more completely. The Evolving Infill team, Deshpande and I provided a social habitat and feedback loops; the four voices stepped into the inquiry and discerned next actions that city government should take to enable the movement articulated in the question.

I have learned that there is room for the four Integral City voices and that they are each longing to be heard. Each voice pays attention to different things, all of which are essential for a city to work well. The more each group knows about themselves the better. The more they know about each other the better. Feedback loops that continue this learning about self and other help the city learn what it needs to do to improve. With feedback, the city system learns to be awake to what the city wants more of, and what it needs of its citizens.

NESTWORK CITY INTELLIGENCE

Humanity is experiencing an evolutionary burst. Our population is growing. The number of cities is growing, and they are bigger than ever before. Technology is changing how we experience the world. Amidst all of the change, two things remain constant: we live together in cities and we want cities that serve us well.

With feedback, the city system learns to be awake to what the city wants more of, and what it needs of its citizens.

So how can humanity successfully ride out this evolutionary burst? Marilyn Hamilton's twelve evolutionary intelligences provide a good start to answering that question.[250] Here they are again, distilled into one sentence:

> *Seeing the entire city as a habitat made up of many alive, evolving "wholes" that need nourishment allows us to create cities that serve citizens well and citizens that serve cities well.*

Hamilton's intelligences have surfaced throughout this book, in explicit and implicit ways, yet one of her intelligence merits further mention: meshworking intelligence.

The "wiring" of the brain and the city are similar. In 2010, *Popular Science* writer Rebecca Boyle shared high resolution, 3-D imagery of the brain and mapped the connections. Stanford professor Stephen Smith comments on Boyle's image:

> *A human cerebral cortex holds about 125 trillion synapses, which are connections among neurons, packed into an ultra-thin layer of tissue. That's equivalent to the number of stars in 1,500 Milky*

Way galaxies...These electrical interfaces are found throughout the brain and control our thinking, feeling and movement.[251]

When I look at cities, I have the same imagery in mind on a different scale. Despite the fact that no one element or person is in charge, clear patterns emerge. Our brains are sufficiently alike that we recognize ourselves as a single species, and our cities also take remarkably similar shapes independently. The pattern that emerges is from the simultaneous existence of chaos and order.

Meshworking is the ability to hold both hierarchies of order and self-organizing systems. Hamilton began using the term meshworking, typically used in brain science, to describe the ways that the city aligns "different capacities, functions, and locations so they can be of service to a purpose and each other."[252] The city, just like a brain, needs hierarchy and order to build itself. Think of order as scaffolding. Once the scaffolding is in place, the city self-organizes in infinite ways by making connections. It is an amazing combination: the ability to forever reinvent as well as the ability to sort and choose.[253]

Meshworking is the ability to hold both hierarchies of order and self-organizing systems.

When applied to cities, meshworking leads us to consider the value of whole-system thinking. This work naturally takes place in our cities, and we can choose to enhance it to nourish our cities' emergence into what they next need to be for us. Meshworking invites us to establish new order when old hierarchies are in need of recalibration and to establish new connections at every turn to nurture our self-organizing. Further, a meshworking stance asks us to be conscious of our collective learning about creating habitats that meet our needs. Cities are full of hierarchies and self-organizing systems. The challenge in our work is to find the balance in each moment that meets our life conditions, and to do so, as these images of the brain and the city and galaxies remind us, at the appropriate scale.

Let's look at a tangible example, with the destination–journey–emergence circles we encountered in Part Two. Imagine a city government that decides to build a new neighbourhood. At first glance, this may seem to be a very linear project that relies on hierarchical decision-making. Before building begins, the city government makes a plan that outlines the roles and tasks that need to happen: engineers look after pipes, roads, drainage, utilities; developers establish the overall character of the neighbourhood, ensure there is a market, line up builders, secure money to build the neighbourhood's infrastructure, and establish a construction schedule; contractors will eventually build the neighbourhood; but first, school boards and parks departments weigh in about how much land they need; city hall makes sure all the policy requirements are met; planners write and review the plan, and move it through to city council for approval as appropriate. The roles are clear and along the way everyone learns, as individuals and hopefully as governments and organizations, about how to build better neighbourhoods and cities over time. They learn as they move toward their destination. From the vantage point of the emergence circle, we know that we never arrive at the exact destination we set out for at the beginning of the journey. But we learn and adapt to situations that emerge along the way.

When we mesh hierarchies and self-organizing systems in our cities, we recognize that building a neighbourhood, for example, involves hierarchical elements, like a construction schedule and clear accountability on money flow. With all the players and organizations involved, a new neighbourhood self-organizes to an extent, especially over time. A plan can never anticipate what the neighbourhood will look and feel like decades down the road—rather it provides the basic structure upon which to build a neighbourhood. A "meshworker" is tuned in to the pattern, the plot, nudging the players to make connections and feel the direction in which the city is growing. In thinking of the city as the nest habitat we build for ourselves, it is the meshworker turned "nestworker" who tunes into citizens' relationships with economic, social, and physical habitats.

The nestworker creates the conditions for citizens, civic managers, the business community and community organizations to see that they are city makers. The quality of their civic practice matters because it makes them evolutionary agents of the city, and they have a hand in charting the direction the city moves by being aware of the city around them and responding with action and inquiry. The nestworker is you.

1.   The city emerges from actions and inquiry. Feedback loops provide the information we need to learn and adjust.

2.   Our relationship with our cities is a mass of feedback loops, of many sizes and scales and at many points in time. The feedback loops connect our economic life with our social and physical habitats.

3.   If we operate out of scarcity and fear, we lose contact with our feedback loops.

4.   Inquiry is a willingness to be open and curious, and to explore our cities in ways that lead us to new work that reshapes the world around us.

5.   Action inquiry transforms our cities. Triple-loop inquiry offers us a way to listen to our own intelligence. At the scale of the city, for citizens, civic managers, community organizations, and the business community:

     a.   Single-loop inquiry invites us to notice gaps and changes needed in behaviour.

     b.   Double-loop inquiry invites us to search for and act on shared goals and strategies.

     c.   Triple-loop inquiry invites us to further organize to support each other's effectiveness, mutuality, and integrity. We choose to learn and transform ourselves to make cities that serve all well.

6. City planning is no longer about plans and rules. It's about supporting the city to be in conversation with itself—and then taking action that enables movement in the direction we choose.

7. The quality of our social habitat, and the quality of our civic practice, allows wise inquiry and action.

8. The key words of Part Two—destination, journey, and emergence—shift slightly, but significantly, to destination, journey, and emergence in service to a direction. Without a clear sense of direction we can easily be thrown off track.

9. Simple ways to help the city see itself will allow us to see the actions that support the movement we desire. Identify what needs to be understood, then measure what matters.

10. Meshworking—or nestworking—is the ability to hold hierarchies of order and self-organizing systems. The nestworker creates the conditions for citizens, civic managers, the business community and community organizations to be evolutionary agents through action and inquiry and to make cities that serve citizens well. The nestworker is you.

NEST-MAKING PRACTICE
Noticing Patterns

I'm doing some work with a municipal government that is annexing the land of a neighbouring municipality to accommodate its physical growth. Over the course of a month, the municipal team met with angry and frustrated landowners and after each meeting took a moment to really listen to their perspectives. I asked a simple question—"With all you have heard, what resonates with you?"—and here's what they noticed:

- Citizens are searching for a place for their voice to be heard.
- Citizens are searching for a place in decision-making.
- Citizens are confused by mixed messages.
- Citizens want to know how the proposal will affect them personally.
- There are many voices among citizens; they are not unified.
- There are varied reactions to the proposal; for some it's a threat, for others an opportunity.

The municipal team moved past the information collected, moved past the process used to collect the information, and landed on something more important: they discerned the undercurrents of the work they were doing. In their inquiry, they learned that their work affects people's lives in real ways and that understanding this shapes what they notice about themselves and how they approach the work they are doing. They noticed this about themselves:

- We are here to serve citizens.
- "Us versus Them" does not serve us—or citizens.
- As an organization, we need to step up.
- When threatened, it is hard to listen.
- We need to demonstrate that we care—saying it is not enough.
- We have a lot of work to do internally to ensure we can deliver what we say we will deliver.

By simply taking the time to inquire, they learned to take a few steps in others' shoes, and they let those steps change how they moved on the dance floor, how they danced with others. When they paused to listen fully, wonderful action inquiry took place.

We place great emphasis on trends, believing that what has happened in the past naturally extends into the future. When the relationships at play are simple, clear, and linear, this may be an appropriate way to operate. But a higher level of operating is needed to discern relationships and patterns. In what ways does your city explore the relationships at play, the patterns in how things come about? Is data available for anyone to find unusual causal relationships, or are you presented with the results? When you meet as a community, do you participate in conversations or do you sit and listen to experts? Are the voices of the city mixing and mingling in their efforts to improve the city or are they separate and distinct, possibly in conflict with each other? In each of these options, the latter is linear, inadequate to the task; the former seeks patterns, acknowledging the complexity of our cities.

REFLECT

Take a moment with a journal or sketchbook and see where the following questions take you. There are no wrong or right answers. Think about the city around and within you.

Self—In what ways do I engage in inquiry?

Other— In what ways do I engage in inquiry with others? What do I see the same and/or different when I collaborate with others and a shared vision emerges?

City— As a city, in what ways do we inquire about the well-being of the city? What supports do we need, as a whole city, to inquire about who we are and where we want to go?

Care—What support do I need to engage deeply in inquiry? What do others need and how can I support them? What does my city need to courageously inquire about itself?

Reminder: "city" means the city-habitat we make for ourselves, the community around us, not our municipal government (often referred to as "the City").

A BIRDS EYE VIEW

> *Every thought we have is a tangible energy with the power*
> *to transform. A thought is not only a thing; a thought is a*
> *thing that influences other things.*
>   *—Lynne McTaggart*[254]
>
> *You are standing on the threshold of the unbounded spa-*
> *ciousness, sensing the invitation to know it ever more deeply*
> *and intimately. Taking up that invitation, you actually extend*
> *your presence, creating a new edge between the known*
> *and the unknown… Like rivers converging, you are not only*
> *renewing and reorganizing yourself but the whole universe,*
> *as it opens infinitely to your touch, to being received by you.*
>   *—Risa Kaparo*[255]

How we think about our cities, and our relationship with them, matters. It changes everything. This book offers a set of nests that form a sweet spot of generative reciprocity, a place for citizens to show up well so the city can serve them well in return.

Let's go back to the concentric circles that form the city habitat (Figure F). At the centre is our economic life, always in response to our physical habitat, the outer circle, and in between, our social habitat. Our physical habitat is the place in which we work—at any scale, that we make and remake. Our social habitat is the social space in which we work—at any scale, that we make and remake. At the centre is our economic life, where our self and our work connect, and from where we interact with our social habitat and physical habitat in a dynamic of three elements: destination/ direction, journey, and emergence. This is the relationship we have with our work—and ultimately with the economic, social, and physical habitats around us. These three habitats comprise our fullest city habitat.

The degree to which we tune into our work is reflected in the Spiral. As our relationship with our work grows, so too does our connection with our self, others, and the places we live and work.

As we move up and down the Spiral, or more appropriately, as the Spiral emerges through us, our energy oscillates between self and others. As we move upwards, we consider self in a bigger "we" way, and we consider others with more "Self." The more authentic the Self, the more authentic the "We," the more authentic the Place. Here's how our relationship with work might show up as the Spiral emerges in us:

1. Work to meet basic needs.
2. Find community in our work.
3. Engage with passion in our work.
4. Pursue a purpose beyond ourselves in our work.
5. Let our creative selves surface in our work.
6. Recognize the connection between our choices and the economic, social, and physical habitats within which we live and work (Part One).
7. Discern the affinity between self and work as it emerges in our economic life, able to see and be in relationship with the direction we are moving in, open to learning, and trust that what will come will unfold, emerge (Part Two).
8. Experience a strong relationship between self and work in our economic life. We are conscious of our civic practices, on an explicit and embodied learning journey, and we choose to be evolutionary agents (Part Three).
9. Live in the sweet spot, embodying the city at every scale.

With the city we grow and evolve into our full potential.

As we fly around, between, and from our city nests, we sort out our relationships with self, with others, and with the nests we've made. We experiment with the ideas, models, and frameworks laid out in this book. I invite you to take what is useful, try ideas that feel helpful. I leave you with ten principles to consider as you practise being a city maker.

1. **Pursue your passion.** It takes practice to follow your passion, so find people who share your passion and spend time with them. In ways you can't imagine, they will support you. They are your collaborators to help you—and the city—make more work you love. (If you don't yet know your passion, follow what interests you and the passion naturally follows.)

2. **Boldly grow your Self**. Listen to the voice of your Higher Self; it knows where you want to spend your time and energy, to best serve self, others, and our places. This is an essential part of how we make cities (and homes, neighbourhoods, organizations, nations, and so on) that serve citizens well—by being citizens that tune into our drive to improve. Boldly grow your Higher Self and you grow a better world.

3. **Think, make, and do new things.** All kinds of work matter; all work reshapes our physical habitat, our economic life, and our social habitat. Volunteering to maintain and create places for neighbours to gather is work. Pursuing your passion in nanotechnology is work. Making art is work. Cleaning the school is work. Fundraising for homeless shelters is work. Our very culture is a result of our work, and as the work diversifies and recombines, we create more opportunities to reshape our city habitats to better serve citizens, but only if citizens jump in and think, make, and do new things.

4. **Focus on what matters.** There is a lot of drama in city life. There's the kind that tells wonderful stories about ourselves, helps us see ourselves, spreads insight, reveals culture, challenges priorities, questions assumptions, and simply entertains. There's another kind of drama that shields us from insight and awareness; I call it "fight drama." When a flood is looming, we fight. When a plant closes and we lose our livelihood, we fight. When the well-being of our loved ones is at stake, we fight. There are other times when we are in fight mode without knowing why, caught in the momentum of the drama. When this happens, we hide what we really want from ourselves, keeping ourselves in a downward spiral away from our fullest potential, away from what matters. When in fight mode, notice if you are in the fight you want to be in, or are caught in the drama, distracted from what matters.

5. **Invite conflict, while nourishing self, others, and our cities.** The city-making exchange is full of conflict, full of value clashes, but we need conflict for our growth and this necessary dance is largely meaningful, even if it doesn't always feel good. Things get ugly and confusing, so make sure you nourish self, others, and the places you inhabit. (Hot tip—feeling good is not a steady state. It comes and goes!)

6. **Set yourself to learning.** The learning in our cities takes place over generations. Our learning partners travel with us, before us, and after us. We will never meet many of these travellers, even those in our lifetime, but that does not mean that we do not travel and learn together. We most certainly do. When we share our love and our work, it shapes our world, how we see it; and it shapes how we learn.

7. **Adjust structures along the way.** Every day we are in relationship with structure. It takes the form of protocols in family life, the policies in our workplaces, the physical design of our cities, and the laws that govern our expectations of each other in cities. Goldilocks knows that there can be too much or too little structure. "Just right" is a balance between chaos and order that is closely tied to context and the purpose of a structure. And as the context changes, the purpose changes. And as purpose changes, so too should our structures. If we don't know what the purpose of a structure is, it won't do what we want it to do. Ask these two questions of any new structure: What purpose needs to be served by the structure? What is the minimal structure needed to serve that purpose? To ask of an existing structure: What purpose needs to be served by the structure now? Does the structure, as it has changed over time, serve today's new purpose?

8. **Know who your city wants to be and where it wants to go.** The city-making exchange means noticing the direction we wish to go and our relationship with that direction, how we'll get there, and who we'll be along the way. Notice what is alive in your city. By naming it, you bring it into being.

9. **Tap into the full range of the city's knowledge.** The perspectives of citizens, our public institutions, the business community, and our community organizations each inform what we know about cities. Together, they give us a full view, yet we keep them separate. Helping these perspectives get to know each other is a vital part of city making. All of them make and remake our cities. Whether we work to improve economic life, social habitat, or physical habitat.

10. **Jump in.** Your contributions matter, to your own personal development and that of your city. It's worth risking an exchange with your city, because all kinds of work matter. Just as your work builds on those who have come before us, the cities of the future need your work to build upon as well. When you wait to be asked, you disengage yourself from the work you really want to be doing, and never offer all you have to the world around you. Meaningful work is what you make for yourself.

The words of Thomas Friedman are fitting: "It is so much easier to venture far—not just in distance but also in terms of your willingness to experiment, take risks, and reach out to the other—when you know that you're still tethered to a place called home, and to a real community."[256] Make yourself at home in your city, make room for others to make themselves at home in your city, and do the never-ending work you know you need to do to make it a place worthy of calling home.

FIGURES AND TABLES

FIGURES

TABLES

ACKNOWLEDGEMENTS

Thank you to the circle of cities, large and small, I've lived in, from Edmonton to Grande Prairie, Amos, Ottawa, Winnipeg, Brandon, Fort McMurray, and back to Edmonton. Everyone everywhere—family and friends, business and community colleagues, and fellow citizens—offers great insight into the work we do for ourselves: for self, others and the places we live.

A few special mentions along my learning journey in chronological order: my parents, Marg and Hugh, for nourishing my adventurous spirit; my brother Scott, for playfulness; Carla Nordby, for teaching me what good listening and unconditional love feels like; my Grade 12 English teacher, for telling me it was a shame I couldn't write well enough to get into university and teaching me that a bad teacher is a good teacher; professor Kent Gerecke, for the gift of many truths; professor Christine McKee, for the gift of shepherding and guiding; professor Ian Wight, for the ongoing gifts of spiritual professionalism and activism and connecting me to the big world out there; Ron McCullough (and BAPD), for nurturing me in my first job and the gift of generosity and shared leadership; Women for Equality, for more nurturing and a warm fire over lunch hour; Marlow Kirton, for the words, "that's why risk is a four letter word"; my team at the Regional Municipality of Wood Buffalo, for support in the challenge of a lifetime; the Ginger Group Collaborative, for all its rhizomes, and the Ginger Saloon rhizome; Marilyn Hamilton, for being ahead of her time and reaching a hand back for me; Michael Keller, for planting seeds wherever he goes; John Dickson, for worldly Spiral stories; Dan McKinnon, for modeling how to care for the introvert in me; Tenneson Woolf, for his support of the rogue host; Christina Baldwin and Ann Linnea, for lighting and tending to the fire; Deborah Greene-Jacobi, for the experience of the wilderness hug; the Integral City Sangha (Alia, Anne-Marie, Cherie, Diana, Ellen, Joan, Linda, Marilyn, and Pieter), for creating a field for this work, and their love and support; Katharine Weinmann, for wise and heartfelt personal and professional friendship; to Maureen Parker, Suzanne Morter and Colleen Van Tighem for open-hearted friendship in turbulent times; and to Heather Plett, for profound friendship and partnership in curiosity about conscientious disruption.

Thanks to Edmonton and all the ways the city I was born in, and circled back to, has birthed me. A big thanks to all the people I work with who love the work they do—and invite me to join them. Just a few: Dnyanesh, Lucas and Micheal; Azkaa, Shelley, Kana, Wesley; Kalen, Charity, Gabrielle, Michael, Trevor, Howaida, Mike and Pablo; Hani, Dan, Anne, and Yvonne; Nancy, Marnie, Kris, Jodi, Shelley and Colleen; and Colton, Anne, Robert and Jeff. Thank you to the first round of participants in the online version of the Nest City Circle in 2018, for playing with me and the manuscript: Andres, Anne, Anne, Ashley, Azkaa, Dan, Dnyanesh, Jane, Kalen, Kana, Mariah, Omar, Laura, Robert, Susan, TR, and Wendy. Thank you to the fulsome Calgary energy of the first face-to-face Nest City Circle participants in 2019: Alkarim, Allan-Cleary, Andrea, Annalise, Cynthia, Garret, Jeff, Kate, Leanne, Madyson, Sherry, and Tylara. Thank you to Aaron Aubin for wise insight.

It seems fitting, after having lived and worked in many Canadian locations, that my return to Edmonton, my original city nest, brought about the writing of this book. Thank you to Edmonton—this place I belong to and belongs to me. It also seems fitting, after lengthy efforts to find a publisher, that this book is made in Edmonton; thank you to editors Margaret Sadler and Theresa Agnew, copy editor Mira Spearey, book designer Judy Armstrong and illustrator Amanda Schutz.

Thank you to Peter for kindness and generosity for many of the years it took for this work to come to fruition. Thank you to Evan for quiet and solid support, with a laugh always timed just right. Thank you to nine-year-old Mira who asked if I was writing a book; ten minutes later I realized I was. Thirteen years later, here it is.

NEST CITY

E N D N O T E S

1 Risa F. Kaparo, Awakening Somatic Intelligence: The Art and Practice of Embodied Intelligence (Berkeley: North Atlantic Books, 2012), xxx.

2 Bruce Grierson, *U-Turn: What if You Woke Up One Morning and Realized You Were Living the Wrong Life* (New York: Bloomsbury, 2007), 223.

3 David Whyte, *The Three Marriages: Reimagining Work, Self and Relationship* (New York: Riverhead Books, 2009), 24.

4 Whyte, *Three Marriages*, 26.

5 Terry Patten, *A New Republic of the Heart* (Berkeley: North Atlantic Books, 2018), 87.

6 Jane Jacobs, *The Nature of Economies* (Toronto: Random House, 2001), 22-23.

7 Annabel Lyon, *The Golden Mean* (Toronto: Random House, 2009), 102.

8 Barbara Marx Hubbard, *Emergence: The Shift from Ego to Essence* (San Francisco: Hampton Roads, 2012), 142.

9 Truth and Reconciliation Commission of Canada, *Honouring the Truth, Reconciling for the Future: Summary of the Final Report of the Truth and Reconciliation Commission of Canada* (Toronto: James Lorimer & Company, 2015), 44. Includes citations of Stephen Howe, *Empire: A Very Short Introduction* (Oxford: Oxford University Press, 2002), 21-22, 57).

10 Truth and Reconciliation Commission of Canada, *Honouring the Truth*, 45.

11 Truth and Reconciliation Commission of Canada, *Honouring the Truth*, 45. Includes citation of Patrick Wolfe, "Settler Colonialism," *Journal of Genocide Research*, 2006, 8(4), December 388, 391, 399.

12 Truth and Reconciliation Commission of Canada, *Honouring the Truth*, 1.

13 Ashley Fitzpatrick, St. John's Changes Pre-Meeting Land Acknowledgement, *The Telegram*, April 16, 2018, https://www.thetelegram.com/news/local/st-johns-changes-pre-meeting-land-acknowledgement-202464/

14 Don E. Beck and Christopher C. Cowan, *Spiral Dynamics: Mastering Values, Leadership, and Change* (Oxford: Blackwell, 2006), 52-56.

15 Beth Sanders, "From the High Water Mark to the Back of the Fish Flakes: The Purposeful Evolution of Cities," *Plan Canada* 51, no. 4 (Winter 2011): 26-31.

16 See Memorial University Digital Archives: Chart of St. John's Harbour in Newfoundland, surveyed in October 1798 by Francis Owen, Master of His Majesty's Ship Agincourt, http://collections.mun.ca/cdm/ref/collection/maps/id/161.

17 See Newfoundland's Grand Banks Genealogical and Historical Data website, and their account of inhabitants residing in the harbor and district of St. John's 1794-1795, as transcribed from a transcription kept at the Newfoundland Archives GN/2/39/A, http://ngb.chebucto.org/C1794/1794-totals-sje.shtml.

18 Newfoundland and Labrador Heritage: Fisheries, www.heritage.nf.ca/society/fishery.html.

19 See Memorial University Digital Archives: Chart of the Harbour and Narrows and Plan of the Town of St. John's, Newfoundland, http://collections.mun.ca/cdm/ref/collection/maps/id/291.

20 In 1857, 30,476 people reside in St. John's. Statistics Canada. Nfld Table I—Dwellings, Families, Population, Sexes, Conjugal Condition, etc., 1857—Newfoundland (table), 1857—Census of Newfoundland (Population/Sexes/Conjugal Condition) (database), Using E-STAT (distributor), http://estat.statcan.gc.ca/cgi-win/cnsmcgi.exe?Lang=E&EST-Fi=EStat\English\SC_RR-eng.htm.

21 "*Total Oil Production, Barrels Newfoundland and Labrador November 1997 to Date,*" Newfoundland & Labrador Statistics Agency, Department of Finance, February 6, 2018, www.stats.gov.nl.ca/Statistics/Industry/PDF/Oil_Production.pdf.

22 See St. John's Port Authority website: www.sjpa.com/pages.aspx?id=35.

23 Thomas Brinkhoff, "*Major Agglomerations of the World: Statistics and Charts in Maps, Diagrams and Tables,*" City Population, accessed November 6, 2019, www.citypopulation.de/world/Agglomerations.html.

24 United Nations, *World Urbanization Prospects: The 2009 Revision, Highlights* (New York: UN Department of Economic and Social Affairs, Population Division, 2010).

25 Brinkhoff, "Major Agglomerations," accessed November 6, 2019, www.citypopulation.de/world/Agglomerations.html.

26 United Nations, The World at Six Billion (New York: UN Department of Economic and Social Affairs, Population Division, 2011).

27 Worldometers.info, Current World Population: World Population Clock: 7.3 Billion People (Dover, DE: Dadax, 2015), accessed November 6, 2019, www.worldometers.info/world-population/.

28 Matt Rosenberg, "Current World Population: World Population and World Population Growth Since Year One." World Population – Current and Historic Counts, accessed January 3, 2016, http://geography.about.com/od/obtainpopulationdata/a/worldpopulation.html. In year "1" we numbered 200 million. It took until the year 1850 to reach 1.2 billion.

29 United Nations, "World Population Prospects – The 2012 Revisions." (New York: UN Department of Economic and Social Affairs, Population Estimates and Projections Section), accessed April 7, 2015, http://esa.un.org/wpp/Other-Information/faq.htm#q4.

30 United Nations, "State of World Population 2011: People and Possibilities in a World of 7 Billion." (New York: UN Population Fund, UNFPA, 2011).

31 Spencer Wells, *The Journey of Man: A Genetic Odyssey* (Princeton University Press, 2002), 85. Wells draws on Jared Diamond's anthropological work around "The Great Leap Forward" and others' work around Diamond. He also draws on Richard Klein's work.

32 Wells, *Journey*, 85.

33 Ronald Wright, *A Short History of Progress* (Toronto: House of Anansi, 2004), 64-65.

34 Geoffrey West quoted by Steven Johnson, *Where Good Ideas Come From: The Natural History of Innovation* (Toronto: Riverhead Books, 2010), 10.

35 Johnson, *Good Ideas*, 16. The sheer force of cities in terms of their role in the recent advancements of the human species is well demonstrated by Johnson.

36 Johnson, *Good Ideas*, 10-11.

37 Resurgence & Ecologist no. 313 (March/April 2019).

38 Connie Walker, "Shooting death of young Indigenous man forces rural community to confront racism," CBC News, last modified November 6, 2019, https://www.cbc.ca/news/investigates/kristian-ayoungman-shooting-strathmore-alberta-1.4866823.

39 See St. John's Port Authority website: https://sjpa.com/about-the-port/.

40 James Lovelock, *The Vanishing Face of Gaia* (Toronto: Penguin Books, 2010). Marilyn Hamilton, *Integral City: Evolutionary Intelligences for the Human Hive* (Gabriola Island: New Society Publishers, 2008). Earth system scientist and writer James Lovelock founded the Gaia hypothesis: Earth as a self-regulating system, a community of living organisms. Earth will self-regulate to survive. Writer Marilyn Hamilton notices that we are becoming a planet of cities, where humans play an even more significant role as the species with the capacity for reflection and self-awareness.

41 Jacobs, *Nature of Economies* and Jane Jacobs, *The Economy of Cities* (Toronto: Random House, 1970).

42 Jacobs, *Nature of Economies*, 24.

43 Jacobs, *Nature of Economies*, 17.

44 A **holarchy**, in the terminology of Arthur Koestler, is a connection between holons— where a holon is both a part and a whole. The term was coined in Koestler's 1967 book *The Ghost in the Machine*.

45 Marilyn Hamilton, *Integral City: Evolutionary Intelligences for the Human Hive* (Gabriola Island: New Society Publishers, 2008), 65.

46 Jacobs, *Nature of Economies*, 54.

47 Jacobs, *Nature of Economies*, 56.

48 Steven Johnson, *Emergence: The Connected Lives of Ants, Brains, Cities and Software* (New York: Scribner, 2001), 108.

49 Johnson, *Good Ideas*, 22.

50 Herbert Giardet, "Regenerative Economics for a Sustainable World," *Resurgence & Ecologist* no. 313 (March/April 2019): 20-24.

51 Lovelock, *Gaia*, 2.

52 Lovelock, *Gaia*, 113.

53 Whyte, *Three Marriages*, 68.

54 Whyte, *Three Marriages*, 68-69.

55 Whyte, *Three Marriages*, 139.

56 Jane Jacobs, *The Death and Life of Great American Cities* (New York: Random House, 1961), 406.

57 Hamilton, *Integral City*, 61-64.

58 Zainab Moghal, PhD, and Shawna Peddle, MSc, At the Front Lines of Flood: How Prepared are Ontario Communities? (Partners for Action: July 4, 2016), ii-iii. Retrieved on Nov 2, 2016. https://uwaterloo.ca/partners-for-action/sites/ca.partners-for-action/files/uploads/files/p4a_front_lines_of_the_flood_04jul16.pdf

59 Brian Robertson, YouTube: What if We Rode A Bicycle Like We Manage Companies? Copyright HolacracyOne LLC, YouTube, retrieved November 2, 2016. https://www.youtube.com/watch?v=7hKtFVlfp4U

60 Jacobs, *Nature of Economies*, 23

61 Patten, *Republic of the Heart*, 87.

62 Spiral Dynamics is one of several windows into our evolutionary intelligence. Others include Suzanne Cook-Greuter's perspectives, Jane Loevinger's ego stages, Jean Piaget's moral stages, and Abraham Maslow's needs. An exhaustive list, and comparison, of this line of work can be found in Ken Wilber, Integral Psychology: Consciousness, Spirit, Psychology, Therapy (Boston: Shambhala, 2000).

63 Beck and Cowan joined Richard Dawkins (The Selfish Gene) and Mihaly Csikszentmihalyi (The Evolving Self) in the use of this language: memes, value memes.

64 Don Edward Beck and Christopher C. Cowan, *Spiral Dynamics: Mastering Values, Leadership, and Change* (Oxford: Blackwell, 2006), 31-32.

65 Beck and Cowan, *Spiral Dynamics*, 11, 45-47.

66 Columns 3-5: Beck and Cowan, *Spiral Dynamics*, 44. Illustrations: Beth Sanders.

67 Beck and Cowan, *Spiral Dynamics*, 50-67.

68 Beck and Cowan, *Spiral Dynamics,* 50-51.

69 Lewis Mumford, *The City in History: Its Origins, Its Transformations, and Its Prospects* (New York: Harcourt Brace Jovanovich, 1961).

70 Mumford, *City in History,* 103.

71 Mumford, *City in History,* 50.

72 Mumford, *City in History,* 131.

73 Beck and Cowan, *Spiral Dynamics,* 56.

74 Beck and Cowan, *Spiral Dynamics,* 56-59.

75 Beck and Cowan, *Spiral Dynamics,* 59.

76 Beck and Cowan, *Spiral Dynamics,* 62.

77 Beck and Cowan, Spiral Dynamics, 66

78 As quoted by Beck and Cowan, Spiral Dynamics, 274. Graves's use of the masculine in this explanation is indicative of his life conditions and the times (post-WW2).

79 Beck and Cowan, *Spiral Dynamics,* 76.

80 Beck and Cowan, *Spiral Dynamics,* 82.

81 Beck and Cowan, *Spiral Dynamics,* 82.

82 Beck and Cowan, *Spiral Dynamics,* 83.

83 Beck and Cowan, *Spiral Dynamics,* 84.

84 Beck and Cowan, *Spiral Dynamics,* 84.

85 Beck and Cowan, *Spiral Dynamics,* 85.

86 Scalar is a physical quantity that only has magnitude but no direction.

87 A fractal is a never-ending pattern. Fractals are infinitely complex patterns that are self-similar across different scales. They are created by repeating a simple process over and over in an ongoing feedback loop.

88 Ben Okri, *Mental Fight: An Anti-Spell for the 21st Century* (London: Phoenix House, 1999), 4.

89 See www.cip-icu.ca/_CMS/Files/ThomasAdams_75article.pdf

90 Thomas Adams, *Present Scope for Practical Work in Improving Civic Conditions,* 1916 (Ottawa: Conference of Civic Improvement League of Canada, 1916). Retrieved from www.urbancenter.utoronto.ca/pdfs/policyarchives/1916ThomasAdams01.pdf

91 "About Planning," Candian Institute of Planners, accessed February 8, 2020, https://www.cip-icu.ca/Careers-in-Planning/About-Planning.

92 Gerald Hodge and David L. A. Gordon, Planning Canadian Communities: *An Introduction to the Principles, Practice, and Participants,* 5th ed. (Toronto: Thomson Canada, 2008), 3.

93 Thomas Adams as quoted in Hodge and Gordon, *Planning Canadian Communities,* 3.

94 Frances Westley, Brenda Zimmerman, and Michael Quinn Patton, *Getting to Maybe: How the World is Changed* (Toronto: Vintage Canada, 2007).

95 Content mostly Westley, Zimmerman, and Patton, *Getting to Maybe,* 9. The "city twist": Beth Sanders.

96 Hodge and Gordon, *Planning Canadian Communities,* 5.

97 Hodge and Gordon, *Planning Canadian Communities,* 5.

98 Thomas L. Friedman, *Thank You for Being Late: An Optimist's Guide to Thriving in the Age of Accelerations* (New York: Farrar, Straus and Giroux, 2016), 310.

99 W. Timothy Gallwey, *The Inner Game of Work: Focus, Learning, Pleasure, and Mobility in the Workplace* (New York: Random House, 2001), 142.

100 Steve McIntosh, Evolution's Purpose: *An Integral Interpretation of the Scientific Story of Our Origins* (New York: SelectBooks, 2012), 13-14. McIntosh, Evolution's Purpose, 146.

101 McIntosh, *Evolution's Purpose,* 146.

102 McIntosh, *Evolution's Purpose*, 13.

103 McIntosh, *Evolution's Purpose*, 88.

104 Rose Eveleth, "There are 37.2 Trillion Cells in Your Body," *Smithsonian Magazine*, October 24, 2013, https://www.smithsonianmag.com/smart-news/there-are-372-trillion-cells-in-your-body-4941473/.

105 McIntosh, *Evolution's Purpose*, 134.

106 McIntosh, *Evolution's Purpose*, 160.

107 Food and Urban Agriculture Advisory Committee, *Fresh: Edmonton's Food and Urban Agriculture Strategy* (Edmonton: City of Edmonton, October 2012). www.edmonton.ca/city_government/documents/FRESH_October_2012.pdf.

108 For more information on the Edmonton Food Council see: https://edmontonfoodcouncil.org/about-2/.

109 Don Iveson, "Final thoughts on the election," DonIveson.ca website, posted October 20, 2013, accessed May 16, 2016, http://doniveson.ca/2013/10/20/final-thoughts-on-the-election/#more-3175.

110 McIntosh, *Evolution's Purpose*, 154.

111 McIntosh, *Evolution's Purpose*, 154.

112 McIntosh, *Evolution's Purpose*, 161 (emphasis mine).

113 McIntosh, *Evolution's Purpose*, 155.

114 Lynn Coady, *The Antagonist* (Toronto: House of Anansi, 2011), 234-235.

115 Coady, *Antagonist*, 235.

116 McIntosh, *Evolution's Purpose*, 161.

117 Shmuley Boteach, 10 *Conversations You Need to Have With Your Children* (New York: Regan Books, 2006), 11.

118 Henning Mankell, *The Man from Beijing*, trans. Laurie Thompson (Toronto: Alfred A Knopf, 2010), 249.

119 Anne Michaels, *The Winter Vault* (Toronto: McClelland & Stewart, 2009), 10.

120 Ronald Wright, A Short History of Progress (Toronto: House of Anansi, 2004), 5.

121 Wright, Short History of Progress, 108.

122 Wright, Short History of Progress, 108-109.

123 Charles Dickens, *Little Dorrit* (London: Penguin Classics, 2004).

124 Will Kenton, "Bernie Madoff," Crime & Fraud, Investopedia, updated February 5, 2020, https://www.investopedia.com/terms/b/bernard-madoff.asp.

125 "United in Science", World Meterological Organization, accessed January 15, 2020, https://public.wmo.int/en/resources/united_in_science.

126 "Journey," Macmillan Dictionary, accessed February 8, 2020, www.macmillandictionary.com/thesaurus/british/journey - journey_13.

127 McIntosh, *Evolution's Purpose*, 106-107.

128 Akrasia: a lack of self-control or the state of acting against one's better judgment. The adjectival form is "akratic". For more information, see https://en.wikipedia.org/wiki/Akrasia.

129 Cindy Wigglesworth, *SQ21: The Twenty-One Skills of Spiritual Intelligence* (New York: SelectBooks, 2012), 12..

130 Wigglesworth, *SQ21*, 13.

131 Wigglesworth, *SQ21*, 12.

132 Wigglesworth, *SQ21*, 13.

133 John Patrick Stanley about his play, Doubt, in the playbill for The Citadel Theatre production, Edmonton, 2008–09 season.

134 Jane Jacobs, *Dark Age Ahead* (Toronto: Random House, 2005), 25, 99.

135 Jacobs, *Dark Age Ahead*, 175.

136 Jacobs, *Dark Age Ahead*, 176.

137 Jacobs, *Dark Age Ahead*, 159.

138 Jacobs, *Dark Age Ahead*, 160.

139 Jacobs, *Dark Age Ahead*, 158.

140 Jacobs, *Dark Age Ahead*, 26.

141 Garr Reynolds, Presentation Zen: *Simple Ideas on Presentation Design and Delivery* (Berkeley: New Riders, 2008), 115.

142 Stanley, playbill for *Doubt*.

143 Whyte, *Three Marriages*, 131.

144 Patten, *Republic of the Heart*, 193.

145 Okri, *Mental Fight*, 57.

146 Peggy Holman, *Engaging Emergence: Turning Upheaval into Emergence* (San Francisco: Berrett-Koehler, 2010), 18.

147 Margaret Wheatley and Deborah Frieze, *Using Emergence to Take Social Innovation to Scale* (Provo, UT: Berkana Institute, 2006), 4. Retrieved from www.walkoutwalkon.net/wp-content/uploads/2011/03/using-emergence.pdf.

148 Patten, *Republic of the Heart*, 93.

149 Ian Goldin and Chris Kutarna, *Age of Discovery: Navigating the Risks and Rewards of our New Renaissance* (New York: St. Martin's Press), 3-4.

150 Goldin and Kutarna, *Age of Discovery*, 168.

151 Goldin and Kutarna, *Age of Discovery*, 176.

152 Jacobs, *Economy of Cities*, 105.

153 Whyte, *Three Marriages*, 32.

154 Grierson, *U-Turn*, 118.

155 Grierson, *U-Turn*, 6.

156 Otto Scharmer and Katrin Kaufer, *Leading from the Emerging Future: From Ego-System to Eco-System Economies* (San Francisco: Berrett-Koehler, 2013), 163.

157 Okri, *Mental Fight*, 15.

158 Alberta Professional Planners Institute conference title: What if we are not planning to survive? And Who's Planning Our Future Anyway?

159 Beth Sanders, "Elephants: Creating the Conditions to Flourish." *APPI Planning Journal* 6 (2010): 10-13.

160 Whyte, *Three Marriages*, 70.

161 Joseph Jaworski, *Synchronicity: The Inner Path of Leadership* (San Francisco: Berrett-Koehler, 1998), 183.

162 Ken Robinson, "Bring on the Learning Revolution," TED video, 20:57. Posted February 2010, http://www.ted.com/talks/sir_ken_robinson_bring_on_the_revolution, and Ken Robinson, *The Element: How Finding Your Passion Changes Everything* (New York: Penguin, 2009).

163 David Bohm, As quoted in *New Scientist* (February 1993), 42.

164 Beth Sanders, "Are Planners Suffering from Akrasia?," *AACIP Planning Journal* 3 (Winter 2009/10), 11–14.

165 In philosophy, systems theory, science, and art, emergence is a process whereby larger entities, patterns, and regularities arise through interactions among smaller or simpler entities that themselves do not exhibit such properties.

166 Grierson, *U-Turn*, 202.

167 Holacracy website, last modified 2016, accessed May 19, 2016, http://www.holacracy.org/.

168 The Art of Hosting is an approach to participatory leadership that scales from the personal to the systemic. It involves personal practice, dialogue, facilitation and the co-creation of innovation to respond to the complex world around us. Chris is an early Art of Hosting practitioner and steward of the global community of practitioners. Years ago he asked this question and it has stuck with me. http://www.artofhosting.org

169 Whyte, *Three Marriages*, 48.

170 C. Otto Scharmer, *Theory U: Leading From the Future as It Emerges; The Social Technology on Presencing* (Cambridge, MA: Society for Organizational Learning, 2007).

171 Scharmer and Kaufer, *Emerging Future*, 22-23.

172 Douglas R. Hofstadter, *Metamagical Themas: Questing for the Essence of Mind and Pattern* (New York: BasicBooks, 1985), xx.

173 Thomas King, *The Truth About Stories: A Native Narrative* (Toronto: House of Anansi Press, 2003), 32.

174 Richard Adams, *Watership Down* (London: Penguin, 1973), 42.

175 Elise Stolte, "Committee endorses plan to buy 100 per cent renewable energy for city operations," Edmonton Journal (May 22, 2018), updated May 22, 2018, http://edmontonjournal.com/news/local-news/committee-endorses-plan-to-buy-100-per-cent-renewable-energy-for-city-operations, Stephen Cook, "Maskwacis teen to pitch sustainable housing plan in Ottawa," Edmonton Journal (May 22, 2018), updated May 22, 2018, http://edmontonjournal.com/news/local-news/maskwacis-resident-invited-to-ottawa, and Su-Ling Goh, "New program makes it easier for people with celiac disease to eat out," Global News Edmonton (May 21, 2018), updated May 2w, 2018, https://globalnews.ca/news/4222453/gluten-free-celiac-disease-health-food-service-businesses/.

176 Charles Montgomery, *Happy City: Transforming Our Lives Through Urban Design* (Toronto: Doubleday, 2013), 40-41.

177 Montgomery, *Happy City*, 39.

178 Montgomery, *Happy City*, 41.

179 *Eudaimonia* (Greek: μ[eudaimonía]), sometimes anglicized as eudaemonia or eudemonia, is a Greek word commonly translated as happiness or welfare; however, "human flourishing" has been proposed as a more accurate translation. Etymologically, it consists of the words "*eu*" ("good") and "*daimōn*" ("spirit"). Retrieved from https://en.wikipedia.org/wiki/Eudaimonia

180 Montgomery, *Happy City*, 36. In Carol D. Ryff and B. H. Singer, "Know Thyself and Become What You Are: A Eudaimonic Approach to Psychological Well-Being," *Journal of Happiness Studies*, 2006:13-29.

181 Christina Baldwin and Ann Linnea, *The Circle Way: A Leader in Every Chair* (San Francisco: Berrett-Koehler, 2010). A wonderful resource for creating more robust social habitats.

182 Figure inspired by a model by Christina Baldwin and Ann Linnea, 2008, shared with me (unpublished). Used with permission. The model is part of Baldwin and Linnea's ongoing exploration of the question: "How do we re-village the world?" Visit www.peerspirit.com.

183 This is my version of the Spiral, merging Baldwin and Linnea's model with others' work highlighted in earlier chapters: Marilyn Hamilton, Christopher Cowan, and Don Beck.

184 "Boteach, *10 Conversations*, 11

185 "About," Trevor Anderson Dirt City Films, accessed May 31, 2016, www.dirtcityfilms.com/about.

186 For the stories of the area's Indigenous peoples and their territories, see https://huuayaht.org/services/language-culture/culture-history/, https://www.nitinaht.com/first-nation/, and http://pacheedahtfirstnation.com/pacheedaht-first-nation-history-and-villages/,

187 "Monto," Spirit of Edmonton, accessed May 31, 2016, http://www.monto.ca/monto/.

188 David Faber and Lewis Cardinal, "Spirit of Edmonton: Reclaiming Monto, a Collective Vision Connecting the River and the People" (December 12, 2011), accessed May 31, 2016, www.scribd.com/doc/83090078/Final-Draft-Spirit-of-Edmonton.

189 Todd Babiak, "Is there an Edmonton story?," *Magpie Town* (blog), September 24, 2012, http://magpietown.wordpress.com/2012/09/24/is-there-an-edmonton-story/.

190 Babiak, "A city story: what the hell does that even mean?," *Magpie Town* (blog), September 26, 2012, http://magpietown.wordpress.com/2012/09/26/a-city-story-what-the-hell-does-that-even-mean/.

191 Babiak, "Audacity in Edmonton," *Magpie Town* (blog), October 1, 2012, http://magpietown.wordpress.com/2012/10/01/audacity-in-edmonton/.

192 Babiak, "Edmonton, the verb," Magpie Town (blog), January 15, 2013, http://magpietown.wordpress.com/2013/01/15/edmonton-the-verb/. Here's a wee video to get a sense of where Babiak went with this: www.makesomethingedmonton.ca/about/.

193 Babiak, "Why did you come back here?," Magpie Town (blog), October 15, 2012, http://magpietown.wordpress.com/2012/10/15/why-did-you-come-back-here/.

194 "Projects," Make Something Edmonton, accessed May 15, 2016, https://www.makesomethingedmonton.ca/about/. The spirit of Make Something Edmonton is now in transition; the "baton" has been passed on to Edmonton NextGen. For more information, visit https://www.makesomethingedmonton.ca and https://edmontonnextgen.ca.

195 "Panic over the Pacific," an episode in television series Mayday, Season 4, Episode 6, originally broadcast May 20, 2007.

196 Whyte, *Three Marriages*, 149-150.

197 Parker J. Palmer, *Let Your Life Speak: Listening for the Voice of Vocation* (San Francisco: Jossey-Bass, 2000), 74.

198 Whyte, *Three Marriages*, 255.

199 Patten, *Republic of the Heart*, 47-48.

200 Scharmer and Kaufer, *Emerging Future*, 152.

201 Marx Hubbard, *Emergence*, 138.

202 Scharmer and Kaufer, *Emerging Future*, 153.

203 Scharmer and Kaufer, *Emerging Future*, 161-163.

204 Scharmer and Kaufer, *Emerging Future*, 162.

205 Kaparo, *Awakening Somatic Intelligence*, 106.

206 Andrew Cohen, *Evolutionary Enlightenment: A New Path to Spiritual Awakening* (New York: SelectBooks, 2011), 122-165.

207 Jacobs, *Nature of Economies*, 29-33.

208 David Whyte, *Three Marriages*, 73.

209 Angeles Arrien, *The Four-Fold Way: Walking the Paths of the Warrior, Teacher, Healer, and Visionary* (San Francisco: Harper, 1993), 7-8.

210 Palmer, *Let Your Life Speak*, 31.

211 Scharmer and Kaufer, *Emerging Future*, 87.

212 Patten, *Republic of the Heart*, 172.

213 Scharmer and Kaufer, *Emerging Future*, 69.

214 Structures 1 to 4 are developed by Scharmer and Kaufer (see *Emerging Future*), and Structures 5 and 6 by Sanders.

215 A reminder that Structures 1 to 4 are developed by Scharmer and Kaufer (see *Emerging Future*), and Structures 5 and 6 by Sanders.

216 Shirzad Chamine, *Positive Intelligence: Why Only 20% of Teams and Individuals Achieve Their True Potential and How You Can Achieve Yours* (Austin, TX: Greenleaf Book, 2012), accessed May 31, 2016, http://positiveintelligence.com/.

217 Shirzad Chamine, *Positive Intelligence: Why Only 20% of Teams and Individuals Achieve Their True Potential, and How You Can Achieve Yours* (Austin: Green Leaf Book Press, 2012), 75.

218 Shirzad Chamine, *Positive Intelligence*, 20.

219 Isabel Allende, Maya's Notebook (Toronto: HarperCollins, 2013), 126.

220 Montgomery, *Happy City*, xx

221 Montgomery, *Happy City*, 43.

222 Montgomery, Happy City, 54.

223 Montgomery, *Happy City*, 69.

224 Montgomery, *Happy City*, 70. He cites Peter D. Norton, Fighting Traffic: The Dawn of the Motor Age in the American City (Cambridge, MA: MIT Press, 2008), 21.

225 The numbers in Table 7 reflect the boundaries of the municipal corporation, or government. Numbers are sourced from Thomas Brinkhoff: City Population, accessed June 5, 2018, www.citypopulation.de.

226 "Dwellings in Canada," Census in Brief, Statistics Canada, May 3, 2017, https://www12.statcan.gc.ca/census-recensement/2016/as-sa/98-200-x/2016005/98-200-x2016005-eng.cfm.

227 Montgomery, *Happy City*, 186-197.

228 Whyte, *Three Marriages*, 287.

229 Whyte, *Three Marriages*, 70.

230 Montgomery, *Happy City*, 316.

231 Whyte, *Three Marriages*, 269.

232 Jacobs, *Nature of Economies*, 145.

233 Whyte, *Three Marriages*, 321.

234 See https://www.100in1day.ca for links to the work in Vancouver, Edmonton, Toronto, Hamilton, Montreal, and Halifax. Accessed May 30, 2016.

235 See https://www.100in1day.ca/#getinvolved for the latest activity in Halifax, Hamilton and Toronto. Accessed March 24, 2020.

236 "About," Global Cities Institute, Accessed February 8, 2020, https://www.global-citiesinstitute.org/about. The Global Cities Institute houses the Global Cities Indicators Facility.

237 "Sustainable Development in Communities: City Indicators for Service Delivery and Quality of Life," International Organization for Standardization, accessed February 8, 2020, https://www.iso.org/files/live/sites/isoorg/files/archive/pdf/en/37120_briefing_note.pdf. A briefing note about ISO 37120, the first ISO International Standard on city indicators.

238 "2017 Dubai Declaration: A Commitment to City Data as a Universal Language," World Council on City Data, accessed February 8, 2020, https://www.dataforcities.org/dubai-declaration.

239 Neal Peirce, "Finally, clear performance data for comparing the world's cities," Citiscope (June 4, 2014), accessed June 4, 2016, www.citiscope.org/story/2014/finally-clear-performance-data-comparing-worlds-cities.

240 "Gould Street in a New Light," Ryerson University, February 5, 2014, http://www.ryerson.ca/news/news/General_Public/20140205_intheair.html.

241 Bill Torbert's book, Action Inquiry: *The Secret of Timely and Transforming Leadership* (San Francisco: Berrett-Koehler, 2004). For more information on the scientific roots of action inquiry, see the appendix.

242 Torbert, *Action Inquiry*, 5.

243 Torbert, *Action Inquiry*, 5.

244 Torbert, *Action Inquiry*, 1.

245 Torbert, *Action Inquiry*, 27-30.

246 Torbert, *Action Inquiry*, 31-32.

247 John Purkis and Beth Sanders, *Awesome Neighbourhoods for a Sustainable Edmonton: Summary Report* (Ottawa: The Natural Step, March 8, 2013).

248 The City of Edmonton's Open City Initiative website can be found at https://www. edmonton.ca/city_government/initiatives_innovation/foundational-elements.aspx.

249 "About," VitalSigns, Community Foundations of Canada, accessed January 17, 2020, https://www.communityfoundations.ca/initiatives/vital-signs/.

250 The twelve intelligences named by Marilyn Hamilton are ecosphere intelligence, emerging wholeness intelligence, integral intelligence, living intelligence, inner intelligence, outer intelligence, building intelligence, story intelligence, inquiry intelligence, meshing intelligence, navigating intelligence, and evolving intelligence. See Hamilton's *Integral City*.

251 Rebecca Boyle, "Video: 3-D Image Shows Brain's Circuitry in Highest Resolution Ever," *Popular Science* (November 19, 2010), November 19, 2010, www.popsci.com/ science/article/2010-11/video-3-d-brain-image-highlights-neuronal-circuits-highest-resolution-ever.

252 Hamilton, *Integral City*, 221-222.

253 Hamilton, *Integral City*, 223.

254 Lynne McTaggart, T*he Intention Experiment: Using Your Thoughts to Change Your Life and the World* (New York: FreePress, 2007), xxi.

255 Kaparo, *Awakening Somatic Intelligence*, 34.

256 Friedman, Thank You For Being Late, 452-453.

Manufactured by Amazon.ca
Bolton, ON

14066393R00155